WILLA CATHER

WILLA CATHER

Edward Wagenknecht

A Frederick Ungar Book
CONTINUUM • NEW YORK

1994

The Continuum Publishing Company
370 Lexington Avenue
New York, NY 10017

Printed in the United States of America

Library of Congress Cataloging-in-Publication Data

Wagenknecht, Edward, 1900–
    Willa Cather / Edward Wagenknecht.
        p.   cm. — (Literature and life. American writers)
    "A Frederick Ungar book"
    ISBN 0-8264-0607-6 (hardcover : acid-free)
    1. Cather, Willa, 1873–1947. 2. Novelists, American—20th
century–Biography.   I. Title. II. Series.
PS3505.A87Z935 1994
813'.52—dc20
[B]   93-26869
                                                                                CIP

In memory of my beloved wife
DOROTHY ARNOLD WAGENKNECHT
Born, Bellingham, Washington, March 3, 1910
Married, Seattle, August 3, 1932
Died, West Newton, Massachusetts, July 7, 1993

"Gott sei dir gnädig, O meine Wonne."

Contents

Preface

In 1938 I conceived the idea of writing an article for *The Colophon* on Willa Cather's uncollected stories. This of course was before Curtis Bradford or anybody else had turned his thoughts in this direction. I drew up a list of all the stories I had been able to find and sent it to Miss Cather with an inquiry as to whether it was complete (it was not). In reply, she wrote me what one Cather scholar has called "a testy letter." I had not told her what I wished to do, but she promptly got it into her head that I wished to reprint some or all of the stories and virtually threatened me with the law should I attempt anything of the kind. Her early stories were worthless. She did not wish to have them reprinted and was taking care to keep all their copyrights renewed in order to prevent this.

I thereupon wrote her that I had never intended reprinting the stories but simply discussing them, to which I added that now that I knew such action would give her pain, I should abandon the idea forthwith. This brought promptly a long and much more pleasant letter, in which she thanked me warmly for my consideration for her; if I had told her what I wanted in the first place, she said, the tone of her first letter would have been very different.

I also told her however that I thought her attitude toward her early work and her attempt to expunge it from her record was completely unreasonable: first, because after the copyrights finally expired, it would be impossible for either her or anybody else to prevent their republication; and second, because she was a sufficiently important writer so that the world had the right to possess her whole oeuvre and thus be in a position to trace the whole course of her development. I did not convert her to my way of thinking though I did score one or two minor points. It happened that at the time I was working on the chapter on George Eliot in my *Cavalcade of the English Novel,* for which I had found useful material in a new book called *Early Essays of George Eliot,* which, wisely or foolishly, I took the liberty of mentioning to her. This she brushed aside peremptorily. Such books, she said, served no purpose except to earn money for those who published them. Now I knew the book in question and she did not, and I am afraid I had a moment of unholy pleasure in rather meanly informing her that it had not been published but only privately printed. This correspondence is now in the Pierpont Morgan Library.

On the question of discussing her early stories, I had carefully reserved my freedom of action on one point. If I should ever write a book about her, I told her, in which all her works would have to be considered, I should hold myself free to include the stories she wished to forget. Here, now, after more than fifty years, is that book. I do not know whether great writers who have passed beyond this mortal sphere are allowed to be aware of what is being written about them on earth. Neither am I sure whether this gives them more pleasure or pain. If they are, I am sure Miss Cather must hate many recent "interpretations" of her work that make her over into what she was not. What she would think of this book, I am probably the least possible competent judge. I cannot honestly think she would hate it as a whole, and I only hope she will forgive me for the appendix.

There remains only the pleasant duty of acknowledging a great obligation. *Willa Cather: A Literary Life,* by James Woodress, seems to me one of the best biographies of any writer I have ever read. Professor Woodress and I live at opposite ends of the continent — California and Massachusetts — and we have never stood face-to-face; he therefore owes me nothing. But he tells me that he has been familiar with my work since he was in graduate school, and he has undertaken the not-inconsiderable chore of reading my manuscript to check it for factual accuracy. This seems to me a fine example of scholarly kindness and courtesy at its best, and I am extremely grateful. For his protection, I suppose I must add that he has no responsibility whatever for any of my literary judgments or critical evaluations.

Edward Wagenknecht
February 1993

Chronology

1912   First trip to Southwest. First novel, *Alexander's Bridge,* published by Houghton Mifflin Company.

1913   June. *O Pioneers!,* first novel making use of her Nebraska memories.

1915   *The Song of the Lark.*

1917   First visit to Jaffrey, New Hampshire; first honorary degree.

1918   *My Ántonia.*

1920   Leaves Houghton Mifflin Company for Alfred A. Knopf, who publishes all her remaining books, beginning with *Youth and the Bright Medusa.*

1922   Publishes *One of Ours,* which wins Pulitzer Prize; first summer on Grand Manan Island in the Bay of Fundy; is confirmed in the Episcopal Church.

1923   *A Lost Lady.*

1925   *The Professor's House.*

1926   *My Mortal Enemy.*

1927   *Death Comes for the Archbishop.*

1931   *Shadows on the Rock.*

1932   *Obscure Destinies* (short stories).

1935   *Lucy Gayheart.*

1936   *Not under Forty* (essays).

1937–   Autograph Edition of collected fiction published.
1938,
1941

1940   *Sapphira and the Slave Girl.*

1947   April 24. Death at 570 Park Avenue, New York City.

1948   *The Old Beauty and Others* (short stories).

Part 1

1

A Writer's Life

Willa Cather[1] was born in Back Creek Valley, near what is now Gore, Virginia, on December 7, 1873,[2] the first child of Charles Fetigue Cather and his wife, Mary Virginia Boak. The Cather family seems to have originated in Wales, but family tradition averred that after the Restoration King Charles II showed his appreciation of their loyalty to his father during the civil war by bestowing a grant of land in County Tyrone, Ireland, upon them, and it was from Ireland that Jasper Cather came to Pennsylvania around 1750 and, after having fought in the Revolution, came to Back Creek Valley. Jasper's son James strongly disapproved of both slavery and secession, but because he believed in states' rights, he took the Confederate side in the American Civil War. James's son William, who built Willow Shade, where Willa Cather lived during her childhood, was however a strong Union man. Two of his sons left Virginia to avoid being forced into the Confederate Army, and his remarkable sister, Sidney Gore, ministered impartially to those on both sides of the conflict. The sympathies of the Boaks, on the other hand, were strongly Confederate, and it was for the South that Willa's uncle, William Sibert Boak, died, though in her "Namesake" story, she considerably transferred him to the Union side.

Charles Cather was a sweet, probably not over-forceful man, whose gentleness his eldest daughter loved. When he was sheep farming in Willow Shade days, he made shoes for the feet of his favorite sheepdog. His wife, Mary Virginia, generally called Jennie, was of sterner stuff, a handsome, proud, imperious Southern lady, capable of disciplining her children with a rawhide whip. She was not a domestic tyrant. Intent upon her children's developing their own individuality, she allowed them more latitude than many parents did in her time, and when Willa wished to go to college, she supported her to the limit, even though her husband had to borrow money to send her. But there were certain things the children might not do, and when they disobeyed she saw to it that they lived to regret it; none of them seem to have held it against her. She bore six more after Willa: Roscoe (1877); Douglass (1880); Jessica (1881); James (1886); Elsie (1890); and John (1892); the first three, like Willa, in Virginia and the rest after the move to Nebraska. If we may trust her daughter's portrait of her as Victoria Templeton in "Old Mrs. Harris," she resented her frequent pregnancies.

The move was made in 1883, when Willa was "going on ten," to a farm in Webster County, where other members of the family, prompted apparently by both health and economic considerations, including Willa's Uncle George and Aunt Franc, had already settled. Charles and Jennie set up a crowded household, which included Jennie's mother, who read the Bible and *The Pilgrim's Progress* with Willa and whose importance to her may be gauged from her portrait as old Mrs. Harris, and Margie Anderson, who became both Mandy in that story and Mahailey in *One of Ours*. But since Charles, who had had two years of legal study, was not the stuff of which pioneers are made, it is not surprising that after some eighteen months he should have moved his family into Red Cloud, a division point on the Burlington Railroad, where eight passenger trains stopped daily on their run between Kansas City and Denver and where he opened an office in which, as James Woodress puts it, he "made farm loans, wrote contracts, and sold insurance."

After Willa Cather had firmly placed Nebraska on the American literary map with *O Pioneers!* and *My Ántonia,* it became so easy to think of her as a "regional" writer that some readers were even disappointed in some of her later books because they did not deal with her "own" material. But she was never in this sense "regional," nor did she think Nebraska superior to other places because she had grown up there; had her lot been cast elsewhere, her materials might have been very different, but her aims and methods would have been much the same. In *My Ántonia* when Jim Burden arrives in Nebraska, he feels as though he had been "erased, blotted out" between earth and sky, and Willa's own experience was much the same. She feared she might die in a cornfield, swallowed up, absorbed in a land "as bare as a piece of sheet metal." She called Nebraska both "the happiness and the curse of my life," and it took her a long time to get it into perspective. It is beautiful in such early stories as "The Treasure of Far Island" and that brief masterpiece, "The Enchanted Bluff," but "On the Divide," "Eric Hermannson's Soul," "The Sculptor's Funeral," and "A Wagner Matinee" are quite bleak enough to remind us that as late as

1898 she headed one of her Nebraska letters "Siberia." As long as
her parents lived, she returned home again and again, often for extended visits, and when her train crossed the Missouri River, "the
very smell of the soil tore [her] to pieces," but she never went back
there to live nor yet to write.[3]

The early reviewer of O Pioneers! who remarked that a scat-
tered effect might have been expected from a novel that took its title
from Whitman but was dedicated to Sarah Orne Jewett had managed the one thing in the world that is only less difficult than being
exactly right; he had managed to get it exactly wrong. Even while
her heart clung most passionately to the Western land, Willa Cather
was hungry for the art, music, literature, and culture then identified
largely with the East, so that when she stepped into Mrs. Fields's
parlor at 148 Charles Street in Boston, she felt like "an American of the Apache period," and if the division in her mind thus
indicated did not always make for her comfort, it did contribute
importantly toward the development of that complex amalgam that
was her art. She once wrote that "the shapes and scenes that have
'teased' the mind for years, when they do at last get themselves
rightly put down, make a much higher order of writing, and a much
more costly, than the most vivid and vigorous transfer of immediate
impressions." For literary purposes Miss Cather treated Nebraska
quite as she treated all the other experiences of her life. None of
them were of use to her as a writer until she had assimilated them
and possessed them in memory and made them a part of herself.
The Nebraska that was real to her was the Nebraska she carried in
her heart.

In a sense she never got out of Red Cloud any more than Mark
Twain got out of Hannibal, for all the small towns in her stories are
Red Cloud, no matter what she calls them or where they are placed.
But Nebraska in the 1880s was not quite the cultural wilderness
Easterners have sometimes assumed. Alfred Kazin startles when he
writes that "Amiel wrote letters to a nephew who died among the
Nebraska farmers; Knut Hamsun worked on a farm just across the
state line in South Dakota; a cousin of Camille Saint-Saëns lived
nearby in Kansas."[4] Willa Cather had more formal early schooling
than she sometimes claimed, and her extracurricular cultural oppor-
tunities were considerably more important. She learned Latin and
Greek from an Englishman named William Ducker, who clerked in
his brother's store, and her Aunt Franc, a Mount Holyoke graduate, organized "cultures" for the study of the standard English
and American writers. The "quality" American magazines had their

subscribers in Red Cloud. The Wieners, a cultured Jewish family
who became the Rosens in "Old Mrs. Harris," and who spoke both
French and German, made young Willa free to use their excellent
library. Mrs. Miner (the Mrs. Harling of *My Ántonia*), a fine pi-
anist who introduced Willa to standard music, was the daughter of a
member of the Royal Norwegian Orchestra. The Red Cloud Opera
House, built about 1885, booked many traveling shows, and after
Willa Cather moved to Lincoln, she had a far better chance to see
all the outstanding actors and actresses of the time than any American outside of New York City has today. Moreover the culture in
which she grew up in Nebraska was considerably more cosmopolitan than what she would have had if she had stayed in Virginia.
Readers of her novels may sometimes assume that the only Eu-
ropeans she knew were Norwegians and Bohemians, but her first
playmates, the Lichtenstein children, were Germans; and Swedes,
Danes, Swiss, and French Canadians were among the others who
came her way. On Sunday church services of various denominations
were conducted in various languages. According to Philip Garber,
no fewer than twenty-three nations were represented among the
purchasers of Burlington land.

In June 1890 Willa Cather was graduated from Red Cloud High
School, fluttering the dovecotes with an oration on "Superstition
versus Investigation" in which she championed vivisection even by
amateurs. In sharp contrast to her later attitude, she deplored glorification of the past and denigration of the present; the nineteenth,
she declared, was the greatest of centuries. "It is the most sacred
right of man to investigate; we paid dearly for it in Eden; we have
been shedding our blood for it ever since; it is ours; we have bought
it with a price." Without scientific research there could be no progress. All the lives lost in scientific experimentation were insignificant
compared to the good done by one great discovery, such as Harvey's of the circulation of the blood. "If we bar our novices from
advancement, whence shall come our experts?"

If this was hardly "womanly," much less girlish, by 1890 standards, to be womanly was at this time the last thing Willa Cather
desired. She professed to dislike all strictly feminine household arts,
and all her aspirations were set upon a medical career. She had
worked in William Ducker's basement laboratory and made friends
with two Red Cloud physicians, one of whom had allowed her to
administer chloroform while he performed an amputation. She dis-
sected frogs and toads and other small animals and professed to
enjoy it, and she distressed her mother by cutting her hair short

and wearing boys' clothes, as some very unattractive photographs of her in Bernice Slote's *Willa Cather: A Pictorial Memoir* remain to testify. When she appeared in amateur theatricals she specialized in male roles.

In the fall of 1890 Willa Cather was enrolled in the University of Nebraska at Lincoln, where she remained for five years, since, the high school preparation available in Red Cloud having been insufficient to equip her fully for college level work, she had to be enrolled first in a preparatory course. Though the University of Nebraska was at this time a fledgling, freshwater institution, there were good scholars on the faculty and distinguished men- and women-to-be in the student body. Dorothy Canfield's father was chancellor. Alvin Johnson, future founder of the New School for Social Research, was a student, and Miss Cather was intimate with Roscoe Pound, future dean of the Harvard Law School, and his sister Louise, who would be an outstanding philologist and folklorist and the first woman president of the Modern Language Association (of which more hereinafter). In her freshman year, Willa, still supposing her main interest to be in science, took chemistry and math (the math earned her a condition she did not succeed in working off until just before graduation). Thereafter most of her work was in English literature, with a sizable amount of Greek and Latin, French, and some German. Yet she had no sympathy with literary scholarship in the technical sense and conducted something of a running feud with the head of the department of English, Professor Lucius A. Sherman.

She herself later gave the credit — or the blame — for her switch from science to the humanities to the instructor who sent her precocious essay on Carlyle to the *Nebraska State Journal* without her consent ("what youthful vanity can be unaffected by the sight of itself in print?"), and thereafter she lived only to write. She abandoned her mannish clothes and short haircut early in her college career and was active in college dramatics and, above all, publications. In 1893 she began contributing to the *Journal* at a dollar a column. "Hard times" had hit Nebraska, and the Cathers did not escape the pinch. Yet though Willa did send some of the money she earned home, it may be that both she and Edith Lewis exaggerated the importance of financial need at the beginning of her journalistic career. She later believed that what the *Journal* gave her was good pay for her "high-stepping rhetoric," and her passion for self-expression being what it was at this time, it seems likely that she would have written for nothing rather than not write at all. In any case, the bulk of her journalistic writing is very large (the best of it has now been gathered in *The Kingdom of Art* and *The World and the Parish*), and she never really abandoned journalism until after she had left *McClure's*.

The twelvemonth following graduation was a difficult time for Miss Cather. She tried to get a teaching position at the university without success; it may be that Professor Sherman prevented this. In June 1896 however she received and accepted an offer to go to Pittsburgh and help edit the *Home Monthly*, a short-lived periodical that aspired to challenge the *Ladies' Home Journal* and, to put it gently, never did. Since she was obliged to supply much copy herself in order to fill up space, it is not surprising that a number of her early stories should have been published here. "Peter," in the *Mahogany Tree* of Boston in May 1892, had been her first story in print, and in June 1896 the *Overland Monthly* published "On the Divide," but it was not until April 1900, when the *Cosmopolitan* published "Eric Hermannson's Soul," that she appeared in a magazine of truly national circulation. But she also filled many *Home Monthly* pages with what must have seemed to her quite meaningless chatter upon various aspects of domestic arts that the readers of women's magazines wished to read about in those days or that their editors thought they did. It is not surprising to find Willa Cather serving the Pittsburgh *Leader* between 1897 and 1900 not only as book and drama critic but also as telegraph editor.

From 1901 to 1906 Miss Cather earned her living in Pittsburgh as a high school teacher, first at Central High School, then at Allegheny. During her first term she was required to teach Latin and algebra as well as English, which nearly killed her: she lost twenty pounds. She had a good working knowledge of Latin, but to teach it was another matter, and mathematics was always her bête noire. Thereafter it was all English, which she seems to have done well, though it is clear that the student responses to her strong personality were varied. Her most illustrious pupil seems to have been Norman Foerster.

Her first two books were published during this period: the first edition of her only volume of poems, *April Twilights,* in 1903, through a better than usual "vanity" publisher, Richard G. Badger, of Boston, and a collection of short stories, *The Troll Garden,* in 1905, through McClure, Phillips & Co. But altogether the happiest event of Willa Cather's Pittsburgh years was her meeting with the friend of friends in her life, Isabelle McClung, who rescued her from boardinghouses and gave her a place to live and to write in the spacious Murray Hill Avenue mansion of her parents, Judge and Mrs.

Samuel A. McClung. In 1902, with Isabelle, Willa Cather made her first trip abroad, to England and France;[5] in 1905 they spent two months in Nebraska, Wyoming, and South Dakota; and in 1908 they would go to Italy together.

What seemed the big chance in Willa Cather's professional life came her way in May 1906, when she moved to New York to become a member of the editorial staff of *McClure's Magazine*, currently notable not only for its sensational exposés of corruption in business and politics but also for publishing first-rate fiction by the foremost English and American writers in a magazine that sold for fifteen cents instead of the twenty-five or thirty-five commanded by *Harper's, Scribner's*, the *Atlantic Monthly*, and the *Century*. Alerted to her by one of his talent scouts, the mad publishing genius, Samuel S. McClure, had been in touch with her since 1903, when he peremptorily summoned her to New York for an interview, during which he practically offered her the world with a fence around it, and she joined him at the right moment, just when John Phillips, Ida M. Tarbell, Lincoln Steffens, and Ray Stannard Baker, weary of his professional and personal idiosyncrasies, resigned in a body to become the founders of the *American Magazine;* in 1908 she would become managing editor, which position she held until 1911, when she took a leave of absence, not definitely resigning until after McClure had lost control. Whether this experience helped or hindered Miss Cather as a writer is debatable. It introduced her to New York, Boston, and London, and established many useful contacts for her. Nor is there any doubt as to her successful performance of her duties; McClure himself called her the best of magazine executives. But though he had been attracted to her by her writing, he had or developed serious doubts as to her literary potential, and all his influence was in the direction of encouraging her to develop her capacities in the sphere in which she could be most useful to him and his far-flung enterprises. As for her, though she was certainly not unaware of her chief's limitations, she was not only fond of him but passionately loyal. As a labor of love she "ghosted" his autobiography,[6] for which she received neither cash nor credit; in his old age, when he was destitute, both she and Ida Tarbell contributed to his support, and in 1944, when both were being honored by the National Institute of Arts and Letters, this reserved, undemonstrative lady astonished everybody by going to him on the platform and throwing her arms about him to embrace him.

After Miss Cather had been working for McClure about eight months, he gave her her first important assignment. One Georgine

Milmine had submitted a manuscript that ultimately became *The Life of Mary Baker G. Eddy and the History of Christian Science*, first serialized in *McClure's* and then, in 1909, published as a book by Doubleday, Page. McClure had recognized it on sight as a potential sensation but also as quite unpublishable in the form in which its author had left it. The subject was highly controversial, and the Christian Science Church was known to be vigilantly aggressive in guarding the reputation of its founder. Miss Cather was therefore despatched to Boston and New Hampshire, where she remained through 1907 and part of 1908, not only to rewrite the text but also to check the author's research. The full extent of the work she did was never acknowledged by her except in one 1922 letter. One Cather scholar, L. Brent Bohlke, believes not only that this "necessitates the inclusion" of the Eddy book in the Cather canon but also that Miss Cather's work on it exercised an important influence upon her fiction.[7] Whether or not one accepts this, it is certain that the New England sojourn, quite apart from the Eddy matter, did importantly influence Willa Cather's career. In Boston she met Mrs. James T. Fields,[8] Margaret Deland, Louise Imogen Guiney, Mr. and Mrs. Louis D. Brandeis, and, above all, Sarah Orne Jewett, who probably more deeply influenced her theory and practice of fiction than any other single person, besides, of course, Ferris Greenslet, the great Houghton Mifflin editor, who published her first four novels.

In 1912 Willa Cather encountered another of the great formative influences of her life. Having gone west to visit her brother Douglass in Winslow, Arizona, she saw the cliff dwellings in Walnut Canyon (Panther Canyon in *The Song of the Lark*), and when she revisited the Southwest three years later, she saw Mesa Verde and traveled to Taos, New Mexico, then still far from having become a tourist center. Though she told Elizabeth Shepley Sergeant that she finally had to "make tracks for home" because she felt the Southwest was consuming her, she seems to have made her vital contact with this region both more quickly and more passionately than she had with Nebraska, and with the beautiful young Mexican, Julio, she seems to have come closer to really falling in love with a man than she ever did again. She never wrote "The Blue Mesa," the novel she once contemplated about the Southwest, nor yet the travel book she perhaps less seriously pondered, but nobody who knows her books needs to be told that she still made distinguished use of these materials in both *The Song of the Lark* and *The Professor's House*. Surely Dorothy Van Ghent did not exaggerate when she compared the "shock of recognition" Willa Cather experienced when she saw the ruins of the cliff dwellers with "that felt by Keats when he first saw the Elgin marbles." Willa Cather "admired the Indians' communal way of life, their respect for the environment, and the organic forms of their dwellings and their arts," and David Stouck too sees the 1912 excursion as "one of the most creative adventures in [Miss Cather's] imaginative life." "These Indians adjusted their lives collectively to the natural laws of the universe, never exploiting their environment nor setting themselves against it, but living very much within it."[9]

In the fall of 1911 Miss Cather, in association with Isabelle Mc-Clung, took a house in Cherry Valley, New York, and henceforth devoted all her working time to the writing of fiction. With this her apprenticeship ends and her serious accomplishment as a writer begins. From here on therefore her biography becomes essentially a record of the publication of her various books. This does not mean that it was roses all the way. Neither her fame nor her vogue were easily or quickly won. She had many painful and trying illnesses, and in her last years especially, many sorrows, when, like all persons who live fairly long lives, she saw her friends and members of her family dying around her. Nor did she escape her own personal maladies of the spirit, some of which shall be noted hereinafter as they seem to be reflected in the changing tones and themes of her books.

In the fall of 1911 however all this was still far away. In August 1912 *McClure's Magazine* published "The Bohemian Girl," in which she made a more extensive and ambitious use of her Nebraska background than anything else she had written yet, and though "The Bohemian Girl" is still far below the level of *O Pioneers!*, with which, in 1913, as most of her interpreters would agree, she came at last into her kingdom, we should remember that she was already writing or pondering "Alexandra," which later, combined with the tragic Emil Bergson–Marie Tovesky story, originally conceived separately as "The White Mulberry Tree," would constitute *O Pioneers!*. Willa Cather never thought very highly of "The Bohemian Girl" nor allowed it to be reprinted during her lifetime. When *McClure's* offered her 750 dollars for it, she refused to accept more than 500 dollars, and once, when I expressed some interest in it, she said that if I were looking for evidence against her, she thought " 'A Death in the Desert' " ought to be bad enough for me. In April 1912, when Houghton Mifflin Company published her first, rather Jamesian novel, *Alexander's Bridge*, probably none of this seemed very important to her. But she soon changed her mind about *Alexander's Bridge,* repudiating it much too harshly as a "studio picture" and not her own material.[10] *O Pioneers!* followed in little over a year later, and its author had known from the first that it was either a total failure or something rather splendid. It was something of a novelty both in form and subject matter (one critic was quoted as saying that he did not "give a damn" about what happened in Nebraska, no matter who wrote about it), but its critical reception was promising and its sales at least good enough to encourage the author and her publishers to go on.

It was suitable therefore that in 1912 Miss Cather should have established herself in her first real home in New York, the large apartment at 5 Bank Street that she shared with Edith Lewis, and from which they were ejected only in 1927 when the building was razed in the name of "progress." Obviously the publication and the success of *O Pioneers!* gave a considerable boost to her morale, and she followed it in 1915 with the most extensive novel she ever wrote, *The Song of the Lark,* in which she combined her knowledge of the West and her passion for music and the theater in a story of the making of a great prima donna, modeled upon Olive Fremstad. It is true that the *Lark,* considerable achievement though it was, was afterwards, like the *Bridge,* though far less harshly, repudiated by its creator on the ground that its Dreiser-like method of telling everything about everybody was not really congenial to her mind or art. What we may call the first phase of the writer's career as a novelist came to a triumphant end in 1918 in *My Ántonia,* in which she returned to and further developed the methods she had used in *O Pioneers!* and which is now recognized as one of the masterpieces of early twentieth-century American fiction.

Meanwhile, in 1917, with Isabelle McClung and the latter's husband, the violinist Jan Hambourg, Miss Cather discovered a new beloved land in Jaffrey, New Hampshire. To the Shattuck Inn there she would often return during the coming years, and it was in Jaffrey's Old Cemetery there that she would choose, when the time came, to be buried, within sight of Mount Monadnock. It was in 1917 too that she received her first honorary degree, from the University of New Hampshire; this would be followed by degrees from Michigan (1924); Columbia (1928); Yale (1929); California and Princeton (both, 1931); and Smith (1933). In 1931 she would receive the Howells Medal of the American Academy of Arts and Letters, to be followed by the Prix Femina Américain in 1933 and the Gold Medal of the National Institute of Arts and Letters in 1944.

After *My Ántonia,* dissatisfied with both the appearance and the exploitation of her books, Willa Cather decided to leave Houghton Mifflin for the then-fledgling firm of Alfred A.Knopf that was destined to become one of the most distinguished of all publishing houses. *Youth and the Bright Medusa* (1920), which reprinted four stories from *The Troll Garden* and added four new ones, was her first book under the Borzoi imprint, followed in 1922 by her World War I novel, *One of Ours,* which received a divided press but sold well and was awarded the Pulitzer Prize. Willa Cather's own account of how she approached Knopf in his office without an introduction and proposed that he become her publisher is another of her fictions; he had been wooing her for some time, and it was not until after he had successfully marketed *Youth* that she decided to give *One of Ours* to him rather than to Houghton Mifflin. After receiving the news, Ferris Greenslet wished her Godspeed and promised to go home and read the Book of Job. What followed was one of the happiest author-publisher relations in American letters, and Willa Cather never published another book except under the Borzoi imprint.

One of Ours is the first of the four Cather novels that I have classified as novels of frustration, following on the heels of three novels of fulfillment. It takes us into the world Willa Cather surveyed in her *Nation* article on Nebraska. The splendid story of the pioneers was finished, and it had been succeeded by nothing worthy of taking its place, so that for Claude Wheeler there was no "out" save death in a war he fought with muddleheaded idealism, whose bright hopes, insofar as they were not moonshine from the beginning, were all destined to be betrayed, and about the most cheerful note struck in *A Lost Lady* (1923), *The Professor's House* (1925), and *My Mortal Enemy* (1926) was Godfrey St. Peter's conclusion that it is possible, when necessary, to learn to live without delight.

The somber tone of these books did not hamper either their creator's sales or the increasing growth of her fame, and if they caused any of her readers to worry about her personally, these fears must have been assuaged by the radiance of *Death Comes for the Archbishop* (1927) and *Shadows on the Rock* (1931). It is true that since both the *Archbishop* and the *Rock* were historical novels, there were some who felt that in her search for peace Willa Cather had retreated further than ever from her own time and achieved a reconciliation only with the past. But she had always been a novelist of memory, viewing her materials as in retrospect, from a considerable distance, after time had mellowed them, softened harsh outlines, and extracted their essence; the break these readers thought they discerned here was therefore less marked than it might have been with another kind of writer. The Southwest she had lived with and possessed imaginatively for a long time before writing the *Archbishop*. The Quebec of the *Rock,* which was set in the seventeenth century, she saw first in 1927; the principal link with the writer's past here must be sought in the long-standing consanguinity she had enjoyed with the French spirit.

For all the serenity of these books, the *Rock* in particular came out of the most troubled period in their creator's private life. In March 1927 Willa Cather's much-loved father died, and in December her mother suffered a stroke that left her helpless and speechless, though fully conscious, until she too died in September 1931. A happier event of these years was Miss Cather's discovery of another unchanging refuge in an unhappily changing world in Grand Manan Island in the Bay of Fundy, where she built a small cottage, the only piece of real estate she ever owned. In 1931 she and Edith Lewis moved their possessions out of the "temporary" refuge they had inhabited in the Grosvenor Hotel upon being ejected from Bank Street and established themselves in their last home at 570 Park Avenue. There Willa Cather enjoyed every material comfort during her last years, though she was never quite easy in her mind, wondering whether the uniformed doorman would have admitted the likes of my Ántonia should she have been able to come to call.

In the thirties too Willa Cather returned to Nebraska as a source of literary material with *Obscure Destinies* (1932) and *Lucy Gayheart* (1935). The former comprises three short stories in her best and maturest vein, and *Lucy Gayheart* is a sad, sweet love story, which, after the *Lark* also marks Willa Cather's most important fictional use of her interest in music. Like the heroine of the *Lark,* the much softer, sweeter, and gentler Lucy goes to Chicago to study. But in 1938 both Douglass Cather and his sister's very dearest friend, Isabelle McClung Hambourg, died, to be followed in 1942 by Roscoe Cather. For such things there was no adequate compensation, not even in the smashing, unexpected success of the *Rock,* in spite of the minor key in which it was played, her all-time bestseller, nor the privilege of numbering such notables as Thomas Hardy, Sir James Barrie, Justice Oliver Wendell Holmes, and President Masaryk among her admirers, nor yet the satisfaction of being "collected" in the limited Autograph Edition of her works, designed by the great American bookman, Bruce Rogers.[11]

Her last published novel, *Sapphira and the Slave Girl,* appeared in 1940; except for two or three inconsequential early tales, this was the only time she had ever gone back as a writer to the Shenendoah Valley of her earliest youth, and nothing could have been more appropriate than that she should have included herself as a child in the epilogue. When she died on April 24, 1947, she left the three stories that Knopf published in 1948 as *The Old Beauty and Others* and the uncompleted manuscript of another historical novel, "Hard Punishments," set at Avignon in the days of the divided papacy.[12] Though she had long been struggling with failing health, her end was sudden and unexpected and her death peaceful. Only twelve days before she had been planning another trip west come summer. She spent her last day in bed and ate her lunch there. Afterwards she slept and woke up with a headache. A cerebral hemorrhage took her without warning about four o'clock in the afternoon.

2

Storing the Well

1

Before writing, reading; for there is an apostolic succession in art as well as in religion. Every now and then we hear of a "natural" or "original" genius who creates directly from life without the intervention of literary antecedents, but further investigation has a way of disproving this assumption. So it has been with Robert Burns and, later, with Mark Twain.

As we shall see in succeeding chapters, much of Willa Cather's best material came from her own experiences and those of her friends. Even such materials were handled however in the light of what the author had learned from her reading and the literary ideals she had thus formulated. It seems fitting therefore that before turning to what she believed about writing and how she tried to write, we should attempt a brief survey of her own reading and her reactions to it.

There were books in the homes in which she lived during her childhood, and she early came in contact with most of what were called classics in her time and with many others whose reputations have now faded. *Robinson Crusoe* and *Gulliver's Travels* are stars that still shine brightly, but *The Swiss Family Robinson, John Halifax, Gentleman,* and *The Prince of the House of David* are now only names even to many well-read persons. Many other titles will emerge in this and succeeding chapters, but no cataloguelike tabulation will be attempted. The books and authors that were really important to her cannot however be left out.

Like most civilized Americans in her time, Willa Cather drank in the Bible with her mother's milk, and one need only read her essay on Thomas Mann's *Joseph and His Brothers* in *Not under Forty* to realize how much it meant to her. But with her as with so many others, Bunyan's *Pilgrim's Progress* was so closely associated with it as almost to share its authority. Bunyan was in her mind all her life; in Europe in 1902 she wrote that "from the terrace at St. Germain, Montmartre, with the purple city below, looks like the city of St. John's vision, or the heavenly City that Bunyan saw across the river." And in the last novel she ever published, Henry Colbert comforts himself by reading not only *The Pilgrim's Progress* but also *The Holy War.* "An honest man, who had suffered much, was speaking to him of things about which he could not unbosom himself to anyone." She had and loved the standard collections of fairy tales and folk tales, and her mythology embraced northern Europe as well as Greece and Rome, but generally speaking she disparaged books written especially for children because she wanted them to get to the classics as early as possible. She loved *Alice's Adventures in Wonderland,* though she got a little tired of it the winter she had to read it sixteen times to a little brother. She blows more cold than hot on Louisa May Alcott and Frances Hodgson Burnett, but she loved Howard Pyle as both writer and artist. She was consistent too in her dislike of "the worst sort of fiction," mystery stories, "which wronged and exaggerated and distorted" human nature, "all for the sake of keeping the web sufficiently tangled."

Though she considered herself a poor linguist, she had pretty good linguistic training, both in the classroom and out of it. Her first important contact with a classical masterpiece was made in childhood, at a considerable remove, through Pope's translation of the *Iliad*. In her college days she appeared in a production of scenes from classical plays, and one of her first published poems, in the *Hesperian* in 1892, was a translation of a Horatian ode. One of her students has recorded that as a high school teacher, she placed great stress on tracing English words to their Latin roots. The importance of Virgil's *Georgics* is obvious to all readers of *My Ántonia,* and, though the story is very different, the Emil-Marie tragedy in the "White Mulberry Tree" section of *O Pioneers!* has clearly been colored from the Pyramus and Thisbe story in Ovid's *Metamorphoses.* Much later, in *Shadows on the Rock,* Plutarch is one of Euclide Auclair's favorite writers, and at least one scholar sees a parallel between the behavior of Odysseus after his return to Ithaca and the way Bishop Latour establishes order in his diocese.[1]

Miss Cather's French and German began somewhat informally through her acquaintance with Mr. and Mrs. Charles Wiener in Red Cloud and with George Seibel and his wife in Pittsburgh. She apparently learned to read French easily but was always timid about speaking it, and I have no idea how much of her reading of French authors was done in the original and how much in translation. A tremendous Francophile, she once wrote that if France "were to take a landslide into the sea some day, there would not be much creative power of any sort left in the world."[2] It is not surprising, then, that when she met Flaubert's niece, Madame Franklin Grout, she should have taken "one of her lovely hands and kissed it, in homage to a great period, to the names that made her voice tremble."[3] This does not mean however that her Francophilia ever blurred her capacity for nice distinctions or tempted her to denigrate English and American writers. In 1898, commenting on an *Atlantic* article by Henry Dwight Sedgwick, she wrote that French was a "totally uninspired language," incapable of "exalted spiritual fervor," and "as barren of reverence as a desert of dew," but rather "the language of sympathetic criticism ... of life, of manners and of art" as against English, "the tongue of prophesy," which is "the most spiritually suggestive language ever written." According to George Seibel, her reading companion in her Pittsburgh days, Willa, like Henry James, remained Anglo-Saxon in her literary ideals, but learned what she knew of critical theory and of fiction as an art from the great French writers.

When she first read Prosper Mérimée's *Colombe,* she thought it about the best piece of writing she had ever encountered. Of *The Crime of Sylvestre Bonnard,* by Anatole France, she wrote, "If there is any book more pure and delicate of flavor, more rich in high sentiment than this one, I do not know it." She loved Daudet, and when she was in Europe in 1902, she found it a relief to turn her back on Monte Carlo and get into the Daudet country. But first and last it was Flaubert who was the king of them all, especially in *Salammbô,* a choice that shows the same basically romantic taste that had made her revel in Hugo and the elder Dumas. In Rouen she thought of Flaubert and Guy de Maupassant (but not of Joan of Arc). Woodress finds that she herself had much in common with Flaubert — "dedication to art, mistrust of science, lack of interest in politics, and a desire for privacy." Verlaine, a "satyr converted to the most ecstatic form of ascetic Christianity," put both her charity and her understanding to a severe test. "He was imprisoned again and again for unmentionable and almost unheard of crimes, but he wrote some of the most beautiful and devout religious poetry in any language. He was a practicer of every excess known to man, yet if ever inspiration and spiritual rapture came from a human pen, it is in his verses on the Christ." But Zola was, if possible, an even harder nut for her to crack, probably because he wrote in prose and brought all the nastiness of life more nakedly before her. *Germinal,* a work of "magnificent genius and titanic power," inspired her to call him "perhaps the greatest mind in France," but she pitied him for his everlasting consciousness of evil.

One of Willa Cather's most interesting references to early European literature is in "The Marriage of Phaedra" (*The Troll Garden*), where she mentions Boccaccio, *The Romance of the Rose,* and *Amadis of Gaul* as having influenced the painter Hugh Treffinger, but whether or not she herself did any reading in this area is speculative. She is said to have discovered Tolstoy in cheap, paperback copies in a drugstore when she was fourteen. In *The Song of the Lark,* Thea Kronborg loved *Anna Karenina,* but, like Theodore Roosevelt, was disgusted by *The Kreutzer Sonata.* In "Old Mrs. Harris," Vickie finds Goethe's *Faust* and *Wilhem Meister* in the Rosens' library; he and Heine, whom she compares to A. E. Housman, were the Germans who meant most to her. She both praised and condemned Ibsen; in 1900 she published a long, detailed report on the production of *Hedda Gabler* in which Blanche Bates starred. In *O Pioneers!* we are told that Alexandra Bergson's mother had long portions of a much older famous piece of Scandinavian literature, the *Frithiof's Saga* of Esaias Tegnér, by heart. In 1898, when all America was reading *Quo Vadis?*, she played it down in comparison to Sienkiewicz's other novels, but it is impossible to tell from the reference whether she had read all the others herself or not. In later years, she greatly relished Thomas Mann, of whom she wrote admiringly in *Not under Forty* as well as Sigrid Undset, who returned her admiration to the extent of keeping Miss Cather's photograph on her writing desk.

Foremost among the English writers in Miss Cather's graces were Chaucer and Shakespeare, and Edith Lewis has recorded that during her last winter, she "turned almost entirely to them." Compared to Shakespeare, she says little about Chaucer, but late in life she wrote Stephen Tennant that reading *The Canterbury Tales* when she was very sick made her wish to get well and live. Shakespeare she almost deified, writing that "for him alone it was worth while that a planet should be called out of chaos and a race formed out of nothingness. He justified all history before him, and sanctified all history after him," and in her reviewing days she described his birthday as the second time "God ... turned his face in love toward man." Twice a week, she, Edith Lewis, and the three Menuhin children read him together, beginning, oddly, with the historical plays. And in *My Ántonia* Myra chooses to die on a cliff that reminds her of Gloucester's in *King Lear.*

With the two greatest English novelists, Scott and Dickens, she did little. In *One of Ours,* however, *Bleak House* is one of Mrs. Wheeler's favorite novels, and in the 1890s Willa herself named *David Copperfield* as her favorite Dickens novel: "But if I were to undertake to enumerate the beauties of *David Copperfield* I should have to write a book almost as long as it is." She could never, she said, read the account of David's return home after the birth of his half brother with dry eyes. After David himself, Sydney Carton was her favorite among "all Dickens' great characters." In judging just such characters God will show how much kinder and wiser he is than man.

The Scott story is more important. Willa's mother was a Scott enthusiast, but since she seems to have read Ouida and Marie Corelli with equal zest, this did not provide much guidance for her daughter. When in 1896, writing of J. M. Battle, Ian Watson, and S. R. Crockett, Willa Cather asks who ever talked of Scottish fiction twenty-five years ago, she makes one wonder whether she had ever heard of Scott. In 1899 she complained of his ponderousness as compared to Maurice Hewlett, but the only examples she cites are from *Ivanhoe,* and one wonders whether she had then read anything else. According to Edith Lewis, she never read the Scotch novels until late in life, when she capitulated completely, read and reread and even planned an essay on Scott to be called "Apologies to Heaven," which it would have been interesting to have alongside what was written about Scott by another, at first sight, unlikely admirer, Virginia Woolf. In *The Song of the Lark,* Dr. Archie loves both Scott and Burns,[4] and in one of Willa's very last stories, "Before Breakfast," Henry Grenfell gets "a great kick" out of "the old fellows: Scott and Dickens and Fielding." But it has remained for David Daiches to find a consanguinity of spirit between Scott and Miss Cather herself: "Scott, too, was concerned with the fate of heroic ideals in an age of commercial progress and in his best novels presented the essentially tragic perception that progress was incompatible with the survival of the ideal of heroic action."[5]

She admired Thackeray ("all the best things" made her think of him), and once at least she paired him with Shakespeare as "the two King Williams." George Eliot she habitually coupled with George Sand as "the two great Georges." She praised Charlotte Brontë, but I have found no reference to Emily; had she perhaps not read *Wuthering Heights?* She admired Hardy's *Tess of the D'Urbervilles,* but when *Jude the Obscure* was running in *Harper's,* she called it "arrant nonsense and driveling idiocy" and compared it to a series of "apoplectic fits." Jane Austen was granted a high place, and Robert Louis Stevenson, whom she adored, especially in her early and most romantic phase, was "the king and father of them all."

To the Romantic and Victorian poets she was well exposed. Of the great nonfiction prose writers, Carlyle and Ruskin were easily the most important to her, end she gave her 1891 essay on Carlyle[6] the credit for turning her primary interest from science to literature. Of Ruskin she wrote in her Pittsburgh days that he had taken "the wild and stirring strains of the peasant philosopher and set them to delicious harmony."

Of her comments on her British contemporaries and near contemporaries only examples can be given here. She lived at the right time to feel the full force of the Kipling epidemic and even interviewed him for the *Home Monthly,* but, though duly impressed, she was not overwhelmed, and by 1899 she was sure he was not growing and that his reputation would rest not on his poetry but on his prose. She admired Joseph Conrad but dismissed Arnold Bennett's *A Man from the North* as "a curious instance of a bad thing well done." Bernard Shaw obviously puzzled her; she appreciated his intelligence, but his methods and his temperament repelled her.[7] She knew that William Butler Yeats was a true poet but objected to his documentation: "poetry that has to be explained...usually would be as well unwritten." She sensed A. E. Housman's quality before he had made his reputation and sought him out when she went to England.

She called Joyce's *Ulysses* a "landmark" and appreciated Virginia Woolf. She met D. H. Lawrence and apparently liked him personally; and though she called him the most gifted writer of his generation, she objected that his books were overcrowded with "sensory reactions" and thought nothing could be worse than *Romeo and Juliet* rewritten in prose by him. When *The Prisoner of Zenda* was published ("not a great book, only a wonderfully charming and clever one"), she loved it enough to try to place Anthony Hope beside Stevenson, but she was disappointed in the author's later work, as she was by that of Maurice Hewlett after having been captivated by *The Forest Lovers,* and she hailed both Gilbert Parker and John Buchan at the beginning of their careers.

In her introduction to the two-volume collection of *The Best Stories of Sarah Orne Jewett* that Miss Cather put together for Houghton Mifflin Company in 1925, she wrote: "If I were asked to name the three American books which have the possibility of a long, long life, I would say at once, 'The Scarlet Letter,' 'Huckleberry Finn,' and 'The Country of the Pointed Firs.' I can think of no others that confront time and change so serenely."

On the first two titles, I venture to say, there could be no serious dissent from anybody whose judgment on such a matter is worth having. As to the third, it was at least an inevitable choice for her, for Sarah Orne Jewett, whom she knew toward the end of that writer's life, was one of the two American writers who influenced her most. The other of course was Henry James, and it may seem odd that she did not mention him in 1925, especially since in 1913 she had called him, Mark Twain, and Miss Jewett the three great American writers. Moreover neither her love for nor her debt to Miss Jewett inhibited her critical judgment in dealing with her work, for she also believed that "she was a very uneven writer. A good proportion of her work is not worth preserving." In fact she thought her own two-volume collection contained all the best stories.

She thought *The Tragic Muse* by Henry James "the only theatrical novel that has a particle of the real spirit of the stage in it," and in 1896 she was greatly impressed by even one of his least significant novels, *The Other House.* But her real commentary on James is her first novel, *Alexander's Bridge,* so plainly written in his manner, as well as a number of her short stories. Because she felt in her maturity that the methods James employed were not for her, it is sometimes assumed that she turned her back on him forever from *O Pioneers!* on, but this is not true; neither did she ever lose her admiration for him. To the very end she was fond of telling her story, as he so often did, from the point of view of an observer. I have commented elsewhere on some of her judgments of Mark Twain; she at least understood him well enough to reject Van Wyck Brooks's interpretation of him in *The Ordeal of Mark Twain* (1920). It is interesting that she should have placed *The Prince and the Pauper* alongside the Tom and Huck books, yet so scornfully rejected *Joan of Arc.* William Allen White must have been pleased that she should have thought his Boyville stories worth mentioning with *Tom Sawyer.*[8]

Naturally she knew all the "classical" American poets. Norman Foerster, who was one of her high school pupils in Pittsburgh, says she considered Emerson the foremost among them, but in 1895 she called Poe "the greatest of our poets," and then added strangely, "with the exception of Lowell, he is our only great poet." That she should have realized that Poe "did not die because he drank too much but because he ate too little" testifies to the soundness of both her heart and her judgment. Since a recitation in costume of *Hiawatha* was one of her war-horses in childhood, she must have responded warmly to Longfellow at this time, and there are two effectively placed quotations from him in *One of Ours*.[9] She is admirably balanced in her judgment of Whitman, being powerfully drawn to him by his stirring affirmation of life but repelled by his formlessness and lack of discrimination.[10] I am surprised to have found nothing on Emily Dickinson. Though Elizabeth Sergeant includes Carl Sandburg and Edgar Lee Masters among the later American poets Miss Cather respected, and though she herself took her title for one of the sections of *One of Ours* from Vachel Lindsay, Robert Frost seems to have been the only one of the stars of the "New Poetry" revival she really cared for. She disliked what she called "the free verse bunch" from the Middle West, and she loathed Amy Lowell personally. When Ferris Greenslet strangely asked her to write Amy's biography, she replied that she would not do it for the whole Lowell estate and would be equally interested in writing a history of the Chinese Empire.

She was kind to Stephen Crane and Frank Norris ("big and warm and sometimes brutal") and even to Ambrose Bierce (*In the Midst of Life*), and thought Harold Frederic a great man. In *McTeague* she thought Norris had carried his method too far in imitation of his French masters, but *Blix* was "an idyll that sings through one's brain like a summer wind and makes one feel young enough to commit all manner of indiscretions." She devoted a whole article to Mary Johnston's first two novels, *Prisoners of Hope* and *To Have and to Hold,* sensing at once their superiority to most of the other historical novels of the turn-of-the-century revival that less discerning critics have often classified with them. Much later she admired Thornton Wilder's *Our Town* so much that she wrote him a fan letter, and at one time or another she said kind things about Theodore Dreiser, Sinclair Lewis, F. Scott Fitzgerald, and Ernest Hemingway, but she was cold to Eugene O'Neill and thought Gertrude Stein too silly to talk about. Some of her choices seem rather odd for her. Probably her praise of H. L. Mencken was at least partly gratitude for the important role he had played in helping to build up her reputation; for all her customary aloofness, she was not above writing letters of thanks to people who had pleased her by intelligent reviews of her books. But Mencken must have squirmed to find himself coupled in her graces with W. C. Brownell.

2

An important supplement to reading was furnished to Willa Cather by the theater, where the printed page was interpreted by the living actor. Her love for the theater was passionate, especially in early life. Much of her journalistic writing was devoted to plays and actors, and her first book, for which she never found a publisher, was "The Player Letters," a collection of open letters, appreciative and evaluative, to various well-known theatrical personalities of the time. The manuscript seems not to have survived, but some portions of what had been published serially have been reprinted in *The World and the Parish*.[11] She had friends in the profession, Lizzie Hudson Collier, notably in Pittsburgh days and George and Florence Arliss in New York. Like Agnes Repplier, she was cold toward the crusade of the Gerry Society to prevent children from appearing on the stage. "It would be much wiser to remove all actresses over fifty than under fifteen." Perhaps no dramatic critic has ever been free of prejudices or idiosyncrasies, and certainly Willa Cather was not, but speaking generally, her work is amazingly competent for so young a writer and highly knowledgeable in its sense of dramatic values. It is not, I think, irrelevant to note in passing that though she was born a little too early to respond to the movies as some of her younger contemporaries did, she was intelligent enough to realize that the silent film was a better expression of the medium than the "talkie" and that Chaplin was the perfect film actor.[12]

Helena Modjeska, Mrs. Fiske, and Joseph Jefferson are about the only actors Miss Cather praised without reservations. Modjeska, in 1894, had "done more to raise the standard of the American stage and the taste of the American people than any other actress." She makes a brief but impressive appearance in *My Mortal Enemy*. In 1899 Mrs. Fiske was the actress "upon whose frail shoulders the hope of our stage so largely rests"; two years before Willa had seen her in *Tess of the D'Urbervilles* four times in one week.[13] Jefferson was praised not only for his technique but for his irresistible humanity; in thirty-five years his Rip Van Winkle had no more gone stale than Schubert's "Serenade."

In 1897 Willa Cather called Sarah Bernhardt "the greatest artist in the world," but though she achieved some excellent descriptions of her performances,[14] she always shows a tendency to sacrifice her to Eleonora Duse, mainly on the ground of the latter's greater spirituality. Oddly enough, she seems to have felt sure of this without having herself seen Duse on the stage. "I do not believe that

Madame Bernhardt could be great in any role which did not contain the quality of evil." There is much contemporary evidence to the contrary however. Miss Cather wrote much that was eloquent about Richard Mansfield, yet in the end she tends to sacrifice him to Jefferson because, being "all nerves and temperament," he lacked Jefferson's winning humanity. Somewhat surprisingly, she thought his Shylock, which she had admired when she first saw it, inferior to that of Henry Irving, whom she elsewhere disparages. She hemmed and hawed over Julia Marlowe at first, but by 1890 she had been completely converted— "I no longer scorn Julia Marlowe because she is so passing fair" — and when she saw her Rosalind, she thought that if she had not "ensnared the very dream of Shakespeare, had he seen her play, he would have forgot the dream." Mary Anderson was "a sane, normal, and highly gifted woman," but, admirable though her relinquishment of the stage for marriage and motherhood might be in itself, it also showed that she had never been really touched by the "mysterious 'madness of art.'" She and Edwin Booth both figure as legends of the theater in "Two Friends."

The tremendous strength and power of Clara Morris greatly impressed Willa Cather at first ("Better work has never been done by any actress in any country"), and when she saw Olga Nethersole she called her "the most promising young actress I have ever seen, the only one I should mention in the same paragraph with Bernhardt." Later she was less enthusiastic about both these ladies, finding Clara Morris not only awkward but "coarse-grained, mentally and physically." E. S. Willard is praised for his ability to lose himself in his role. Nat Goodwin represents a class of young men with "more vitality than brains," but the critic does not seem to have held this against him. William H. Crane is admired for the same quiet, sane, decent American realism that she admired in James A. Herne but which for some strange reason seems not to have impressed her in Howells.

3

But it was not only literature and the theater upon which Willa Cather drew to store her well. Yet in view of her own marked ability at picture making in prose, she seems to have taken somewhat less from painting and sculpture than might have been expected. She reviewed art shows along with much else in her journalistic days, but her use of El Greco in *Death Comes for the Archbishop* is the most significant reference to a painter in her canonical works. She took the title for *The Song of the Lark,* which, as she afterwards found it necessary to explain, did not fit the book very well, from a painting by Jules Breton that she did not much admire. She did admire a much more precious treasure of the Art Institute of Chicago, Lorado Taft's fountain outside on Michigan Avenue, where the Great Lakes are personified in five beautiful girls, and used to stop off to see it every time she passed through the city. When she went to Europe for the first time in 1902, she visited the studios of Rossetti, Burne-Jones ("master of all English painters") and of Watts and Leighton, for whom she cared much less. In 1925 Walter Tittle reported that she was fond of the impressionists, especially Manet. For some reason she seems to have been less unfriendly to the modernists in painting than in the other arts, as witness her sympathetic handling of Don Hedger in "Coming, Aphrodite!," and Elizabeth Sergeant even says that at one time she had been interested in cubism and the Fauves. If this is true, however, these interests do not seem to have long survived.

But whatever the plastic arts may or may not have given Willa Cather, nobody doubts that music gave her more. She once declared that music was "just a little above" everything else, at the same time oddly calling Beethoven "the Shakespeare of music."[15] Her reverence for music was so great that she thought it inappropriate to sit down to hear the Boston Symphony on the radio without dressing for the occasion, a quaint touch that recalls how both Keats and Buffon put on their best attire to do their work. She made enough use of music in her writing to enable Richard Giannone to devote a whole book and a very good one to the subject. *The Song of the Lark,* in which Thea Kronborg becomes a Wagnerian prima donna, and *Lucy Gayheart,* in which the heroine falls in love with a great Lieder singer in Chicago, are the most obvious examples, but there are other, sometimes subtler examples: witness the memorable performance of *Mignon* in *The Professor's House,* the singing of the "Casta diva" from *Norma* in *My Mortal Enemy,* the use of the *Ring* in "Uncle Valentine," where the threatened industrialization of the valley is seen as a kind of *Götterdämmerung,* and, perhaps best of all, the distinguished use made of *Parsifal* in *One of Ours.*

It may seem surprising that a person to whom music meant so much as it did to Willa Cather should have been so completely indifferent to its technique and so completely free of any desire to produce it herself. When as a child she took piano lessons from one Professor Schindelmeisser, the original of Professor Wunsch in *The Song of the Lark,* she wanted neither to learn nor to practice but only to question him about his musical contacts and experiences in Europe. It seems odd that in "The Affair at Grover Station" (1900) she should have written that "the telegraph poles scored the sky like a musical staff as they flashed by, and the stars, seen between the wires, looked like the notes of some erratic symphony." Her own musical interest at this period was almost wholly in opera, where the personalities of the great singers interested her quite as much as the music they sang, and she certainly had not spent much time over scores. To what extent, one wonders, was her special enthusiasm for Olive Fremstad determined by Fremstad's being primarily a Wagnerian singer or, on the other hand, was Wagner endeared to her by her affection for the singer, both as an artist and a friend?

I have not found many comments on individual operas. One of the most interesting is her comment on Giuseppe Campanari's singing of the great baritone aria in *Hérodiade,* which she finds, "like all Massenet's music, full of [his] ever present sensuous spirituality...hinting of the warfare between the flesh and the spirit but giving the victory quite frankly and joyfully to the flesh." In 1895 there was a splendid description and evaluation of Verdi's *Falstaff,* both in itself and in comparison with the composer's other work. In 1900 she denigrates *The Barber of Seville* as lacking in "dramatic coherency," as against *Cavalleria Rusticana,* which means more than pleasing sound. Probably no reader of *My Ántonia* ever forgets the performance of *Camille* that Jim Burden and Lena Lingard attend in Lincoln, obviously by Clara Morris, though the actress is not named, in which the entr'acte music is from *La Traviata,* "so joyous and sad, so thin and far-away, so clap-trap and yet so heartbreaking."

Though Willa Cather never lost her interest in opera, in later years she seems to have become more concerned with Lieder and instrumental music. Her interest in Josef Hofmann, Josef Lhévinne, Myra Hess, Harold Samuels, and of course the Menuhins undoubtedly exercised some influence here, and certainly no reader of *Lucy Gayheart* needs to be reminded of her interest in the Lieder. Her enthusiasm for Ethelbert Nevin's music was influenced by her affection for the man, upon which I comment elsewhere; his death in 1901 inspired three poems: "Sleep, Minstrel, Sleep," "Arcadian Winter," and "Song." At least in early life, she seems to have preferred Edward MacDowell's instrumental music to his songs, but that is a blind spot she shared with the whole musical world, which persistently neglects the only composer who, in this aspect, can reasonably be compared to the great song writers of Germany and France.

As all the world knows, Willa Cather's favorite singer was Olive Fremstad, of whom more hereinafter, but her best critical writing about a singer was inspired by Victor Maurel, whom she heard in Chicago in 1895, as Falstaff and, with the trumpet-toned Heldentenor, to end all Heldentenors, Francesco Tamagno, in *Otello*. She was properly appreciative of Tamagno's "fire and fury" and "passion and tenderness," but her real enthusiasm was reserved for Maurel, whom she found perfect, as singer, actor, and personality.[16] Lillian Nordica she judged "proficient but spiritless." Emma Eames's power was largely intellectual and her charm that of "a certain dignity and severe, patrician beauty." Both Nellie Melba and Emma Calvé drew mixed notices. Melba's was "the greatest voice in all the world" ("O, the flawless perfection of her method, the magnificent certainty of her execution"), but if she was perfect, she was also colorless. Calvé of course was exactly what Melba was not, and Miss Cather praised her for her "magnificent, dramatic impulses, her abounding vigor, her warmth, her power, her caprices, her whole dynamic personality."[17] Perhaps Willa Cather's most curious treatment of a singer is that of the great English contralto, Clara Butt, another singer who was a law unto herself but in a totally different way from Calvé's. Sir Thomas Beecham said of her that when she sang "Land of Hope and Glory," she could be heard across the Channel. Willa Cather thought her voice magnificent but judged her to lack mind and soul. Those who did not like Clara Butt's voice called her a female baritone, but to find so devout a lady lacking in soul seems very odd.

3

How to Write Fiction

1

Like most young writers, Willa Cather began to produce fiction without any very clear-cut ideas about how stories should be told. As she observed in her essay on Katherine Mansfield, a writer must begin with a long period of writing for writing's sake, and the reader who runs through the notes on her early stories in the appendix to this book will quickly perceive that she tried almost every type of story and experimented with various ways of telling it. Later she developed and proclaimed some positive notions about what a writer should and should not do, but she never wholly ceased to experiment. Her canonical works are far indeed from being carbon copies of each other.

Her range has often been called a rather narrow one, and since her collected edition consists of only thirteen volumes, she is not generally rated a very prolific writer. Yet she set her scenes in the Midwest and the Southwest, Pittsburgh, New York, Chicago, Virginia, seventeenth-century Quebec, France during World War I, and, in her last uncompleted and unpublished novel, fifteenth-century France. As for her fecundity, James Woodress has conjectured that between 1893, when she began to contribute to the *Nebraska State Journal* and the year 1912, she "probably turned out more copy than appears in all her collected works of the following thirty-five years." Between September and January of her senior year in college she published ninety-five pieces. Moreover, even during the years of her fame, she wrote more than she published. Sometimes, she said, the Lord gave her the grace to tear up and destroy.

She usually worked at her writing two or three hours in the morning, doing her first draft by hand, very rapidly, according to Edith Lewis, "not stopping to change a word or phrase, intent only on capturing the flow of her ideas," and when she continued her work next day, she never went back over what she had written "until the whole thing was completed." She then proceeded to make a second draft on the typewriter, not always following the handwritten version. This second draft was then typed by her secretary, after which it was copied and revised by the author; sometimes there were several typed drafts. "For the most part," writes the Houghton Mifflin editor, Ferris Greenslet, "the style is toned down [in revision] rather than toned up.... Sentences are trimmed, words, phrases, even paragraphs omitted. The purgation of superfluities is structural as well as stylistic"[1] Nobody who has ever seen one of Miss Cather's letters or even the few pages of manuscript reproduced in the Autograph Edition can need to be told that the simple, graceful, flowing style of her best writing was not dashed off but hammered out.

Her principal idiosyncrasy in connection with writing was an inability to write except in congenial surroundings. In this connection she almost suggests the German poet who could compose only with the odor of decaying bananas in the room. When the Hambourgs prepared what they thought an ideal place for her at the Ville d'Avray while they were living in France, she found it impossible to work there. She once explained: "I cannot produce my kind of work away from the American idiom.... I must be where the stream of that [American] life flowing over me touches springs that release early caught and assimilated impressions." But the home of her brother Douglass in Arizona was very American and she could not write there either.

This does not at all mean that she demanded luxurious surroundings. When a fine desk was provided for her at Mount Desert Island, she had it replaced by a plain wooden table. At the Shattuck Inn in Jaffrey, New Hampshire, she and Edith Lewis lived in a small attic room that probably reminded her of what she had had in Red Cloud; there and in a tent a mile from the inn, she wrote in peace, and in the little cottage she built on Grand Manan Island she also wrote in an attic room, furnished with one chair and a table but giving a view of cliffs and the sea. But the scenery must not be too entrancing either, or it would distract her from her work. For some strange reason she preferred to correct her proofs out of doors. She did not do much public speaking, but upon at least one occasion her insistence upon congenial surroundings seemed to carry over into this area. When she gave the William Vaughn Moody Lecture at the University of Chicago, she disliked Mandel Hall so much that she declared she could not speak effectively in it and that she would never again accept an invitation to speak in such an unattractive auditorium!

James Woodress has said of Willa Cather that "she turned her own life and experiences into literature to a degree uncommon among writers." She stated repeatedly, not always in exactly the same form, that a writer "acquires" his "thematic material" before the age of fifteen. Once she made it twenty and at least once she said between eight and fifteen, thus ruling out her Virginia years. Her authorized biographer, E. K. Brown, believed that "there is very little sense or feeling" in her books "of what it means to be a very young child." Until she wrote *Sapphira and the Slave Girl,* she had used her Virginia memories only in four short stories. This, I believe, was not only because she believed with Virgil and Jim Burden that "Optima dies . . . prima fugit" [The best years are the first to go] but because she was so constituted that it took time for impressions to sink in with her; she needed distance to get them in perspective and make them ready to be recharactered in art. Joseph Wood Krutch seized unerringly upon this aspect of her art when he wrote that in her pages "events are seen frequently through the haze of distance; the thing immediately present is not these events themselves, but the mood in which they are recollected; and the effect is, therefore, not the vividness and harshness of drama but something almost elegiac in its softness."

Insofar as the sources of particular incidents and characters are concerned, this aspect of Miss Cather's work may best be considered in connection with the stories themselves, but some general characteristics do call for consideration here. All the small Midwestern towns in her fiction are Red Cloud, Nebraska, no matter what she calls them: Hanover in *O Pioneers!,* Moonstone in *The Song of the Lark,* Black Hawk in *My Ántonia,* Frankfort in *One of Ours,* Sweet Water in *A Lost Lady,* and Haverford in *Lucy Gayheart,* and the description of Black Hawk will do for all of them. It was "a clean, well-planted little prairie town, with white fences and good green yards about the dwellings, wide, dusty streets, and shapely little trees growing along the wooden sidewalks. In the center of the town there were two rows of new brick 'store' buildings, a brick schoolhouse, the courthouse, and four white churches." Young Willa's attic room, which must have been associated in her mind with the sewing room she used at the McClungs', survives in "The Best Years" and in the study St. Peter cannot bear to leave in *The Professor's House.* Willa's maternal grandmother, became both old Mrs. Harris and Rachel Blake in *Sapphira.* Margie Anderson, the "hired girl" the Cathers brought with them from Virginia, gave Willa both Mahailey in *One of Ours* and Mandy in "Old Mrs. Harris"; and both Uncle Valentine and Adriance Hilgarde in " 'A Death in the Desert' " have been derived in part from Ethelbert Nevin.

Her use of people she had known sometimes roused anger against her or raised ethical problems. She asked Dr. Julius Tyndale's permission before using him as a model for Dr. Engelhardt in "Double Birthday" (he said he was still "vain enough to feel flattered"), but she was not always so considerate nor her models so agreeable. Olive Fremstad too was delighted with the use made of her in *The Song of the Lark,* saying she could not make up her mind where she ended and Willa began, but Dr. Frederick Sweeney is said to have resented the use made in "The Voyage of the Anchises" section of *One of Ours* of the troopship diary he had permitted her to read, and Mencken rejected "A Diamond Mine" when she submitted it to the *Smart Set* because he feared it suggested Lillian Nordica's last husband sufficiently so that he might bring a libel suit (which indeed he considered doing). Miss Cather's use of her Aunt Franc as a model for Aunt Georgiana in "A Wagner Matinee" displeased their relatives enough to cause the author to tone down her description of what the years in Nebraska had done to her aunt in later printings of the story. Willa professed and I am sure felt great affection for Mrs. Silas Garber, the original of her lost lady, but she presented her in some situations much too unedifying to be relished by her surviving friends or Governor Garber's. But perhaps the most incredible thing she ever did along this line was to give the stupid and insensitive heroine of "Flavia and Her Artists" the very unusual first name and apparently some of the physical characteristics of her friend Dorothy Canfield's mother; it is not strange that, having done this, she should have told Mariel Gere that she wondered when she should be finished with making a fool of herself.

2

In English-speaking countries at least, there has always been another possible conflict in the realm of the arts — that between art and morality. Like Poe and like Henry James, Willa Cather rejected the idea that it is the function of the artist to teach. Of course an artist reveals his sense of values in what he writes and thus teaches incidentally, but he should not propagandize. "An artist should have no moral purpose other than just his art." He does not do his thing "because it is noble or good; he does it because his mind is so made that perfection in something or other is his chiefest need." And she took an even dimmer view of political or social propaganda. She had no desire to hear "economic symphonies and sonatas."

This never became a really serious problem for Willa Cather, however. Like both the masters I have here invoked, in refusing to view art as the handmaid of morality, she was never tempted to use her, instead, as the handmaid of immorality. She granted that, in her first phase, Yvette Guilbert was a perfect artist within her range. "But here is a singer who is a realist, who simply knocks the varnish off, who tells the truth and the most brutal form of the truth at that." But Willa Cather will not stop there. Guilbert may be as representative of her time as Rachel was of her own, but "if we have descended from the tragic muse to a grisette it is time to reflect." For being an artist involves having "ideals and...human worth" and conceiving "lofty things." "There is such a thing in life as nobility, and the novels which celebrate it will always be the novels which are finally loved." In her later years Miss Cather rejoiced that the novel was becoming more experimental, but she deplored the repeal of reticence that somehow seemed to go along with this. Different as they were, she loved *John Halifax, Gentleman, The Prisoner of Zenda, Trilby,* and *Shore Acres* for the same reason: they were all warm, human, sympathetic works that showed the good hearts of their writers and their faith in life. And when it comes to *Camille,* she even tends, I feel, rather to force the note: "There is only one great tragedy in life, the tragedy of sin, and no play has told it better than the lady of the camellias."

Probably few writers have ever been successful at every point in adjusting the respective claims of art and morality. Willa Cather's own decency certainly enters into her early judgments of Zola and Oscar Wilde. Browning himself shocked her with *A Blot in the 'Scutcheon.* "We have become accustomed to seeing the sins of men and women enacted, but who cares to witness the mistakes and tortures of children? Sins of innocence are not subjects for dramatic treatment." On occasion she was capable of even being shocked by a bare-legged Topsy and of finding so innocent a comedienne as Anna Held ("Won't You Come and Play Wiz Me?") "frankly sensual." Certainly she is absurdly severe in judging what she considers the sins of *The Yellow Book* and *The Chap-Book.* Nor is her judgment purely aesthetic when she praises François Coppée because "his stories have a purity which is unusual in France, and a freshness which is unusual anywhere." More importantly, however, she was no mincing Miss Nancy moralist who refused to look life in the face. She never thought of morality as something imposed upon life from without but as something intrinsic that squared with the plumb line of the eternities. So, as she saw it, art itself was moral, and, as Professor St. Peter puts it, art and religion were one. She even thought that "no thoroughly evil woman can ever act," because "acting postulates an appreciation of goodness, greatness, and truth." Margaret Mather, for example, had "marked histrionic talent" but because she was a superficial person, she was incapable of really great acting. To fail to realize these things is not to transgress some code that either you, I, or the cat has set up but to falsify life, and the artist who falsifies life creates bad art. "The greatness of a great artist is his mastery of the truth, which is like the great bow of Odysseus, responsive only to the touch of giants."[2]

<h2 style="text-align:center">3</h2>

For Willa Cather, then, morality was something much larger than mere decency in books. She was not starry-eyed about money. She wanted her books to support her comfortably. She took immense interest in format (not many writers are allowed as much say about this as Knopf allowed her), advertising, reviews, and general exploitation. She had no hesitation in rejecting a translation of one of her books that had not pleased her, even when the translator was so accomplished a writer as Marguerite Yourcenar. But the monetary was by no means the most important reward she received for her writing. She was only with reluctance persuaded to let the Book-of-the-Month Club have *Shadows on the Rock,* on which she had already lost money by refusing to let it be serialized because she did not believe it was the kind of story that could be effectively presented in that form. Metro-Goldwyn-Mayer made a desperate effort to get *Lucy Gayheart* for Norma Shearer, but Miss Cather had so much disliked the 1924 Warner Brothers production of *A Lost Lady* that she could not be moved. Essentially she wanted her books only in the hands of people who really wanted them; for this reason she even refused to sanction school editions of her novels and allowed only a few of her stories to appear in anthologies. She did not want boys and girls to grow up hating her because her books had been forced upon them. But it is only fair to add that she was far more consistently high-minded about all these matters *after* Knopf had made her financially independent than she had been before.

Her tastes and temperament as a writer were essentially romantic.

"Romance is the highest form of fiction." Even such great writers as Zola and Ibsen were "temporary" because they gave no scope to the imagination. In the early days her romanticism linked up with the strain of primitivism in her as well as with her obsession with youth,[3] and it never ceased to tie in with her faith in life and in destiny, thus acquiring a religious significance.

Yet, though she was not incapable, especially at the beginning, of reveling in derring-do, she was never in great danger of writing it. "Obscure destinies" were more in her line. She wrote a good deal about artists, whom she saw as pioneers of the spirit, yet she feared the danger of fiction becoming too ingrown through emphasis upon such types. She believed that "the average person has just as interesting emotions and experiences as public personages" and that art must be based on "the common passions and the common sorrows of the common man." Ántonia is an ignorant Bohemian farmer's wife when Jim Burden sees her as an earth mother, a "battered woman" now, "not a lovely girl," who has lost her teeth but still retains the fire of life and can still "stop one's breath for a moment by a look or a gesture that somehow revealed the meaning of common things."

Miss Cather admitted that she could write successfully only about people and places she cared for. "We are what we love, that is all we are." "To know is little and to feel is all." "To feel greatly is genius and to make others feel is art." The influence of Sarah Orne Jewett was very strong at this point: "The thing that teases the mind over and over for years, and at last gets itself put down rightly on paper — whether little or great, it belongs to Literature." "You must find your own quiet centre of life, and write from that to the world," but "one must know the world so well before one can know the parish." Such advices helped her to learn that while "a reporter can write equally well about everything that is presented to his view, . . . a creative writer can do his best only with what lies within the range and character of his deepest sympathies."

This leads inevitably to the question of the nature of Willa Cather's imagination. In her essay on Miss Jewett (in *Not under Forty*), she denied that a writer, "if he is talented enough," can achieve poignancy "by improving upon his subject-matter, using his 'imagination' upon it and twisting it to suit his purpose. The truth is that by such a process (which is not imaginative at all!) he can at best produce only a brilliant sham, which, like a badly built and pretentious house, looks poor and shabby after a few years." Leon Edel thought he was indicating Miss Cather's limitations when he wrote that "unlike some other writers, she could create only from what had happened to her or what had happened in a history to which she was personally attuned," but, as both she and Miss Jewett knew, to indicate a writer's limitations is only to define the nature of his gift. Willa Cather once told Elizabeth Sergeant that a writer of fiction does not need imagination but only insight and style. My own feeling is that, unlike many writers, she used her imagination not primarily to invent but rather to interpret, and I believe that the most illuminating commentary upon this is what Bishop Latour says in *Death Comes for the Archbishop* about an entirely different matter: "The Miracles of the Church seem to me to rest not so much upon faces or voices or healing power but upon our perception being made finer, so that coming suddenly near us from afar off, for a moment our eyes can see and our ears can hear what there is about us always."

4

Willa Cather knew of course that art represents a selection from nature, which differs from art in that there is no selection in it. In a flash of insight Thea Kronborg thinks of it as "an effort to make a sheath, a mould in which to imprison for a moment the shining, elusive element that is life itself." Jim Burden too has such a moment when he realizes that if there were no girls in the world like the farm girls he had known in Nebraska, there would be no poetry, and Lucy Gayheart has another when it comes to her that the only way to keep what she learned from Clement Sebastian is not to allow his death to crush her but to go out into the world herself and possess that which had made him what he was.

Obviously to realize these things and to use that knowledge calls for the insight of the mystic, and it is in this connection that it is correct to call Miss Cather a religious writer. She knew that "the world was made by an Artist, by the divinity and godhead of art, an Artist of such insatiable love of beauty that He takes all forces, all space, all time to fill them with His universes of beauty, an Artist whose dreams (that is, ourselves, and especially those among us who are what we call artists) are so intense and real that they, too, love and suffer and have have dreams of their own," and this of course is true whether God made the world out of nothing, which is the orthodox view, or whether, as Milton believed, He made it out of Himself. So goodness and beauty become one, art and religion are opposite sides of the same coin, and the human artist's task becomes a self-dedication to something greater than himself: "he fades away into the land and people of his heart, and dies of love only to be born again." The artist who fails to achieve this must in the end find his "success," however great it may be in the world's eyes, at last "empty and unsatisfying." Only "complete self-abnegation" can turn "promise" into "fulfillment."

But art requires not only vision but also form. Without vision the form is only a straightjacket but without form the vision remains uncommunicated. Willa Cather's fullest statement on how she had come to believe that fiction should be written was made in "The Novel Démeublé," first published in the *New Republic* on April 12, 1922, and collected in *Not under Forty* and again, posthumously, in *Willa Cather on Writing*. The heaviest stress here was on simplification. This was not, in 1922, a new idea with her. Even as a fledgling drama critic she had repeatedly complained that plays had too many characters and too much plot, fortifying herself by quoting the elder Dumas to the effect that the dramatist needed "only a stage, four walls, two characters, and one passion." Now she complained that the novel was "overfurnished" and that the time had come to throw the furniture out the window. Cataloguing was not "realism," and a description of physical sensations was no closer to reality than a catalogue of objects. This must be sought rather in "an attitude of mind on the part of the writer toward his material, a vague indication of the sympathy and candour with which he accepts, rather than chooses, his theme." The author of *The Scarlet Letter* understood and achieved this; D. H. Lawrence did not. "Whatever is felt upon the page without being specifically named there — that, one might say, is created." Suggestion therefore should replace portrayal wherever possible. As she says elsewhere, "felicitous description is almost always accidental or incidental. It is not at all a question of presenting information, but of suggesting the character of a place, or reproducing an atmosphere." Thus she accepts Tolstoy's descriptions of clothes, dishes, and interiors because they "seem to exist not so much in the author's mind as in the emotional penumbra of the characters themselves." In *A Lost Lady* the Forrester house is not a rich or beautiful place in itself but is only made to seem so by the atmosphere its inhabitants create. Miss Cather's pictorial sense is always keen, but even here her selectivity appears, in her tendency, as Merrill Skaggs has noted, to "freeze" the action of a scene into a "still," as with the famous picture of the plow outlined against the sun in *My Ántonia*. Some of her minor characters are only vaguely outlined, but there are vivid, quick, impressionistic sketches of others; that of Harry Maxey in *One of Ours* (book 4, chapter 7) is a good example of this.[4]

As early as 1921 she told Latrobe Carroll[5] that in *O Pioneers!*, which she always regarded as the book with which she found her way, she tried not to "write" at all. She did not wish to "arrange" or "invent" anything but to stand aside and let her materials find their own right, spontaneous, inevitable place, instead of being wrenched out of shape and forced into a pattern she had sought to impose upon them. Though the idea for a story generally came to her full-blown, she rarely plotted in advance; once she described her aim as that of making "things and people tell their own story simply by juxtaposition, without any persuasion or explanation on my part."

This does not mean that she failed to realize the need for emphasis in fiction. She praises Bunyan because he creates "scenes" and criticizes Defoe, at least in *Roxana*, to which she wrote what must be one of the most unsympathetic prefaces ever written for a book when it was reprinted in the Borzoi Classics series, because she thought he did not. Nor was she indifferent to unity. She tried to put into *Death Comes for the Archbishop* "what I thought was the best chapter I had written for that story, but it didn't fit. I left it out. A novel should be like a symphony, developed from one theme, one dominating tone. That chapter was out of tone." But the unity she sought was that of impression, not necessarily of action. "For me the important thing is never to kill the figure you care for for the sake of atmosphere, well balanced structure, or neat presentation." It followed naturally then that her characteristic structure should be loose or episodic, nor should one be surprised when she includes inserted tales or holds up the story to fill in the background for one of her characters, nor yet that she is fond of epilogues. It is worth noting too that she sometimes used epilogues not only in her novels but sometimes in pieces as short as "Coming, Aphrodite!" and "The Best Years."

It is equally important to remember however that as a writer of fiction Miss Cather always refused to wear a straightjacket, even when that garment was of her own making. That she cherished the "démeublé" ideal to the end of her life seems obvious from her telling Elizabeth Sergeant that she had cut six pounds from the manuscript of *Sapphira and the Slave Girl*. Yet immediately after having found her way with *O Pioneers!*, she used the Balzacian method in *The Song of the Lark*, returned to the *Pioneers* method in *My Ántonia*, and then returned to Balzac again with *One of Ours*. Probably her most perfect example of "démeublé" writing was *A*

Lost Lady, and in *My Mortal Enemy* she pushed it to its utmost limits. *Death Comes for the Archbishop* she preferred to call not a novel but simply a narrative. She was sufficiently sophisticated to describe the structure of *The Professor's House* in terms of a sonata[6] and to justify the inclusion of "Tom Outland's Story" in it by invoking the influence of Dutch painting of interiors. Yet at the same time she was capable of writing in *A Lost Lady,* "But we will begin this story with a summer morning long ago, when Mrs. Forrester was still a young woman, and Sweet Water was a town of which great things were expected." The truth is that she takes up her place inside or outside her story at will. She might be Mrs. Behn, at almost the beginning of the history of the English novel when she writes in "Coming, Aphrodite!" that "Eden Bower was at twenty very much the same person that we all know her to be at forty, except that she knew a great deal less" and in "The Diamond Mine" that "Cressida Garnet, as all the world knows, was lost on the *Titanic.*" But there are also passages, one of which, from the technically expert *Lost Lady,* has already been quoted in this paragraph, in which she seems to be reminding the reader that she is telling a story and deliberately manipulating its materials to please herself.[7]

So far I have outlined Willa Cather's life, glanced at the roots of her writing in life, literature, and the other arts, and tried to formulate some aspects of her literary creed and practice. The time has now come to proceed to a survey of the writings themselves.

4

The First Books

1

The first book Willa Cather managed to get into print was *April Twilights,* published in Boston in 1903, at the author's expense, by Richard G. Badger, one of the better "vanity" publishers of the time. It might seem that in beginning thus with a collection of poems she was starting out on the wrong foot, for nobody except Gamaliel Bradford, who preferred her verses to her fiction, has ever taken her very seriously as a poet. Certainly she herself did not. Indeed she took a very dim view of the ability of women in general to write first-class poetry. In the years following *April Twilights,* she not only virtually stopped writing verses altogether but even bought up all the copies of that first opus she could find that she might have them destroyed. Yet in 1923 she allowed Alfred Knopf to bring out a new edition, *April Twilights and Other Poems,* which dropped thirteen of the pieces in the 1903 edition and added twelve new ones, and when this was reprinted in the Autograph Edition in 1937, two more had disappeared, and one new one, "Poor Marty," had been added.[1]

In a deeper sense, however, Bradford's judgment, eccentric though it may seem, was penetrating. As Mildred Bennett observed, Miss Cather's temperament was essentially that of a poet rather than a novelist. One does not read her stories for their plots, and her characters are rather evoked than constructed; what one remembers are the feelings they awaken and the atmosphere in which she clothes them. Mrs. Bennett even explained on this basis her passionate clinging to youth and the emotions of youth, an attitude of mind much more characteristic of a poet than of a novelist like Henry James, whose influence shows so plainly in the first Cather novel, *Alexander's Bridge.*

Speaking of Miss Cather's poems in general, one would have to say that they divide into two classes, those derived from her reading and those based on experience. The former predominate in the 1903 edition. The pastoral tradition from Virgil on down is very strong, blending with that of the late nineteenth-century English poets, especially Swinburne and the Pre-Raphaelites, with some influence from Heine and a great deal from A. E. Housman, who was probably the poet more on the author's mind when she published her first book than any other. "London Roses" and "Poppies on Ludlow Castle" seem direct echoes of her 1902 excursion to Europe. "Thine Advocate," however, is more like the cerebral trend in modern poetry than it is like the lyrics that sing more successfully. Did she get it from Donne, I wonder, to whom Mrs. Fields introduced her during her first trip to Boston? There is some of the same quality in "Sonnet," but here it seems more Elizabethan than modern.

Most of the poems use forms and diction that would have been familiar to cultivated late nineteenth-century readers. "Night Express" "Prairie Dawn," "Macon Prairie," "The Swedish Mother," "Spanish Johnny," and "Going Home" are all clearly Western Americana, and generally speaking she may be said to have shown a preference for retaining or adding to the number of such poems in the later editions over the more derivative or allusive "literary" poems, obviously directed toward more conventionally cultivated readers.

The best-known poem is unquestionably the first in the collection, "Grandmither, Think Not I Forget," a dramatic monologue in which a tortured woman whose love has been frustrated or forbidden bewails her sad lot. This, along with a number of other pieces in which sexual motivation is strong, might well be pondered by those critics who contend that normal sexuality in literature lay beyond Willa Cather's range. The most unpleasant poem by far, first published in the *Century* in 1923, is "Street in Packingtown (Chicago)," in which a nearly naked "Polack's brat" tortures a cat in the wilderness of the Stock Yards district. This poem would not surprise those who complain of what they call the sadistic scenes in some of Miss Cather's novels, but the hint of social criticism thrown out here never got very far in her work.

Willa Cather finds herself in comfortable command of all the verse forms she chooses to employ and achieves with ease the singing quality she obviously valued in poetry. Sharon O'Brien complains that "she mixes Greek and Latin references with fin-de-siècle ennui, Provençal spring with Celtic twilight," but whether or not this is a fault must remain a matter of taste. My own feeling is that if she is to be faulted it must be because, though she wrote a number of lovely poems, she did not develop a distinctive poetic voice of her own. Whether she might have done this had she gone on with poetry, developing some of the suggestions she had thrown out in her Western American poems, instead of channeling her energies into prose fiction, is something none of us will ever know.

2

In 1905 McClure, Phillips & Co. published Willa Cather's first collection of stories. It was called *The Troll Garden,* and it contained seven tales in the following order:

> Flavia and Her Artists
> The Sculptor's Funeral
> The Garden Lodge
> "A Death in the Desert"
> The Marriage of Phaedra
> A Wagner Matinee
> Paul's Case

There are two epigraphs. One is from Charles Kingsley's *The Roman and the Teuton:*

A fairy palace, with a fairy garden ... inside the trolls dwell ... working at their magic forges, making and making always things rare and strange.[2]

The other is from Christina Rossetti's "Goblin Market":

> We must not look at Goblin men,
> We must not buy their fruits.
> Who knows upon what soil they fed
> Their hungry thirsty roots?

In Christina Rossetti's poem the Goblin fruits are forbidden fruits, which do not nourish but destroy. In Kingsley's context the trolls are the Romans — civilized, accomplished, sophisticated, the masters of arts and crafts, and the forest children are the barbarians, who finally break into the garden, as historically the Teutons broke into the Roman Empire, seizing the things they coveted but also destroying them. Yet the antithesis between the two groups is not a straight contrast between good and evil, for the cultivated trolls are also more corrupt; along with their arts and crafts, they have acquired vices from which the rough but vital forest children have hitherto been free but which they will now acquire along with the beautiful things "rare and strange," which, at the outset, they can only cheapen or destroy, yet which ultimately their rude, barbarian force is destined to enrich. In other words, art, which, as we know, Willa Cather believed is the best proof we have that man shares in the creative nature of God, can also, when perverted, betray and destroy.

Critical ingenuity has been exercised considerably in analyzing the structure of *The Troll Garden* and the manner in which the stories have been arranged so that they reinforce the author's theme and enrich each other through what Sharon O'Brien calls "juxtaposition and contrast."[3] I shall first discuss the three Henry Jamesian stories — "Flavia and Her Artists," "The Garden Lodge," and "The Marriage of Phaedra" — the three whose dramatis personae are most clearly trolls, which are also the three Willa Cather chose not to retain in her second collection of tales (which see hereinafter) and then proceed to the other four, all but one of which are set in the Middle West.[4]

Flavia Hamilton is quite as ignorant and stupid as Mrs. Leo Hunter in *The Pickwick Papers*. She has seen, heard, and read everything and understood nothing, and she fills her house at Tarrytown with all the celebrities she can muster without ever catching a single glimpse of the realization that they feel only contempt for her. Imogen Willard, from whose point of view the tale is told, who had adored Flavia's husband, Arthur Hamilton, when she herself was a child, wonders (as does the reader) why he ever married Flavia; another puzzle is why the lions ever come to Flavia's house parties. Arthur is a wealthy industrialist, sensitive, intelligent, and unselfish, whom his wife regards as completely incapable of understanding anything related to the arts. After leaving the party at which the reader attends, the biggest lion, M. Roux, a French novelist, gives an outrageous interview, in which he paints an unmistakable satirical portrait of his hostess. The article in which this interview is recorded comes to the attention of her husband and her guests before Flavia has had a chance to see it, and he covers for her by burning the journal in which it appears and then delivering a brief speech at table that gives her a chance to believe that the hegira of their guests that shortly follows is due to his inconceivable gaucherie rather than to her own shortcomings.

In connection with this story, I have already referred to Willa Cather's own bad taste in giving her fool heroine the very unusual first name and possibly some of the characteristics of her friend

Dorothy Canfield's mother. More recently Woodress has suggested that Imogen Willard may have been drawn from Dorothy herself, who had a Ph.D. in Romance languages. But the most interesting thing about this story is the way in which a wealthy businessman, a member of a class that both Miss Cather and Henry James generally either ignored completely or took a dim view of is here made a gentlemen of the first water, while the artists, however able some of them may be in their professions, lack both human feelings and decent manners.

In "The Garden Lodge" Caroline Noble, reared in poverty, is the daughter of a music teacher who neglected the pupils who supplied his livelihood to devote himself to the composition of music that nobody wished to play or hear and the sister of a freckless brother who fancied himself a painter but was too lazy ever to produce anything and who shot himself in a frenzy at twenty-six. Caroline pulled herself up by her own bootstraps and is now the adored wife of a rich man, and herself a superbly disciplined woman. The story deals with a crisis in which the ghost of her past rises and threatens to undo all her hard work. The leading tenor of the Metropolitan is a guest in her house, and she plays the accompaniments for his practicing sessions. This renewed contact with great music nearly sweeps her off her feet, and she is tempted to follow in her family's footsteps and become a dreamer reaching for the stars that are utterly beyond her. The description of her night alone in the lodge, where she had played for the great singer and where she now confronts her temptation and puts it decisively behind her is an impressive piece of writing, possibly inspired by James's account of Isabel Archer's musing before the fire in *The Portrait of a Lady,* and there is also a penetrating passage on the opera star mystique. In this story, though Willa Cather had yet to use that figure, the Medusa aspect of the arts is dominant. She had not read Bunyan devotedly without learning that there is a way to hell even from the gates of the Heavenly City.

"The Marriage of Phaedra" is, I believe, the best of these three tales, though it is much less tightly focused than "The Garden Lodge." The late Hugh Treffinger was both a "brigand" and a genius, one of the forest children (except that his forest was the London slums) who broke into the troll garden and himself created "things rare and strange," though without finding happiness for himself. When, after his death, MacMaster visits his studio, he is so much impressed by his unfinished masterpiece, "The Marriage of Phaedra," that he determines to write the painter's biogra-

phy, but Treffinger's Philistine widow, Lady Ellen, now planning
her remarriage, presents the entire contents of the studio to the
"X——gallery" except for the "Marriage," which she sells, for an
enormous sum, to an Australian dealer as money-minded as herself.
Treffinger's valet is so horrified that he steals the painting from the
studio and brings it to MacMaster, who persuades him to return
it. Miss Cather's portrait of this devoted man is both amusing and
touching, and quite unparalleled in her other work. John H. Randall III has plausibly suggested that the character may have been
derived from Henry James's Brooksmith in the story by that name.
Was the fact that his first name is James intended to suggest this?

The other four stories — "The Sculptor's Funeral," " 'A Death
in the Desert,' " "A Wagner Matinee," and "Paul's Case" — their
creator evidently liked much better than the three I have already
discussed, for she chose to reprint them all in 1920 in *Youth and the
Bright Medusa,* though she afterwards came to dislike " 'A Death in
the Desert' " too, and when the time came to reprint *Medusa* in the
Autograph Edition, she left that story out.

There can be no doubt in anybody's mind that both "The Sculptor's Funeral" and "A Wagner Matinee" came out of Miss Cather's
years in Nebraska and that they are her "own" material. They may
even be seen as anticipative of what later came to be called the "revolt from the village" theme that was destined to be developed more
intensively later in the work of writers more socially conscious than
Willa Cather.

In "The Sculptor's Funeral" the body of Harvey Merrick, dead in
his forties, is brought back to be buried by his imperceptive family
in the little Kansas town of his birth. Though he is the only man
of distinction who ever came out of this miserable place, his old
neighbors, who in their thickheaded materialism are sure he never
amounted to anything, are allowed to talk about him sufficiently to
reveal their own meanness and stupidity, only to be denounced in
an eloquent philippic by Jim Laird, a lawyer who once reached for
the stars but has now been reduced to hopeless alcoholism by the
despair engendered in him by his soul-crushing surroundings. The
entire story is built up to Laird's denunciation, which is as much a
set piece as Mark Antony's oration in *Julius Caesar.* In "A Wagner
Matinee" the male narrator's Aunt Georgiana, once a teacher at the
Boston Conservatory of Music, comes back to Boston after thirty
years in Western parts, and he takes her to an afternoon concert
by the Boston Symphony Orchestra. The result is mingled ecstasy
and agony — rapturous appreciation of the music and agony over

what she has missed for all these years and will probably never hear again. "I don't want to go, Clark. I don't want to go." Her nephew understands. "For her, just outside the concert hall, lay the black pond with the cattle-tracked bluffs; the tall, unpainted house, with weather-curled boards, naked as a tower; the crook-backed ash seedlings where the dish-cloths hung to dry; the gaunt, moulting turkeys picking up refuse about the kitchen door."

"The Sculptor's Funeral" was suggested by the death of a painter and illustrator, Charles Stanley Rinehart, whose funeral Willa Cather attended in Pittsburgh when his body was returned to an indifferent native city in 1896. It is worth noting that Rinehart hailed not from a small town in the Middle West but from one of the great centers of Eastern industrialism and "ruthless individualism," and that the story Miss Cather wrote about his funeral excoriates Pittsburgh, or, if you prefer, what Virginia Woolf might have called "Pittsburghism" as mercilessly as Jim Laird flays his fellow townsmen in the other story. I speak elsewhere of the trouble Willa Cather got herself into by giving Aunt Georgiana some of the physical characteristics of her Aunt Franc, a Mount Holyoke graduate who tried her best to bring the graces of Mount Holyoke to the Divide. The Medusa aspect of art is not stressed in either of these stories. In the first, it is those whose lives have not been sweetened by art who behave like snakes or worse, and Aunt Georgiana's sufferings in the second are caused not by art but rather by having been so long compelled to live without it.

Willa Cather put quotes around the title of " 'A Death in the Desert' " because she had borrowed it from Browning. The desert is Wyoming, where, after a brief successful career as a singer, cut short by tuberculosis, Katharine Gaylord has come home to die, "spent by the race-course, listening to the feet of the runners as they pass, ah, God! the swift feet of the runners!" Art was her triumph and its withdrawal her destruction, but in her case disease and unrequited love have proved even more lethal agents. I find it difficult to account for Miss Cather's later dislike of this story. It is by all means my favorite among the *Troll Garden–Medusa* lot. The time is 1893, for the World's Columbian Exposition is on in Chicago, but the story was first published in *Scribner's Magazine* in January 1903. The author revised it extensively before reprinting it in *The Troll Garden* and then cut it down by about one-third before using it again in *Youth and the Bright Medusa*. It is by all means much the subtlest and most emotionally complicated of all her early stories. It may well be therefore that she saw unrealized possibilities in it that she did not think she had been able to develop satisfactorily; it may be also that by the time the Autograph Edition was being prepared in the 1930s, in the literary atmosphere that then prevailed, she thought too many readers were finding it impossible to distinguish between genuine feeling and sentimentality to give the piece a fair chance.[5]

The story concerns the relations between three persons: Katharine Gaylord, the dying woman; Adriance Hilgarde, a famous composer, who had been her teacher, with whom she had toured as a singer, and whom she had fruitlessly loved; and his brother, Everett Hilgarde, who, like the other two, knows what it means to have the soul of an artist, but who, when we meet him, has ceased "to beat...at doors he could not enter," and whose physical resemblance to his brother is so great that he is sometimes stopped by strangers who have mistaken him for Adriance. To complicate the situation further, as a youth Everett had adored the then-glamorous Katharine at a distance, to such an extent that he has never been able to care for any other woman since. When Katharine is within weeks of her end, chance brings Everett into Cheyenne and gives him the painful privilege of easing Katharine's last days. The irony of the situation is deepened by the fact that he is several times the man, as distinguished from the artist, that his brother is, and in a way Katharine comes to know it and acknowledge it, yet, even as she dies, she whispers in her confusion, "Ah, dear Adriance, dear, dear!"

Except for his faintly sinister aspects, Adriance seems to have been suggested by Ethelbert Nevin, whom Willa Cather knew and, in some sense of the word, loved. Of Everett's ministrations to Katharine we read that this was "not the first time that his duty had been to comfort, as best he could, one of the broken things his brother's imperious speed had cast aside and forgotten." This does not necessarily mean that Adriance was a Don Juan. It was not his duty to love Katharine because she loved him. Nor was it his fault that even his mother, when Everett was a boy, had done her duty by all her children, yet could not help making it clear "that she'd have made burnt-offerings of us all for him any day." He was merely a "whirlwind of flame...consuming all in his path, and himself more resolutely than he consumed others," and in a way this was his misfortune as much as theirs, though there is no indication that he ever recognized it as such. If you wish to force the note, you might even argue that this is the artist's nature and that the concentration art demands of those who have themselves been touched by the divine fire is that they must have no room for anything else in their lives. Indeed Willa Cather has herself argued elsewhere that art is a more jealous god than Jehovah, for while he says, "Thou shalt have no other gods before me," she commands, "Thou shalt have no other gods at all." Yet the same concentration and the same egotism, if that is the word to use, can appear in persons who have no trace of either artistic talent or interest in the arts, while on the other hand, some very great artists have been wholly free of it. There is no trace of it, for example, in Sir Walter Scott. Only one thing, however, is indubitably clear; there is no sadder story anywhere than " 'A Death in the Desert,' " and no young writer could have chosen a more audacious theme.

I must try to be entirely frank about the one remaining *Troll Garden* story, "Paul's Case." If " 'A Death in the Desert' " has been, as I believe, generally underrated, then it seems to me that "Paul's Case" has been as unwisely overrated. That it is well done for what it is, I do not deny, but it is the one story of Willa Cather's that leaves a bad taste in my mouth, and I see no particular reason why it should have been done at all. Perhaps the basic difficulty is that Paul is a "case" and his story "a study in temperament," and that "cases" belong in medical reports, not in literature. For some reason best known to herself, "Paul's Case" was the only story that at the close of her life Willa Cather permitted to be reprinted in anthologies. If I had encountered it in a collection of stories intended for study in high school, without having read anything else by its author, as many young people must have done, I doubt that I should have done anything further to develop our acquaintance.

Paul is a Pittsburgh high school boy, at odds with his family, his teachers, and his surroundings, who finds satisfaction only in association with members of the stock company at the local theater and in the music he hears and to the (to him) glamorous personalities he encounters through his ushering at Pittsburgh's Carnegie Hall. When he is expelled from high school for insolence and his father puts him to work, he absconds with a thousand dollars from the firm where he is employed, which furnishes the wherewithal to put him up in a suite at the Waldorf, where, solitary as he is, he can see himself as one of the glamorous metropolitans he has always envied and admired. When he learns that his theft has been discovered, that his father has refunded the stolen sum, and that the prison shades of Cordelia Street are threatening to close around him again, he performs the Anna Karenina act in the path of an approaching locomotive.

Paul is one of the forest children who break into the troll garden without the vaguest idea of what they are to do with any of the things "rare and strange" that they find there. Actually he does not wish to "do" anything; spongelike, he wishes only to absorb. Not only is he completely without talent; he lacks even the desire to create any of the things he admires. He has very little taste; he gets the same thrill out of a tune on the barrel organ and a symphony. Art does not help him to understand life; it is only an anodyne and therefore fundamentally destructive. Potentially his is a tragic situation, but its cold presentation as a "case" leaves the reader unmoved.

"Paul's Case" is the only story in which Willa Cather drew upon her experience as a teacher. A boy in her Latin class (who fortunately did not come to a bad end) suggested some of Paul's traits, and she either heard or read of two Pittsburgh boys who stole some money and went to Chicago, where they were apprehended at the Auditorium Hotel. She also admitted that her own early bedazzlement by glamour and fashion had added something. The most interesting reference to literary sources is Randall's suggestion that the uncharacteristic detached, aloof tone of the tale was derived from Flaubert and especially from *Madame Bovary*.[6]

When *Youth and the Bright Medusa* appeared in 1920, it presented its readers with the following bill of fare:

> Coming, Aphrodite!
> The Diamond Mine
> A Gold Slipper
> Scandal
> Paul's Case
> A Wagner Matinee
> The Sculptor's Funeral
> "A Death in the Desert"

The last four stories, reprinted from *The Troll Garden*, have already been discussed; the first four were new.

The title of the collection was more clever than accurate. The bright Medusa is obviously art, and the adjective *bright* indicates bedazzlement, which may deceive or betray. But the sight of the Gorgon Medusa in Greek mythology turned the beholder into stone, and that, obviously, art cannot do.

All four of the new stories are about singers and one painter, and all are very competent and entertaining, but no one is especially significant. "Coming, Aphrodite!" is much the longest and most ambitious, and what everybody remembers about it first of all is that it is Willa Cather's only "French postcard" story, for the aspiring young painter, Don Hedger, peeps through a hole in the wall separating his quarters in a Washington Square boardinghouse from those of Eden Bower, an aspiring singer, to watch her going through her exercises naked in a pool of sunshine. Here again the title is clever, perhaps too clever. "Aphrodite" is presumably a reference to the opera by Camille Erlanger that was one of the more sensational items in Mary Garden's repertoire. Since "Eden Bower was, at twenty, very much the same person that we all know her to be at forty," "Coming, Aphrodite!" must mean that at the time of the story she is just the kind of person who might be expected to specialize in material of the kind here indicated.

The essential purpose of the story is to contrast the Eden Bower kind of artist — competent, flamboyant, sensational, and very much interested in "success" — with the avant-garde painter, Hedger, who regards his gift as a sacred trust, and the public be damned. Eden and Hedger have a brief, passionate affair, but quarrel and part when she angers him by trying to put him in touch with some people who can turn his gift into a paying proposition. "After years of sensational success in Paris," Eden Bower brings her Aphrodite to New York. Still sufficiently interested in Don Hedger to wish to know how he has fared, she inquires about him at an art dealer's. Hedger, she learns, "is one of the first men among the moderns. That is to say, among the very moderns." But successful, as Eden Bower understands success, he is not. Miss Cather leaves the reader no choice but to realize that Hedger exemplifies the idealist in art while Eden Bower does not, but whether he thinks the sacrifice the painter has made was worth making will probably be determined by what he thinks of the kind of art he exemplifies. I must say however that I think he treats Eden rather shabbily at the time of their break. Of course she was materially minded, and of course she was imperceptive in what she did. But within the limitations of her temperament and her understanding, she was still trying her best to help a man for whom she cared.

Perhaps the principal source of charm in "Coming, Aphrodite!" today lies in the atmosphere it exudes of the Washington Square district in the days when "Signor Puccini" was "comparatively new in the world." It is amusing that when Miss Cather sent the story to the *Smart Set,* the editors, who liked it immensely, were sufficiently afraid of Anthony Comstock not to permit Eden Bower to do her exercises nude in his magazine's chaste pages, and sufficiently cautious about possible difficulties with Mary Garden to change the title to "Coming, Eden Bower!" On the second point at least, they need not have worried. Miss Garden was much too sensible a woman to concern herself with such trifles.[7]

Two prominent singers are the subjects of the other three stories — Cressida Garnet in "The Diamond Mine" and Kitty Ayrshire in both "A Gold Slipper" and "Scandal." But though we attend one of Kitty Ayrshire's recitals, the stories deal less with what these singers do as artists than with what their art does to their private lives. The editors of the *Smart Set,* who, as we have seen, tinkered with "Coming, Aphrodite!," refused to publish "The Diamond Mine" at all, because they feared the characters sufficiently suggested Lillian Nordica and her last husband so that the latter might embrace the opportunity to file a libel suit. Both these singers are admirable people, and both find fulfillment and satisfaction in their art; it is the inability of others to meet them on their own ground that causes trouble. Cressida, to be sure, has had four husbands, but her first happy marriage ended only with the man's cruelly early death, and her union with the others showed no fault in her except poor judgment in choosing unworthy men, while Kitty Ayrshire is completely innocent in the scandal that besmirches her name, which has been deliberately concocted by a loathsome creature who believed that to have it bruited about that a famous singer was his mistress would redound to his glory. Cressida is exploited by her rapacious relatives, a worthless son, and her husbands, to none of whom neither her art nor her success mean anything but the money they have earned. "A Gold Slipper" is the more substantial of the two Kitty Ayrshire stories. After having observed on the stage at one of her recitals an aggressively insensitive Philistine businessman, who does his best to ruin the occasion by showing how bored he is and how much he disapproves of Kitty and all her kind, the singer is accidentally thrown into contact with him in a Pullman car and improves the occasion by rebuking him with an analysis of him and all his kind that is a considerably more sophisticated, though also a much less impassioned, version of the tirade delivered by Jim Laird in "The Sculptor's Funeral." With this passage Willa Cather must certainly have squared accounts with all the materialistic, self-righteous bourgeoisie whose attitude she so much resented during her Pittsburgh years. If there are suggestions of Mary Garden in "Coming, Aphrodite!" the program Kitty Ayrshire sings in "A Gold Slipper" and her behavior on the concert platform are not without suggestions of Geraldine Farrar. The dressing down Kitty gives

Marshall McKann is well done, but though it is possible that she might mischievously annoy him by leaving her slipper in his berth, that this should have penetrated his thick hide to such an extent that he would preserve the slipper and brood over it in later years quite passes the bounds of credence.

3

When Ferris Greenslet advised Houghton Mifflin Company to publish *Alexander's Bridge,* he stressed its "excellence of workmanship," "perceptiveness," "actuality," and "the spiritual sense of life that informs it." As "Alexander's Masquerade" it was serialized in *McClure's Magazine* in February, March, and April 1912, and the book appeared in April. It was a tightly knit, very Jamesian novel (or nouvelle). Its scenes were laid in Boston, London, and New York, and its characters were sophisticated, cultivated, prosperous people of the kind readers of the best fiction of the time were accustomed to meeting in the pages of James and Edith Wharton. As such, Willa Cather soon came to disparage it, as a "studio picture," contrived and superficial and characteristic of neither her style nor her method.[8] For all that, Bartley Alexander (named after the Macedonian world conqueror), the greatest bridge builder of his time and the one whose picture the Sunday supplements always chose to run when bridges were under consideration, with his Faust-like, fruitless yearning for his lost youth, *is* an authentic Cather character. She would be haunted by such figures all her life, and in her subtlest novel, *The Professor's House,* she would study one of them in much more definitive fashion and in a form more in harmony with her mature aesthetic convictions. It is not surprising therefore that, despite everything she says against it, she should have defended *Alexander's Bridge* when her Aunt Franc criticized it and included it in the Autograph Edition.

The known and conjectured sources of this brief novel are many. The collapse of the Moorlock Bridge, which provides such a smashing and well-managed climax and solves (or evades) all Alexander's problems by killing him is the collapse of the great bridge under construction over the St. Lawrence River on the afternoon of August 29, 1907.[9] The Boston and London backgrounds make use of the knowledge the author gained of these cities while on assignment there for *McClure's Magazine.* The theater in which Hilda Burgoyne performs is the Abbey Theater, which the author came to know well, and Hilda's stage personality is unmistakably that of

Maire O'Neill, of that organization. When, in 1912, Miss Cather was asked whether Alexander was "meant to be a portrait of a noted New York architect," she denied it, saying rather that she had given him "some of the characteristics which I have noted in a dozen architects, engineers, and inventors."[10] Obviously the questioner's reference was to the great Stanford White, whose interest in show girls was well-known and who was murdered in 1906 by Harry K. Thaw, the demented husband of Evelyn Nesbit, who resented White's attentions to his wife before her marriage.[11] More recently, Susan J. Rosowski has nominated Hartley Burr Alexander, a member of the University of Nebraska faculty, as the model not only for Bartley Alexander but for Godfrey St. Peter in *The Professor's House*.[12] Virginia Faulkner and the late Bernice Slote went back into Greek mythology to compare the relations between Alexander and his two loves to those of Paris (who was also called Alexander) with Oenone and Helen, and Miss Slote was also impressed by the resemblance between what Alexander feels when he takes on what he himself describes as a second personality with what Dr. Jekyll felt when he became Mr. Hyde.[13] Ibsen's *The Master Builder* has been invoked, as has Kipling's poem "The Bridge Builders."

Alexander is a big Westerner, who, in his youth, had worked his way across the Atlantic on a cattle boat so that he might study in Paris. His old teacher, Lucius Wilson, says of him that he was never introspective, but always tremendously sensitive to stimuli. When we meet him, he is forty-three years old, spectacularly successful, and ideally married, but everything is wrecked by his uncontrollable passion to "live out his [other] potentialities" and go after "the birds in the bushes." His wife, Winifred, is a Boston aristocrat, rich, cultured, and a gifted musician. Her face is "very, very proud, and just a little hard." Hilda Burgoyne, who "always had that combination of something homely and sensible, and something utterly wild and daft" that many find irresistible, has all the charm of the Irish and has become a skilled and highly respected actress during the dozen years that have passed since Bartley had loved and left her in Paris.

Whether the reader prefers Winifred or Hilda will probably depend upon whether his taste runs to the great lady or the soubrette. There is nothing whatever to be said against Winifred, and she wins both our admiration and our sympathy by her behavior at the time of Bartley's death; until then she had seemed too perfect and self-sufficient to need anything from us. But we see much more of Hilda than we do of her and consequently come to feel much closer to her. Certainly the author was right to give her the last word in the story, for she knew what Bartley had been going through before his death, which Winifred did not, since the letter he had written her was never mailed and, mercifully for her, was too water-soaked to be read when his body was recovered.

Two other points must be made about Hilda however. Though she is the "other" woman of all triangle situations, and an actress to boot, no woman was ever less wanton. She is the kind of woman who can only love once, and if she is to be faulted, it must be on the ground that she is unable to distinguish between fidelity and fixation. Her claim on Bartley had antedated Winifred's, and he had jilted her when he married Winifred, but once she had loved him, she was never able to forget him or to love anybody else. The last words spoken in the novel are hers, and her whole soul is in them: "Yes, nothing can happen to one after Bartley."

The other point is that though the action of the novel centers around Bartley's renewed affair with her, and though Willa Cather's account of the divided mind this creates in him ("I feel as if a second man had been grafted into me"), is by far the best thing in it, Hilda is not herself the cause of his problem; neither did it begin with her. He had never loved her as she loved him. If he had, he would never have left her; and even now her hold upon him is mainly that she was a part of the lost youth he has never ceased to yearn for. The author spells this out for the reader very carefully. He had not thought of Hilda for years, indeed had nearly forgotten her when chance threw her in his way again. Even now "he walked shoulder to shoulder with a shadowy companion — not little Hilda Burgoyne, by any means, but one vastly dearer to him than she had ever been." Even when he writes Winifred the letter she never saw, he knew that she, not Hilda, was the woman he really loved. He proposed leaving her only because he could no longer endure dividing himself and knew no other way of resolving his difficulty. Indeed the most despicable action he ever performs is that he tries to avoid making his own decision by trying to persuade Hilda to promise that if he should come to her, she would not accept him, which she indignantly refuses to do. In a sense, then, though in a vastly different sense, he "uses" Hilda as well as his wife.

At the very beginning of the novel, Professor Wilson says that he "always used to feel" that there was "a weak spot" in Bartley and that, successful though he was, "some day the strain would tell. Even after you began to climb, I stood down in the crowd and watched you with — well, not with confidence." To thrust this upon the reader in the very first chapter is not exactly subtle; neither can one easily believe that Wilson would have said it to Alexander under the circumstances posited. Nevertheless it does suggest that this is to be the theme of the book and thus gives authority to those who see the collapse of the bridge as closely related to the moral collapse of the man. That this was the author's intention is at best only speculative, for even at the end she writes, "Even Lucius Wilson did not see in this accident the disaster he had once foretold." But if it was not, the first chapter was somewhat misleading.

If Bartley Alexander is to be held responsible for the collapse of Moorlock Bridge, this had nothing to do with his affair with Hilda Burgoyne. He might have loved a dozen women and the bridge would still have been intact. What he was responsible for is that he had undertaken to build the "longest cantilever in existence" under the inadmissible limitations as to both money and materials imposed by those who were financing the project. When he accepted these conditions, he knew he was skating very close to the danger line. Would he have done this, being the man he was, with both his reputation and his prestige at stake? If Miss Cather's Hawthorne-like study of Alexander's agonies of conscience is the best thing in the book, her handling of the matter indicated here is certainly the weakest.[14]

Part 2

5

Novels: Studies in Fulfillment

1

Cather scholars have been telling us for more than a generation that the widespread assumption that *O Pioneers!* (1913) marks their author's discovery of Nebraska as literary material,[1] is not correct. A better case can be made however to support the view that this book was her first Nebraska *novel* and that with it she also discovered her natural *form* for fiction. Unless "The Bohemian Girl" is to be called a novel, this view must stand. "The Bohemian Girl," to be sure, is almost as long as *Alexander's Bridge* and of course longer than *My Mortal Enemy*. But Miss Cather never allowed it to be reprinted from *McClure's Magazine* during her lifetime, and it has never appeared between independent covers. The truth of the matter is that as literature is considerably less complicated than life, literature in turn is considerably more complicated then criticism, for our schemes of classification and clarification (and this is as true of this book of mine as of any others of its kind), both simplify and falsify. I have called *O Pioneers!* and its two succeeding novels "Studies in Fulfillment," and I have called the four novels that followed "Studies in Frustration," and I am prepared to go to the barricades to contend that in essence this is correct. But surely frustration is also important in *Alexander's Bridge,* and even in the novel that is now our immediate concern, while *fulfillment* is the right word for Alexandra's story, the love story of Emil Bergson and Marie Shabata ends not only in frustration but in tragedy, in both of which indeed Alexandra shares, for the victims are her beloved brother and her closest friend.

Nevertheless, *O Pioneers!* is very nearly a perfect book. David Daiches, to be sure, complains that it lacks unity, but he seems to be asking for a different sort of unity than Miss Cather was trying to give. The beautifully balanced opening sentence captures our attention at once — "One January day, thirty years ago," the little town of Hanover, anchored on a windy Nebraska tableland, was trying not to be blown away." "Thirty years ago," indicates 1883, incidentally the very year the Cathers came to Nebraska, and the novel ends about 1900, when "The Wild Land" had become "Neighbouring Fields," with an interval of about sixteen years to bring about the change. The land has been called the real hero of the book: there is none other, though Alexandra Bergson is certainly the heroine. And that opening sentence, as masterly as those that introduce *A Lost Lady* and *Lucy Gayheart*, also achieves an excellent selective evocation of the town.

Willa Cather thought that in a book like this everything "took its own place, right or wrong." There was no "arranging or 'inventing'; everything was spontaneous." From the beginning she tried "not to 'write' at all" but simply to surrender "to the pleasure of recapturing in memory people and places I had believed forgotten." Books in which everything finds its own place may not have been organized according to formal rules, but there is not likely to be anything about them that any reader would like to change. Probably this is the only kind of unity that could have been achieved in a book whose writing history was curiously intertwined with those of both *Alexander's Bridge* and "The Bohemian Girl" and that was itself formed through the coalescence of "Alexandra" and "The White Mulberry Tree," originally conceived as separate stories. It is not surprising that though Miss Cather knew from the beginning that she had either done something rather fine or else that she had failed utterly, she was also afraid that not more than a dozen people would care for it.[2]

Willa Cather also said that the book interested her tremendously "because it had to do with a kind of country I loved, because it was about old neighbours, once very dear, whom I had almost forgotten in the hurry and excitement of growing up and finding out what the world was like and trying to get on in it." But though Alexandra may have been suggested by Hilda Kron, who, with her husband's help, developed one of the great farms in Webster County, many literary influences were also brought to bear upon *O Pioneers!* Though Alexandra is something of an epic heroine in her taming of "the wild land," the pastoral tradition, reaching back to Virgil's *Eclogues* was probably more important, and, as has been noted elsewhere, Ovid's story of Pyramus and Thisbe was used for the tragic love story.[3] The wild duck is clearly from Ibsen, and Susie Thomas has suggested that the style may have been influenced by Turgenev's *Sketches from a Hunter's Album*.

Her creator writes of Alexandra that "her mind was slow, truthful, steadfast. She had not the least spark of cleverness." Of cleverness, especially in the superficial or tricky sense, no, but she does not lack imagination. She is the kind of person Captain Forrester has in mind when he speaks of the West as having been developed out of dreams — "the homesteader's and the prospector's and the contractor's. We dreamed the railroads across the mountains, just as I dreamed my place on the Sweet Water." She becomes the head of the family after her father's death, and it is her vision and her faith in the land that keeps her dull and her vacillating brother tied each to his task during the hard times when they are asking only for release. Her self-denial stands in sharp contrast to their selfishness, and their greed for the land that she has won postpones her finding marital happiness for years. But perhaps Willa Cather's happiest touch in showing us her mettle comes in connection with Alexandra's response to the stars. "She always loved to watch them, to think of their vastness and distance, and of their ordered march. It fortified her to reflect upon the great operations of Nature, and when she thought of the law that lay behind them, she felt a sense of personal security." This is a passage that makes the reader think of Thomas Hardy's use of the stars in *Two on a Tower* and elsewhere and of Walter de la Mare's in *Memoirs of a Midget*. And surely Miss Cather never achieved anything more touching in any of her books than her picture of Alexandra at the close trying to get a pardon for the man who killed her brother. This killing is as carefully prepared for as it could be in a tightly patterned novel, and it is interesting that we are not allowed to be with Alexandra when she first hears the news but only some time afterward, when she has had time to adjust herself to it and to achieve this divine compassion. As usual in Willa Cather's books, we are not denied the advantage of backward glances into the lives of her characters; a particularly memorable one in *O Pioneers!* is that concerning Marie in section 7 of part 2. Later there is a briefer but poignant example of the less frequently employed device of a glance ahead: "Later in the winter, Alexandra looked back upon that afternoon as the last satisfactory visit she had had with Marie."

The quicksilverish Marie is the most vivid character in the book. From her introduction as a petted, indulged little girl to the time when her loutish husband kills both her and Emil when he finds them making love for the first and only time in their lives, she never forfeits the reader's sympathy, even when he knows she shows lamentably bad judgment. We meet her lover, Emil, as a small child also, in the very first chapter, where the kitten he had insisted on bringing to market with him and his sister had been chased up a telegraph pole from which Carl Linstrum had to rescue her ("My kitten, oh, my kitten! Her will fweeze!"), but we do not know much about him until, in an unusually formal character sketch for Miss Cather, he is reintroduced, after his return from college, whistling the Jewel Song from *Faust* as he whets his scythe, "a splendid figure of a boy, tall and straight as a young pine tree, with a handsome head, and stormy grey eyes, deeply set under a serious brow." Carl himself ultimately becomes Alexandra's husband after what one must acknowledge was a very tame wooing. David Stouck calls him a "weak, sensitive man, ill-suited to the life of the pioneer." His creator, I think, must have viewed him more sympathetically, for she made him one of her chorus characters, and his tastes are much like her own. A skilled wood engraver, he despises the cheap metalwork that is replacing it, and he feels much as she did about big-city dwellers: "We are all alike, we have no ties, we know nobody, we own nothing. When one of us dies, they scarcely know where to bury him." The other chorus character is the mad Russian saint, Ivar, who has great skill as a healer, although his disparagers say that he takes the medicine meant for the horses himself and then prays over them. Alexandra protects him against those who would have him confined, and it is to her that he leaves his testament: "I am despised because I do not wear shoes, because I do not cut my hair, and because I have visions. At home, in the old country, there were many like me, who had been touched by God, or who had seen things in the graveyard by night and were different afterward. We thought nothing of it, and let them alone. But here, if a man is different in his feet or in his head, they put him in the asylum."

In the last analysis however, the land is the real hero of the book. Willa Cather was right about that. She did not sentimentalize the land. Its "genius" was unfriendly to man. It needed to be broken, like a recalcitrant horse. But at the same time it must be submitted to. You cannot use wood effectively by planing against the grain or the earth by polluting it. Alexandra conquers it because with her, "for the first time, perhaps, since that land emerged from the waters of geologic ages, a human face was set toward it with love and yearning." And if this is not the first chapter in the Gospel according to Willa, it must certainly be the second.

2

In Willa Cather's books, pioneers and artists are close kin. Instead of living mindlessly or traveling blindly along familiar paths, each in his own way lives creatively, reaching out for new experiences, creating new forms of expression. Of all her stories about artists, *The Song of the Lark* (1915) is much the most significant. It followed *O Pioneers!* after two years, and, as I have already noted, though she believed she had found the method that was right for her in that book, she departed from it at once in the *Lark,* which her official biographer, E. K Brown, called an *Entwicklungsroman* in the style of Arnold Bennett's *Clayhanger* and the early Theodore Dreiser.[4] She was hurt when the London publisher William Heinemann, who had published both *Alexander's Bridge* and *O Pioneers!,* rejected the *Lark* because, as she summarized his letter, "he thought that in that book I had taken the wrong road, and that the full-blooded method, which told everything about everybody, was not natural to me and was not the one in which I could ever take satisfaction," but she later came to agree with him and herself criticized the *Lark* only less severely than the *Bridge.* Most readers however are not much concerned about method (which should be the artist's servant, not his master) as such. If a novel has a good story to tell, and if that story is acted out by convincing, well-rounded characters in whom the reader is able to become sufficiently interested to care what becomes of them, that is all he cares about. Though nobody would claim that the *Lark* is a perfect novel or that it is equally successful in all its parts, it certainly passes that test.

The book opens in Moonstone, Colorado. There is a real Moonstone in Colorado, but it is a desert town, west of Denver, and Miss Cather's Moonstone, except for its Mexican settlement, is essentially Red Cloud, Nebraska. From the very beginning, through Doctor Archie's solicitude for little Thea Kronborg, ill with pneumonia, we are prepared to expect something splendid from her. This first section is rich in portraits of the many who influence the burgeoning artist: Doctor Archie himself; the Kohlers, with their quaint German ways, forever planting trees to make shade; Professor Wunsch, the derelict German music master, who first awakens her musical aspirations; Ray Kennedy, the ill-starred young brakeman, who worships her from afar, and whose life insurance is the means of starting her out as a student; and Spanish Johnny, with his sensitive spirit and his disreputable ways.

It is interesting to compare Willa Cather's treatment of Thea's career with what it would have received at the hands of some cheap, romantic "lady novelist." The life of an opera singer — to the uninitiated this is precisely what appeals to those who write for what Gamaliel Bradford called "the vast acceptance of those who are wept over at lone midnight by the shop-girl and the serving-maid." Such a treatment would of course have been wholly external; all Thea's difficulties would have been passed over quickly, so that the reader might revel in the glad, gay triumph of a petted darling. There could have been no such study as Willa Cather made of the artist's inner life or her actual process of creation. Success is not easy for Thea. Even after she has established herself, she has difficulties in getting into a new role; there is a stage when she can only confront it dumbly. The "popular" novelist's prima donna would probably be bawdy, which Thea is not, but all her shortcomings would be picturesque and "interesting" shortcomings, such as her readers would have liked to have themselves. Thea's quarrelsomeness and impatience, her dislike, even hatred, of singers who cut corners and win a surface triumph dishonestly — there could have been no room for these things. Nobody who was not passionately fond of music and who understood the temper of its great interpreters could possibly have written *The Song of the Lark*.

The book is a novelist's tribute to her favorite singer, Olive Fremstad. The idea of the novel antedated Miss Cather's meeting with Madame Fremstad, and save that it was the singer, not the writer, who emerged from a Midwestern parsonage, everything about Thea's early life except her study of the voice and the piano and her teaching of the latter came from the writer's life and not from the singer's. The book had other sources also. The title came from a painting of the same name by Jules Breton in the Art Institute of Chicago, which depicts a French peasant's girl pausing in her way to work in the fields to listen enraptured to the lark's song overheard. Miss Cather was not always fortunate in her choice of titles, and it was characteristic of her that she should afterwards need to explain of this one that it "was meant to suggest a young girl's awakening to something beautiful" and not to Thea's own song, which "was not of the skylark order." The new vision of art as an expression not only of an individual but of the life of a people that Thea achieves in Panther Canyon was Willa Cather's own experience in Walnut Canyon, Arizona, when she first visited there in 1912.[5] Doctor Archie is Dr. McKeeby of Red Cloud, with whom young Willa made house calls during the time she thought her interest was in medicine. Ray Kennedy is from a man named

Tooker, who was the companion of Willa's brother Douglass when she visited him in Winslow, Arizona, and, according to Edith Lewis, Spanish Johnny was derived from the young Mexican Julio, by whom for a time Willa Cather seems to have been swept off her feet. Mrs. Kronborg's rawhide whip is Mrs. Cather's own whip, and Thea's agony over "tree-diagramming" poems reflects the author's own running feud with Professor L. A. Sherman at the University of Nebraska.

There are passages in *The Song of the Lark* that might fairly be called artless: "Thea and Mrs. Kronborg had many friends among the railroad men, who often paused to chat across the fence, and of these we shall have more to say." Yet Ray Kennedy's death is carefully prepared for, and Thea's rivalry with Lily Fisher, the pride of the Moonstone Baptists, who has no real talent and no generosity of spirit, foreshadows her attitude toward other singers later on. The atmosphere of Chicago when Thea goes there to study in the days when Theodore Thomas is developing what was to become the Chicago Symphony Orchestra is successfully evoked, as is Thea's ecstasy upon hearing Dvořák's New World Symphony for the first time. "As long as she lived that ecstasy was going to be hers. She would live for it, work for it, die for it, but she was going to have it, time after time, height after height." In one of the interesting backward glances Willa Cather did so well we are reminded that Theodore Thomas himself had had a similar experience when he was "awakened...by two women who sang in New York in 1851 — Jenny Lind and Henrietta Sontag. They were the first great artists he had ever heard, and he never forgot his debt to them." Equally impressive in a totally different way is the presentation of Thea's contacts with her generous and discerning piano teacher, Andre Harsanyi, and the very capable but mean-spirited Madison Bowers, the best voice teacher in Chicago. It is Harsanyi who, in one of the novel's most quotable passages, defines Thea's "secret" when he comes to New York to hear her after she has established herself as a great singer: "It is every artist's secret — passion. That is all. It is an open secret, and perfectly safe. Like heroism, it is inimitable in cheap materials."

Like Alexandra Bergson's mating with Carl Linstrum, Thea's with Fred Ottenburg is handled fairly casually, and there is general agreement that it is the weakest thing in the novel, not because it is unconvincing in itself, but because it is never made to interest the reader very much. Nor can one easily believe that it interested either Thea or her creator very much in comparison to the girl's career.

But perhaps, after all, that was the impression Miss Cather wished to convey.

Besides her rejection of "the full-blooded method, which told everything about everybody," Willa Cather disparaged *The Song of the Lark* on another ground: "The story set out to tell of an artist's awakening and struggle; her floundering escape from a smug, domestic, self-satisfied provincial world of utter ignorance. It should have been content to do that. It should have disregarded conventional design and stopped where my first conception stopped, telling the latter part of the story by suggestion merely." This point of view is wholly characteristic of the author, and its implications reach far beyond *The Song of the Lark* and indeed of literature itself. It ties up with her obsession with youth ("Optima dies ... prima fugit"), and it explains why she enjoyed quoting Jules Michelet to the effect that the goal of the journey is nothing but the road itself is all. It seems therefore that it calls for some consideration at this point.

My principal difficulty with this is its tacit assumption that the goal is not really worth attaining, which would seem to reduce all human activity to a kind of shadowboxing. We only make believe we wish to arrive in order to keep ourselves occupied and to give us the zest we need to keep going in order to achieve something we do not really want. We function under the stimulus of what Ibsen called "vital lies" and Conrad "dynamic illusions."

In her article on "Three American Singers,"[6] Miss Cather rather sacrificed Geraldine Farrar and Louise Homer to Olive Fremstad on the ground that it was Fremstad who was trying to scale what Miss Farrar called the "frozen heights." This was probably fair enough if one identifies the operatic heights with Wagner, as I believe Miss Cather was at this time inclined to do. Elisabeth in *Tannhäuser* was the only Wagnerian role Miss Farrar ever sang, and though she regarded it as one of her finest achievements, she was not allowed to sing it often, and, though she had also prepared Eva, Elsa, and Sieglinde, she never had a chance to sing them at all.[7] Yet at the height of her career, she declared (contra Miss Cather) that she now found it all quite as wonderful as she had expected it to be in the days of her aspiring girlhood. To be sure, even Miss Farrar found it necessary to qualify, warning unthinking aspirants that "art is not the medium stratum of life but its flowered inspiration and emotional poetry; it demands and obtains its sacrifices and sorrows which modify and chasten its glory, and your own soul best knows the toll you pay." Moreover the operatic contemporary who in some ways came closest to Miss Farrar, Mary Garden, sounds more like

Thea when she tells us that she poured everything she was capable of giving into her work and that off the stage, consequently, her life was empty. Yet Miss Farrar also said that "if those who come in contact with me find a sense of encouragement and enrichment, that is all I ask of life. Far more important to me than to have succeeded in being a great artist will be to have succeeded in being a great human being." Geraldine Farrar honored me with her friendship over forty years, and I am sure that nobody who ever had the privilege of knowing her could possibly doubt that she succeeded in achieving this ambition. Mary Garden I met only twice, though, being a Chicagoan, I saw much more of her on the stage, but this was enough to make me sure that she seriously underrated herself in the statement I have quoted. She was vital, outgoing, and dynamic, and though she was a tireless self-advertiser in the newspapers, out of the spotlight she had that rarest gift among celebrities, always to give the impression of being more interested in the person she was talking to than she was in herself. Olive Fremstad I never either saw or heard, and unfortunately her few recordings are not good enough mechanically to make a fair estimate of her capacities possible.[8]

3

In *My Ántonia* (1918), the unquestioned masterpiece of Willa Cather's first period as a novelist and one of the most luminous and enduring works of modern American fiction, she returned to the material and the method of *O Pioneers!* "Here, unless I err greatly," wrote H. L. Mencken, "we have the best piece of fiction ever done by a woman in America."[9] If anything, the fabric seems even more loosely woven here; later, of course, one perceives a basic, subtle, underlying unity. Only, as E. K. Brown observes, "Everything... is there to convey a feeling, not to establish a social philosophy, not even to animate a group of characters. The feeling attaches to persons, places, moments: if one were to pin it in a phrase it might be called a mournful appreciation of 'the precious, the incommunicable past.'"[10]

The story opens in the fall of 1885, when the narrator, Jim Burden, is ten years old, and Ántonia fourteen, and closes in 1916. Jim is now a prosperous New York lawyer, childless, not too happily married, and unfulfilled in his personal life, who looks back upon his childhood days with Ántonia on the Divide, despite all their hardships, as his season in Arcadia. Miss Cather afterwards spoke of Ántonia's original, Annie Sadilek, as "a Bohemian girl who was

good to me when I was a child. I saw a great deal of her from the
time I was eight until I was twelve. She was big hearted and essentially romantic." But she also said she preferred to have Ántonia's
story told by Jim Burden because much of what she knew about
her came from young men. "She had a fascination for them, and
they used to be with her whenever they could." As the title warns
us, the book not intended to give its readers an objective view of
Ántonia or, for that matter, of anything else. It is "my," that is,
Jim's Ántonia that he gives us. A very clear line of demarcation was
drawn between Ántonia and the other immigrant "hired girls" of
the area and the "town girls," who were what later came to be
called "WASPs." But as Frances Harling tells Jim of the former,
"You always put a kind of glamour over them."

The use of the narrator is not significant for this reason alone
however. It makes Jim Burden much more important in the story
than its early critics realized, thus serving, in at least a measure,
to undercut the objection that in such sections as book 3 ("Lena
Lingard") unity was violated because Ántonia disappeared for the
time being from the narrative. Willa Cather believed that novels of
feeling were best told by a participant and novels of action by an
omniscient author. The early critics sometimes observed that the
book was not "really" a novel — "Why should it be?" asked the
author. Actually it *is* a novel, but it is a novel in the form of memoir,
and memoirs do not naturally take on a tightly knit form. "I knew
I'd ruin my material if I put it into the usual fictional pattern. I just
used it the way I thought absolutely true." Ántonia is lured away
from Black Hawk by a promise of marriage from a rascally railroad
conductor named Larry Donovan, who betrays her and leaves her
with a baby to support. If the book is a memoir, it is completely natural that Jim should not know about this until, after his return to
Black Hawk, the Widow Steavens ("The Pioneer Woman's Story")
should cue him in on what happened after his departure. More important still is the fact that the author's method of narration suits
the tone and the mood of the story even more decidedly than it af-
fects its structure. As Terence Martin puts it: "We are never really
on the prairie with Jim, nor does he try to take us there. Rather,
he preserves his retrospective point of view and tells us what it was
like for him to be on the prairie."[11]

It was ironical that Ántonia should be the "hired girl" to suffer a
sexual mishap, for it was she, not Lena Lingard nor Tiny Soderball
nor the "Three Bohemian Marys," who was a strictly moral girl.
From the time her child was born "she loved it . . . as dearly as if she

had had a ring on her finger, and was never ashamed of it." Many years later she says that she would never have married Cuzak if he had objected to the baby, but that he had loved her from the first as dearly as if she had been his own. None of this means however that, in the ordinary sense of the term, Ántonia is idealized. She does not see the future of the land like Alexandra Bergson and lay her plans accordingly. Rather she is a part of it. She feels; she does not plan. But her roots run deeper than Alexandra's and one feels that she has even more depth. She comes of a family that lives in what is virtually a dugout and that might well have starved without the generosity of Grandmother Burden. Her mother and her brother are mean, grubbing, grasping people, and her father, whom she adores, a man of considerable cultivation, kills himself to escape from conditions he has never been made qualified to endure.[12] When, after his death, his daughter works in the fields like a man, she loses her "nice ways," as Jim's grandmother had foreseen she would: "Ántonia ate noisily now ... and she yawned often at the table and kept stretching her arms over her head, as if they ached." Later, when the Vannis come to Black Hawk and set up an itinerant social parlor, she develops the dance craze and everything that goes with it. But when, after a twenty-year absence, Jim encounters her again as the mother of many children, an aging woman, who has lost her teeth but not "the fire of life," she has become the earth mother, "a rich mine of life, like the founders of early races." In a worldly sense, both Lena Lingard and Tiny Soderball, who have escaped all her responsibilities, have been much more successful in the world than she, but hers is the fulfilled life.

There remains one interesting, though perhaps unanswerable, question about Jim's relationship with Ántonia. If she meant as much to him as his memoir seems to indicate, why did he never attempt to establish a love relationship with her? Was it because, like so many of his fellow townsmen, he was too much of a snob to marry a "hired girl"? When they were both children, she once tried to give him a ring, which he refused to accept. Later on he tells her, "I'd have liked to have you for a sweetheart, or a wife, or my mother or sister — anything a woman can be to a man." Possibly Ántonia appealed to him less sexually than that "fair Norwegian," the luscious Lena Lingard, of whom he used to dream that she came to him across the field, half-naked, with a reaping hook in her hand, saying, "Now I can kiss you as much as I like." Jim may possibly have had intercourse with Lena, when she came to him in Lincoln; Willa Cather apparently preferred not to tell us, one way or the other. Yet

he says, "I used to wish I could have this flattering dream about
Ántonia, but I never did." A complete and authoritative answer to
the question I have asked is probably impossible, but Jim does say
that it was the "idea" of Ántonia that was a part of his mind, and
John J. Murphy very likely comes about as close as we can come
to answering our question when he sees him "restricting his pos-
session" of her "to the imaginative realm, where she can be refined
and idealized," which would be quite in harmony with the relaxed
and nostalgic tone of the book in general and may even have some
bearing on the comparative failure of his own marriage.

As a novel of memory, *My Ántonia* naturally draws most of its
material from what the author remembered of her own Nebraska
childhood. If the land is not quite so all-important here as it was
in *O Pioneers!*, the terrain itself is not therefore less clearly envi-
sioned and described. Willa Cather first encountered Annie Sadilek
the Miners' "hired girl" in Red Cloud. Mr. Harling is Mr. Miner,
who, with his brother, owned the leading store in town. His wife,
Julia, was an accomplished musician, who introduced Willa to standard music. Frances Harling is their daughter Carrie, to whom and
her sister Irene, the novel was dedicated "in memory of affections
old and true."[13]

Jim's ride to the farm on the night of his arrival in Nebraska
comes close to being a record of the author's own experience. His
grandparents are Willa's own, William and Caroline Cather, and
the cane Grandmother uses to protect herself against rattlesnakes
is Caroline's own cane. The account of Jim's stay at the University
of Nebraska was obviously based upon Willa's own, and Gaston
Cleric is Herbert Bates, her favorite instructor in English. It is interesting that Jim's stay at Harvard is passed over; was this because
here Miss Cather had no memories of her own to draw upon? Even
the appalling Wick Cutter had an original in a loan shark, M. R.
Bentley. The murder and suicide at the Cutters' really happened,
but in Arkansas, after they had left Red Cloud, and some of the
more dramatic details, as well as the wife's fantastic appearance,
were apparently Miss Cather's own invention.[14]

But there were literary sources also. Curtis Dahl calls the book
"a genuine *Georgic,* but an American rather than a Roman *Georgic.*" Virgil's words echo through it: *Optima dies...prima fugit*
and *Primus ego in patriam...in patriam meum...deducam* (I shall
be the first to bring the Muse into my country). Virgil's Mantua,
like Willa Cather's Nebraska, was a new land in the writer's time.
Recently Susie Thomas has also suggested that the *Aeneid* may

have exercised some influence.[15] Even aside from such specific references however, the whole tone of the book makes it clear that it came from a mind attuned to the classics and disciplined by their austerity.

Of other sources the Bible is the most important, especially in the section dealing with Shimerda's suicide and burial and in the association of the huge rattlesnake that Jim kills with "the ancient, eldest Evil," but this latter incident also involves the whole world of Northern myth and folklore in its echo, its modernization, and, in a way, its parody of the story of St. George and the Dragon. Here already in Willa Cather's writing, all the glamour belongs to the past, for Jim's snake, disgusting as it is in its obscene bulk, is old, fat, lazy, and not very dangerous. Bernice Slote mentions both George Sand's *Antonia* and Browning's "Ivan Ivanovich" as possible sources.[16] As for possible influences from other arts than literature, Murphy has suggested that the tone of the narrative has been colored by the work of the Barbizon painters and the impressionists and luminists influenced by them, especially in many impressionistic renderings of landscape, and finds Jim arranging what he sees in the manner of genre paintings, beginning with the description of the newly arrived Shimerdas huddled on the station platform.

There are at least three outstanding images in *My Ántonia*. The first, that delight of the Freudian critics, Lena Lingard's reaping hook, has already been mentioned.[17] The second is the most famous image in the whole Cather oeuvre, the picture of the abandoned plow, magnified and silhouetted against the descending sun. The third and the most satisfying to my way of thinking comes near the end of the book, where Jim sees Ántonia's children bursting from the cave where they store provisions, "big and little, tow-heads and gold heads and brown, and flashing little naked legs, a veritable explosion of life out of the dark cave into the sunlight." Woodress calls this "a modern enactment of the ancient Eleusinian Mysteries, that celebrated the earth's fertility two thousand years before Christ."[18]

In the last analysis however, the book must stand or fall with the heroine — "my Ántonia," Jim Burden's Ántonia, Willa Cather's Ántonia, and now the world's Ántonia. If Willa Cather cannot persuade her readers to accept this woman at the author's valuation, nothing else will much avail.

To understand this we must remember that Miss Cather, who had as much respect for the carpenter who made good bookshelves for her as she had for the authors of the books she placed upon them, and who ranked among artists "the German housewife who set be-

fore her family on Thanksgiving Day a perfectly roasted goose,"
saw her Ántonia — and Annie Sadilek Pavelka too — as "one of
the truest artists I ever knew in the keenness and sensitiveness of
her enjoyment, in her love of people, and in her willingness to take
pains." Her career, as Philip Gerber sees it, "was to live merely for
the rich experience of living." She reminds him of Thoreau "with-
drawing to Walden purposely to confront life, drive it into a corner,
and derive its essential quality." But perhaps Richard Giannone is
the one who puts it best of all when he describes her gift as that of
"absolute love."[19]

6

Novels: Studies in Frustration

1

Willa Cather discovered her method in O *Pioneers!* only to depart from it immediately in *The Song of the Lark;* then, having perfected it in *My Ántonia,* she departed again in her World War I novel, *One of Ours* (1922), much her longest work after the *Lark,* which it resembled not in subject matter but in its accumulation of detail and its development.

It was four years in the making, and, according to the author, took more out of her than any other book. Writing began in the fall of 1918. In the spring of 1920, with the book two-thirds done, she felt that she could not handle the French part without renewing and extending her impressions of France, and in June she went to Paris for a rather extended stay. The novel was completed in the spring of 1922. After reading the manuscript, Alfred Knopf telegraphed her enthusiastically that it was the best thing she had done (which it was not), but he thought her proposed title, "Claude," quite impossible. She at first refused to change it, then agreed to let her friend, Fanny Butcher, literary editor of the Chicago *Tribune,* decide. Miss Butcher agreed with Knopf,[1] and the book appeared in the autumn.

With fifty thousand copies sold during the first year and the Pulitzer Prize in the bag, there could be no question as to the book's "success." It was its author's first "best-seller." But critical opinion was sharply divided. Practically everybody agreed that the Nebraska part was vintage Cather. But the war part raised issues that carried far beyond "mere literature." Perhaps the sharpest expression of dissatisfaction came from Heywood Broun: "It seems to Miss Cather that the war was not without purpose, since it gave significance to the life of farm boys in Nebraska. The hero of the book loses his life and finds his soul. We happen to believe that there is such a thing as setting too high a price even upon souls, and war is too high a price." When her next novel, *A Lost Lady*, appeared, Broun welcomed Miss Cather back from the war, safe and sound.

To be sure, it was not only because of her treatment of the war (of which more later) that Miss Cather was taken to task. She was accused of having started out to write one kind of book and ending up with another, of writing outside her range, and of setting up a problem she did not even attempt to solve. Her great admirer Mencken compared the book to a serial in the *Ladies' Home Journal*. Ernest Hemingway accused her of having got her war out of *The Birth of a Nation*.[2] Sinclair Lewis saw her indulging in "all the commonplaces of ordinary war novels." When she received the Pulitzer Prize, William Lyon Phelps wryly defended the award on the ground that though *One of Ours* was her poorest novel, it was still better than any other writer's best. As late as 1941, Stephen Vincent Benét thought the novel its writer's only failure. For once "the clear eye did not see and the architecture is confused."

The author's reaction to all this is interesting. In 1925 she declared that *One of Ours* "had more of value in it" than any other of her books. "I like best of my books the one that all the highbrow critics knock." But the record is not quite clear. She conferred with Dorothy Canfield, whose knowledge of France she respected, to help her get things right, arranged for her friend to review the book in the *New York Times*, and admitted privately that she feared it was a failure. When it appeared, she sent copies to Mencken and Carl Van Doren, with letters explaining what she had tried to do. All in all, I think this is a case of the lady protesting too much. She was not a fool. She could not help knowing that what needed to be checked and rechecked or experienced for the purpose of writing about it could not possibly have the authenticity of what she had lived with for years with no ostensible purpose in mind or that the latter and not the former was what Sarah Orne Jewett had taught her was the kind of material a creative writer, as distinct from a journalist, needed. *One of Ours* is a tour de force and for Willa Cather a highly creditable performance, revealing aspects of her talent not elsewhere exploited. But it is not her masterpiece.

What sparked the book was the death, at Cantigny, in May 1918, of her cousin, Grosvenor P. Cather, the son of Uncle George and Aunt Franc. He was ten years her junior, and she had had a share in looking after him when he was little, but there is no indication that he meant very much to her emotionally while he was alive. They were not altogether congenial; he shared none of her special interests; and he seems to have been even more of a misfit in life than

Claude is in the book. After his death, Aunt Franc allowed Willa to read his letters; from here she went on to David Hochstein's letters[3] and to such classics of the hour as Victor Chapman's letters and Alan Seeger's poems and to extensive interviews with soldiers. It seems hardly an exaggeration to say that she became obsessed with her cousin — or rather, perhaps, with her idea of him — to such an extent that she could not bear to let him go even after she had finished her book. According to David Stouck, she wrote Dorothy Canfield "that she had conceived of Claude as herself, and through him she was reliving vicariously the painful experience of being a misfit in a small town and of being culturally ill at ease in the larger sophisticated world."[4] If this is true, there must be at least as much Willa Cather in Claude Wheeler as there was in Thea Kronborg, which would bring *One of Ours* and *The Song of the Lark* even closer together than one had thought, and in this light it may well be that Miss Cather's protestations of special closeness to *One of Ours* deserve to be discounted less heavily than it has been customary to do.[5]

As already noted, hardly anybody has found any fault with the Nebraska portions of the novel. In this book even the war is more exciting in Nebraska than in France. The frantic reading of newspapers, the hunting for old neglected maps, the wonder of a world expanding, for the first time in American history, to the breadth of the world itself — that all this is authentic must be realized by everybody who lived through those harrowing days. But the Nebraska of *One of Ours* is far from being the Nebraska that Alexandra and Ántonia knew. It is rather the Nebraska of Miss Cather's *Nation* article, "Nebraska: The End of the First Cycle."[6] The spiritual life of man has been shrunken to the lazy, ignorant dogmatism of "Brother" Weldon, and religion is not "the practice of the presence of God" but instead a mechanical "accepting Jesus Christ as your personal Savior" and observing a table of "thou shalt nots." Claude's father, Nat Wheeler, is a rich farmer, whose idea of a good joke is to chop down a beautiful cherry tree, loaded with fruit, because his wife has complained that the cherries are too high for her to reach. Claude is not allowed to attend the state university because "Brother" Weldon has said that there are men on the faculty who are not "professing" Christians. When his father needs him on the farm, he is even withdrawn from the third-rate denominational college he has until then been permitted to attend. His older brother, Bayliss — greedy, intolerant, narrow-minded, "thin and dyspeptic" — is appropriately engaged not in producing but in buying and selling, while the younger, Ralph, is enamored of machines to such an extent that he has no energy left to have much interest in anything that is alive.

Enid Royce, the frigid girl Claude marries, is admirable in the performance of every wifely duty except the one that makes a woman a wife. "She was proud of Claude, was glad to see him when he came in from the fields, and was solicitous for his comfort, [but] everything about a man's embrace was distasteful to Enid; something inflicted upon women like the pangs of childbirth — for Eve's transgression, perhaps." On their wedding night she shuts him out of their stateroom on the train, telling him to find a berth for himself somewhere in the car because she thinks something she ate has disagreed with her. Willa Cather said afterward that she would not have dared to use this incident without knowing of a case in which it had really happened. It is a little difficult to see why Enid should have married at all, especially an "unsaved man." It is easier to see why Claude should have married her, for she is not unattractive personally, and she has been very attentive to him during a period of disablement, though it is harder to see how he could have passed over the schoolteacher, Gladys Farmer, obviously a much more suitable choice, who is condemned by public opinion for her extravagance when she goes to a neighboring city to hear opera. The objection that Miss Cather leaves Claude's marriage hanging in the air is unfair however, for that is just where Enid leaves it when she goes off to China to nurse a sick sister in the mission field, and there is very little likelihood that she will ever return to Claude. The book is in no sense a study of marriage. Marriage is only an incident in Claude's career, marking one more step in his disillusionment with all his peacetime activities.

Though their characters, temperaments, and circumstances are entirely different, Claude is almost as maladjusted on the farm as the hero of "Paul's Case" was in Pittsburgh. Sympathetically as he is presented, one cannot but wonder how much better he would have done under more favorable circumstances. "I don't believe I can ever settle to anything. Don't you feel that at this rate there isn't much in it?" He is twenty-one when we meet him. His brother Bayliss thinks he is secretly a dangerous rebel, and his mother thinks his difficulty is that he has not yet "found his Saviour." He hates his "chump" name, and he hates his appearance. With blue eyes in a red head shaped like a block, he is "exactly the sort of looking boy he didn't want to be." As a child he had had a violent temper and a habit of imposing "physical tests and penances upon himself," but at present one can hardly think him capable of putting up a fight for anything. He had also feared death and hell, yet clung to his own individuality enough to prevent his yielding himself up to the "mysterious change called conversion." Though he "believed in God, and in the spirit of the four Gospels, and in the Sermon on the Mount," he had given up theology as "something too full of evasions and sophistries to be reasoned about." If, on first consideration, it may seem unbelievable that such a young man should fit into the army as well as Claude does and find contentment and fulfillment there, actually this is not the case. The war gives him his first opportunity to identify himself with something he believes in completely and puts him into a position where all his decisions are made for him until he himself acquires a command and finds himself giving orders to a group of men who have no choice but to obey him. For him and his like the war was made. Though Theodore Roosevelt was far from being the fire-eater that many persons who know nothing about him suppose him to have been, he was not exactly a pacifist either. Yet when his oldest son was flirting with the idea of making a career out of the army, he told him that no man should do that unless it had been made clear that he was not capable of making it in civil life.

This brings us at last to the question by which the reviewers of 1922 were so much agitated: What does the book say about war in general and about World War I in particular? Is Claude Wheeler Miss Cather's spokesman? Or is Jean Schwind right when she sees her rejecting Claude's "soft" idealism and all his "beautiful beliefs" by making her last chapter "a devastating punchline to the black joke of Claude's 'heroic' death"?[7]

The author herself would seem to have regarded such questions as pretty much beside the point. She claimed that her focus was not on war or the war but on Claude himself, who was not meant to represent the American soldier in general to say nothing of any particular cause or philosophy. There is enough to this so that it needs to be taken into serious consideration, and it has been accepted, though sometimes with significant modifications, by a number of writers. "When Claude embraces the war," writes Susan Rosowski, "he is as willfully uncritical as he was earlier of Enid." But I do not believe that the matter can be dropped quite there.

In *The Song of the Lark,* Willa Cather writes of Thea Kronborg, who, as we have seen, was partly herself, that she "loved to read about great generals" and cherished a photograph of the Naples bust of Julius Caesar, and Napoléon himself was a great hero of

Willa Cather's in her youth. In 1898 she praised William Gillette's play, *Secret Service,* because it made "no appeal to the gallery through cheap patriotic sentiment," but this, I think, is rather exceptional; only a year before she had seemed to regret that the Greco-Turkish War had been stopped by negotiation. She cherished and cultivated the fiction that she had been named for her soldier uncle, William Sibert Boak, who had been killed in the Civil War, and in her early rebel days, she had herself photographed in what looks like a military uniform and cap. She even liked to think of great writers as conquerors, as Sharon O'Brien has shown.

Miss Cather gave no Christmas presents in 1914, preferring to use the money for Belgian relief, and the next year, if Judge McClung had not put his foot down, she and Isabelle might actually have gone to Germany by way of the Scandinavian countries to interview German leaders for the *New York Evening Mail.* Finally, as late as 1921, when the postwar disillusionment had already set in, she is reported to have declared in a speech at Omaha that "the war developed a new look in the faces of people, a look that the pioneers used to have when they were conquering the soil. A new color was over the land. I cannot name it. But it was the color of glory." In the novel itself, the Germans are "Huns," and the Allied soldiers are idealized, even when they are not high-minded people like Claude and David Hochstein. Even Victor Morse, the ace of the Royal Flying Corps, is admired by Claude, though his off-duty conduct has been far from admirable. The only real pacifist in the book seems to be Claude's hateful brother, Bayliss.

It is true of course that the epilogue is steeped in the disillusionment and disappointment that had gripped the world by the time the novel appeared, so that even the hero's mother, the gentle Mrs. Wheeler, who had thought that the United States ought to get into the war long before such an idea can have occurred to many persons of her temperament and in her station and had lamented that we must have a Democrat in the White House at such a time as this, is driven to comfort herself after Claude's death by rejoicing that he has escaped the anguish he must have suffered had he lived. "He died believing his own country better than it is, and France better than any country can ever be." But this is clearly meant to indicate not that the cause was not worth dying for but rather that it had been betrayed by those who could not sustain the noble idealism in which Claude had died. "It seemed as if the flood of meanness and greed had been held back just long enough for the boys to go over, and then swept down and engulfed everything that had been left at home." Moreover such reports as we have of Miss Cather's own views, as expressed in unpublished letters written during the period under consideration, would seem to me to support what I have written here. Much as I should like to report otherwise, I must therefore reluctantly conclude that on the war issue, Heywood Broun was essentially right in what he wrote of *One of Ours* in 1922.

2

Nobody has ever called *A Lost Lady* (1923) Willa Cather's greatest novel, but many have considered it the most perfectly wrought. T. K. Whipple praised its "classical severity," and E. K. Brown called it the "first of her novels to be wholly uncluttered." Though the author fumbled more in her first attack than was her wont, beginning the story in three different ways and discarding her rejected attempts, once she had found her way, it was written in about five months in 1922. It was a short novel, much like what the French call a nouvelle, the third shortest in her oeuvre, 173 pages in the Autograph Edition, as against 139 for *Alexander's Bridge* and 93 for *My Mortal Enemy,* and when she had finished it, the author at first feared it was too short to be published by itself. Fortunately her publisher knew better. The book was serialized in the *Century Magazine* in advance of book publication.

It is Willa Cather's Portrait of a (Somewhat Soiled) Lady. Its Nebraska is the Nebraska of Claude Wheeler rather than Ántonia Shimerda, and the deterioration of the heroine, Marian Forrester, runs along with the decline of the town, here called Sweet Water, and with young Niel Herbert's painful initiation into some of the truths concerning the complexities of human character. Marian was based upon Mrs. Silas Garber, whom Willa Cather had known as a child, first the wife, then the widow of the founder of Red Cloud, an ex-Union officer, who moved from a dugout to the governorship of Nebraska in four years. Their house, which was "well known from Omaha to Denver for its hospitality and for a certain charm of atmosphere" stood until it was destroyed by fire the very year before it was made to live again in *A Lost Lady.* Willa Cather said that her heroine had lived as "a beautiful ghost in [her] mind for twenty years" before she thought of the book, which was sparked by her reading of the death of Mrs. Garber, then Mrs. Lyra Anderson, in Spokane, Washington, on March 21, 1921. The shock of the news sent her to her room, and when she emerged an hour later, she had her story.[8]

As her reflecting consciousness, Miss Cather used Niel Herbert, as boy and man, who loves and idealizes Mrs. Forrester only to be cruelly disillusioned about her when, approaching her house one summer morning with a bouquet of flowers in his hand, he hears Frank Ellinger's "fat and lazy" voice floating out from her bedroom window. Marian is never presented to us directly or from her own viewpoint. At one time the author planned to write the whole story in the first person with Niel as narrator and indeed began a draft in this way, but she soon became convinced that this would not work out satisfactorily. She once said that Niel was not a character but only a "point of view," but this is an overstatement. He is a very real character in his own right, and the reader is interested in him for his own sake, but by using the method of the omniscient author, winding in and out of Niel's consciousness at will, using his insights and special privileges of observation when she needs them, but not confining herself to them, Miss Cather makes it possible for herself to secure a more comprehensive view of Marian and of her story than would otherwise have been at her command. One chapter begins: "But we will begin this story with a summer morning long ago, when Mrs. Forrester was still a young woman, and Sweet Water was a town of which great things were expected." Call this naïveté or a divine simplicity as you please, the fact remains that it does give the writer elbowroom. She can have Adolph Blum, not Niel Herbert, see Mrs. Forrester and Frank Ellinger emerging together from their tryst in the woods. She can use a flashback to describe the courtship of the Forresters before the story begins, and she can avail herself of a time lapse whenever this suits the needs of her story. She can even have Neil himself weave backwards and forwards in time, giving us his impressions now in the fullness of the tick and then from the more reflective standpoint of later years: "Long, long afterward, when Neil did not know whether Mrs. Forrester were living or dead, if her image flashed into his mind, it came with a brightness of dark eyes, her pale triangular cheeks with long earrings, and her many coloured laugh." If Miss Cather had been more strict about method, she would have had to omit much that she wished to give or else to present it in an awkward, round-about, or second-hand fashion, and she would also have been compelled to make Niel more important in the action of her story than she had planned he should be.

Though there are other vivid characters in *A Lost Lady*, it is of course with Marian herself that the story stands or falls. Willa Cather insisted that she had not attempted a character study of either Marian or her original. "I wasn't interested in her character when I was little, but in her lovely hair and her laugh which made me happy clear down to my toes.... The question was, by what medium could I present her the most vividly, and that, of course, meant the most truly. There was no fun in it unless I could get her just as I remembered her and picture the effect she had on me and the many others who knew her. I had to succeed in this. Otherwise I should have been cheating."[9]

Character study or no, there can be no question that a character was created, and of this the creator must have been fully aware. The secret of Mrs. Forrester's charm is that she is a genius in the field of personal contacts. "If she merely bowed to you, merely looked at you, it constituted a personal relationship." Like all such people, she had immense vitality. "One could talk with her about the most trivial things, and go away with a high sense of elation." Moreover she had an immense interest in people, "even very commonplace people." She is as gracious to the boys who are picnicking near her house when she comes out to bring them cookies as she is to her husband's wealthy and distinguished guests, and when Niel breaks his arm, she has him brought inside and placed on her own bed until he can be looked after. Unlike Alexandra Bergson, Ántonia Shimerda, and Hilda Burgoyne, she is volatile, capricious, and complex, but it is not only in Niel that she inspires loyalty. When Adolph Blum sees her emerging from the woods with Frank Ellinger, it never occurs to him to pass on what he has learned, and when, in the last chapter, Ed Elliott learns that Niel rejoices she was well cared for in her later years he exclaims, "I knew you'd feel that way. I did."

Her great weakness is her dependence upon men, which is much more than mere sexuality or a craving for admiration. Unsure of herself, she depends upon male support; in this respect she is frankly an old-fashioned woman. While her husband is alive, she draws her strength from him, even to the extent of sharing his nobility of spirit. When the bank fails and she learns that he has impoverished himself and her to insure that the depositors shall not lose their savings, she says, "I wouldn't for the world have had him do otherwise for me. He would never hold up his head again. You see, I know him." But with Forrester gone, she drifts like a ship without a rudder until at last she even finds it possible to surrender not only her financial affairs but even herself to such scum as Ivy Peters.

This loathsome creature exemplifies what Willa Cather thought

of as the decline of standards in both personal and business relationships during Marion Forrester's later years. The author takes care
of him once and for all in her first chapter by having him wantonly
blind a woodpecker for the pleasure of seeing it fluttering and floundering about; it was while climbing a tree to catch it and put it out
of its misery that Niel fell and broke his arm. As a business man, he
specializes in chicanery, of which Marian is fully aware, and when
she takes her business away from her husband's old friend, Judge
Pomeroy, and entrusts it to him, she shares in his guilt. It has been
urged by Joseph Wood Krutch and others that in such actions, along
with her drinking and her choice of such lovers as Frank Ellinger
and Ivy Peters, she fails as an artist, but there has been a tendency
to overstress the aesthetic as opposed to the moral element in Niel's
disillusionment in her. Perhaps Miss Cather herself was partly responsible for this by writing that "it was not a moral scruple she had
outraged but an aesthetic ideal." Certainly this element is not only
present but bulks large, but not to the extent that the moral element
is crowded out. Niel quotes Shakespeare to himself — "Lilies that
fester smell far worse than weeds" — and ponders darkly, "Beautiful women, whose beauty meant more than it said...was their
brilliancy always fed by something coarse and concealed? Was that
their secret?" There is both aesthetic and moral outrage in Niel's attitude toward Mrs. Forrester when he learns that she has a lover,
and there is a touching young idealism too, but idealism can be
cruel, and self-righteousness can corrupt it: "It was what he most
held against Mrs. Forrester: that she was not willing to immolate
herself...and die with the pioneer period to which she belonged,
that she preferred life on any terms. In the end Niel went away without bidding her good-bye. He went away with weary contempt for
her in his heart."

Marian fails in much, but it is a mistake to think of her as
wholly an immoralist. After Forrester has been rendered helpless
by a stroke, she looks after him devotedly until he dies, and it never
occurs to her that she could do anything else. After having left Sweet
Water, she sends money every year to purchase flowers for his grave.
Only, the tides of life are still running high in her: "I could dance all
night and not feel tired. I could ride horseback all day and be ready
for a dinner party in the evening." Ellinger becomes her lover before the captain dies, and although the matter is never mentioned
between husband and wife, it is clear that the old man knows how
she conducts herself, and that this knowledge does not, in his mind,
cancel out his gratitude for her services to him nor destroy his love

for her. If this makes him a contemptible cuckold and an immoralist, then that arch-Puritan, John Milton, was an immoralist also, for he wrote in one of his divorce pamphlets that a "good" wife may wrong her husband in other ways even more deeply than an adulteress, for in adultery "nothing is taken from the husband which he misses, or enjoys the less," to which he added that unchastity does not automatically cancel out all other good or womanly qualities: "she may be otherwise loving and prevalent."

An apologia for Marian Forrester does not necessarily have to stop here however. The nobility of self-immolation may easily be overestimated, especially when it thrills those who prefer to have somebody else exercise it. Does survival itself have no moral value? (There are no morals in the grave.) One need not denigrate the martyrs because one perceives that the admiration they have always elicited has been partly inspired by the perverse and unhealthy obsession humanity often cherishes with death. To say that "the blood of the martyrs is the seed of the church" sounds very fine and very noble, but it has one drawback: it does not happen to be true. The most that the blood of the martyrs can have achieved is to have watered that seed. The church survived not in those who died but in those who lived and carried on its work in a humdrum, often compromising world. If all Christians had been martyred, there would have been no church and nobody left to honor them.

3

Willa Cather began writing *The Professor's House* (1925) late in 1923 and completed her work in the winter of 1924–25. *Collier's* paid ten-thousand dollars for the serial rights. Miss Cather later refused to allow *Shadows on the Rock* to be serialized because she did not believe it could be presented effectively in that form. It is a little difficult to see why she could have thought *The Professor's House* better adapted to serialization, nor yet why *Collier's* should have been willing to pay ten-thousand dollars for a novel that one would think must have been caviar to most of their readership. The book, which was dedicated "To Jan [Hambourg] because he likes narrative," sold better than had been expected, but the author's attitude toward it seems to have wavered. At one time she called it "nasty" and "grim," but later she seems to have looked at it more favorably.

In a letter written to a friend in 1938, which she permitted to be published in Knopf's newsletter,[10] Miss Cather managed to suggest a number of sources for her novel. Like "the early French and Spanish novelists," she wished to try fitting the nouvelle (in this case, her book 2, "Tom Outland's Story") into the roman. But she also wished to try to use in fiction "the sonata form" as it appeared in the work of composers who handled it "somewhat freely." Finally, in an exhibition of Dutch paintings she had seen in Paris, she had noticed that though the foreground might be occupied by an interior as "overcrowded and stuffy" as Godfrey St. Peter's house, there would often be in the background "a square window, open, through which one saw the masts of ships, or a stretch of gray sea." In the Dutch paintings the breath of fresh air that blew into these houses came from the ships of the Dutch explorers and traders, but in *The Professor's House* it would come from the Blue Mesa.

She did not particularize the French and Spanish novels she had in mind. Woodress calls her vague about the sonata form, which she is, and suggests that she may have "meant no more than the use of a three-part form based on contrast." But Edward and Lillian Bloom attempt a suggestive analysis in terms of exposition, development, and recapitulation. "Thinking of Beethoven's mastery of form, Miss Cather permits the shape of the structure to be determined by the themes themselves. In the novel again, as in the sonata, mood is a controlling link."[11]

The Blue Mesa business can be better documented. We have already seen the use Willa Cather made of her 1912 visit to Walnut Canyon in *The Song of the Lark*. She returned to the Southwest here and handled it much more impressively: "Such silence and stillness and repose — immortal repose. That village sat looking down into the cañon with the calmness of eternity."[12] Because the cliff dwellers made even their every day utensils beautiful, Tom feels that they must have "lived for something more than bread and shelter," and Willa Cather responded to them almost as eagerly as she had responded to the Nebraska pioneers in her childhood. Father Duchene, who derives from the Belgian priest, Father Haltermann, whom she met in the Southwest, tells Tom, "Like you, I feel a reverence for this place. Wherever humanity has made that hardest of all starts, and lifted itself out of mere brutality, is a sacred spot." Harry Atkins, the Englishman who cooks for Tom and Rodney Blake, is the cockney who was serving Douglass Cather when his sister visited him at Winslow, but the rough elements in the old West, as shown in Blake's background before he teamed up with Tom, like the war scenes in *One of Ours*, show Willa Cather handling material beyond the range of her own experience. How much of her own personality and experience got into this book must depend in part upon the reader's own interpretation,[13] but certainly her devastating picture of Washington bureaucracy, when Tom goes there to report his discoveries, must have come straight out of her own observation when she worked there in her journalistic days, and whether or not she shared St. Peter's malaise, she must at least have felt herself sufficiently close to him to understand his problem and present it sympathetically.

There are several interesting literary references in *The Professor's House* — to *Amis and Amile,* "The Pit and the Pendulum," and *The American* by Henry James, and one interesting quotation from Longfellow.[14] Most interesting of all this however is the use made of Anatole France in connection with the dress forms in St. Peter's study. These forms obviously have some symbolic significance (one suggests maternity, the other a younger, perhaps flashier type), but just what this is, is never spelled out. St. Peter himself gives the source hunters their lead here when he says of the forms that "if they were good enough for Monsieur Bergerat, they are good enough for me."[15]

In considering *The Professor's House,* any discussion of sources must be very closely related to structure. As we have seen, Miss Cather's structure had long before now caused her admirers problems, but nowhere else had she been so daring as here, where the whole of the magnificently written book 2, which is Tom Outland's own first-person account of his adventures in the Southwest before the novel begins, breaks into St. Peter's story. This does considerably more however than to bring into the novel the breath of fresh air that was promised with the reference to the Dutch paintings. St. Peter's contacts with Tom Outland, the most brilliant pupil he ever had, had brought him both great stimulation and an enlarged vision of both history and life. When Tom was killed in World War I, he was engaged to St. Peter's older daughter, Rosamond, to whom he left the patent of an aircraft engine that has since earned considerable money. Ironically it has also corrupted not only Rosamond but everybody else who has come within the sphere of its influence except St. Peter himself, who has refused to profit financially by his association with Tom, and even he has been estranged from his family by its effects. Book 2 then is the "turquoise set in dull silver" referred to in the book's epigraph, the contrast being that between Tom's selfless purity and disinterested idealism and the materialistic commercialism of the world from which he escaped through death but into which St. Peter has been compelled to survive. This is brought out through "an intricate network of correspondences, part relating to part," which produces a story that does not chronicle an "imaginative escape from the unsatisfactory modern world into a vision of past but inconceivable beauty and harmony," but concerns itself rather with "fallen man's failure to integrate his vision of harmony with the realities of his emotional nature."[16]

Except for "Tom Outland's Story," *The Professor's House* is a curiously static novel, for nearly the whole drama is played out in St. Peter's mind. He is in his early fifties, a professor, presumably of history, in a state university in sight of Lake Michigan. There have been two great passions in his life — his love for his wife Lillian and his association with Tom Outland. Now Outland is dead, and Lillian feels that at St. Peter's age it is "more dignified" for him to have a bedroom of his own. His eight-volume work on the Spanish explorers has been recognized as a distinguished piece of scholarship, and with it finished, he feels pretty much at a loose end. The prize money he received for his history has enabled his wife to build a fine new house; only he cannot bear to tear himself out of his uncomfortable study in the old one, where his most important work was done and he and his family were happy. At the university he seems to have lost his fight against the forces in the legislature and even on the faculty who would like to turn an institution of learning into a trade school by stressing utilitarian, commercialized rather than cultural courses.

Rosamond is married to Louis Marsellus, who manages her financial affairs with what may be regarded as either admirable or appalling efficiency.[17] Her trip to Chicago to buy furnishings for the Norwegian manor house that is being built with Tom's money, for her and her husband, and which they have had the appalling gaucherie to call "Outland," is an "orgy of accumulation" that her father can only compare to Napoléon's looting of the Italian palaces. The younger daughter Kathleen is married to Scott McGregor, who was a classmate of Tom's. Scott would like to do important work as a writer, but so far he has been successful only with newspaper verses and "uplift" editorials, which he hates. By nature Kathleen is a much sweeter person than Rosamond, but she has allowed her resentment against her sister to proceed to such lengths that her life is being poisoned. "When she comes toward me, I feel hate coming toward me, like a snake's hate."

Louis Marsellus himself is far from being a bad man. He would gladly have given St. Peter a share in Tom's riches had the professor not steadfastly refused to accept it. When St. Peter and Lillian go to Chicago with the Marselluses, Louis puts them up in an expensive suite at the Blackstone, and he would gladly have included them both in a European jaunt had St. Peter been willing to go. But the insensitivity he shows toward the feelings of others is amazing and the innocently boastful way he shows off his and Rosamond's possessions, which might be endearing in a child, is exasperating in a grown man.

Lillian St. Peter however has so wholeheartedly accepted both her son-in-laws (and Louis's munificence along with them) that her husband not unreasonably feels that they have taken over his old place in her affections. "With them she had begun the game of being a woman all over again." Some readers, especially James F. Maxfield,[18] have gone so far as to blame him, not her, for their estrangement, and there can be no doubt that there is a case here. Lillian has obviously loved her husband deeply, taken good care of him, and devoted herself to his interests. Even now she is sensitive enough so that her heart can still bleed for him when she senses how Rosamond has hurt him, and when he tells her that they ought to have been "picturesquely shipwrecked" when they were young, she replies, "How often I've thought that!" She is justified too in her feeling that her husband is foolishly, even irrationally, stubborn in refusing to move out of his old study, even though to retain it he must rent the whole house in which it is contained. When the family members are in Europe, he reads their letters carelessly and looks forward with dread to their return. "He loved his family, he would make any sacrifice for them, but just now he couldn't live with them." Like other Cather characters, he would really like to return to his boyhood ("Optima dies... prima fugit"), but with him the thought had become an obsession. Youth had been the only real time of his life; all the rest had been "accidental and ordered from the outside." Lillian is correct also when she accuses him of turning into himself and shutting himself off from the rest of them. During the last summer of the novel, he does not expect to live to teach in the fall term, and at the end he escapes suicide by only a hair. Finally, though we are not told that Lillian resented it, in his own way, he displays an insensitivity almost equal to Marsellus's own when he compares himself to Euripides, in his old age, going to live in a cave by the sea. "It seems that houses had become insupportable to him. I wonder whether it was because he had observed women so closely all his life."

In the last analysis nevertheless, any attempt to exalt Lillian at Godfrey's expense must be rejected as clearly opposed to the tone, temper, and intent of the book. Lillian had never really understood the importance of Tom Outland in her husband's life; in a sense she had been jealous of her husband's friendship with him from almost the inception of their acquaintance, and when she is embarrassed by the lecture in which her husband bares his heart, telling his students that only art and religion, which are basically the same thing, have ever satisfied man's basic needs and that technology has never done anything for him beyond helping to make him feel more comfortable, one wonders whether she understands anything else much better. ("You cheapen yourself, Godfrey. It makes me a little ashamed. It is in rather bad taste.") She berates him at length when she thinks he has not been sufficiently genial at a dinner party. After all has been said and done, it is she, not he, who has surrendered to the basic materialism of the time.

None of this means that St. Peter has not failed to make the adjustment to life that a man must make if he is to be either happy or useful in his later years. What happens at the end when the wind blows out the gas stove while he is resting in his study is that he half wakes and smells the gas but sinks back into slumber. He does not deliberately seek death; he is simply too tired to muster the energy needed to get up and turn the stove off. He settles down and accepts what fate deals out to him, and when that turns out to be the sewing woman Augusta, he accepts her too. Yet his traumatic experience has also been in some sense creative; if St. Peter will never again be what he was when he courted Lillian or even when he wrote about the Spanish explorers, neither will he be what he has been this last lonely summer. It is all a little like what Henry James had happen to Spencer Brydon in "The Jolly Corner." Moreover, as in that story itself, there is some room for difference of interpretation about what actually happened. Taking her figure from one of Robert Frost's poems, Willa Cather told the poet that her novel had nothing to do with "a system of philosophy" but only deals with "letting go with the heart." But not all readers have been content to leave it there.

Dorothy McFarland speaks eloquently for those who see the "emergence of St. Peter's boyhood self [as] indicative, not of his regression to a more primitive kind of consciousness, but of his incipient rebirth." As she reads the novel, his near asphyxiation is a "spiritual experience, the death that is necessary for the birth of the new man." The resemblance to what I think it fair to call the majority interpretation of "The Jolly Corner" seems very close at this point.[19] And, in her own way, Susie Thomas comes even closer when she discerns kinship between St. Peter and Bishop Latour, reminding us that though Latour finds rich fulfillment, in his time he too had "known blackness and despair." Both men are "fastidious, cultured, tolerant, humane and lonely," but, above all, they are "artists." Whether we accept this interpretation or prefer instead to stop with the simpler, bleaker conviction that St. Peter had now learned to "live without delight," there seems no reason to doubt that he had passed through the crisis in which we have seen him immobilized since the beginning of our acquaintance with him. He may never again scale the heights, but at least we need no longer fear that he may destroy himself. Instead he will come to some sort of terms with himself, with his family, and with life. And surely it is no accident that it should be the faithful, matter-of-fact, unimaginative Augusta, whom he had used to tease about her comfortably settled religion, who should save his life and see him through.[20]

Whatever other meanings may be found in — or read into — *The Professor's House,* the book does involve ideas that are basic in Willa Cather's reading of life. Money corrupts, and redemption must be sought through the humanities, not science. Rodney Blake's selling for profit the Indian remains that Tom had regarded as a sacred trust for posterity may be excused on the ground that Blake is only an ignorant cowboy with a spotty past, but what shall be said of academics who themselves worship the Golden Calf? Professor Crane has been one of St. Peter's strongest allies in his fight for high academic standards, yet, because he had aided Tom Outland in his research, in the end both he and his wife find their fingers itching for a share in his riches.[21]

Different as the two books are, *The Professor's House* seems to occupy much the same place in Willa Cather's oeuvre as does *The Blithedale Romance* in Hawthorne's. By no means her greatest novel, it is in a way the most interesting, certainly the subtlest and most teasing, capable of yielding fresh suggestions upon every reading. It is interesting that Woodress should have called its hero a Hawthornesque character and that Alfred Kazin should find it "one of those imperfect and ambitious works whose very imperfections illustrate the quality of an imagination."

4

Willa Cather wrote down her most austere literary convictions in "The Novel Démeublé" in 1922, but only in 1926 in *My Mortal Enemy* did she achieve a completely logical realization of them. The book runs to less than one hundred pages in the generously, even luxuriously spaced pages of the Autograph Edition, with every chapter beginning on the right-hand page. The story is stripped to essentials beyond anything else its author ever wrote, with suggestion taking the place of portrayal wherever possible and of analysis throughout. In these pages, Myra Driscoll's hometown in Illinois, from which she runs off from her grim, rough old Irish Catholic great-uncle, who promptly disinherited her, to marry "a German freethinker,"[22] is only a house and a name, and the place on the Pacific Coast where she dies is a cliff overlooking the sea and a cheap hotel of which we learn nothing except that the rooms above the Henshawes' are occupied by "cattle" who torment Myra with their endless tramping back and forth over her head. More is made of setting to be sure in the Washington Square portion of the story, where the young narrator, Nellie Birdseye, and her Aunt Lydia visit Myra and her husband at Christmastime. Miss Cather once said that what she tried to catch here was the New York atmosphere as it was about 1904, but most of this too is given by suggestion. All the rest is from what Nellie saw or heard from Aunt Lydia, for in *My Mortal Enemy,* for once, we find Willa Cather using a female narrator. Nellie is only fifteen when she meets Myra, who has already become a legend to her, upon the latter's return to Parthia for a visit. Shortly after, Nellie and her aunt go to New York at Christmas, and we do not meet any of these people again until ten years later, when Nellie comes upon the Henshawes in "a sprawling overgrown Western city which . . . ran about the shore, stumbling all over itself and finally tumbled untidily into the sea." Myra is now a sick, bitter woman, and Nellie does not lose sight of her again until she dies.

The only date given in the book is the "1876" Oswald had written in a volume of Heine's poems he had given "Myra Driscoll," obviously in the days of their courtship. The novel is as cryptic as they come; there have even been different views as to the identity of the "mortal enemy" of the title. The heroine is "difficult," complex, perverse far beyond Marian Forrester, and hard to describe fairly. The novel was serialized in *McCall's Magazine* in advance of book publication; it is amusing to speculate on what the average reader of serials in women's magazines made of it. Alfred Knopf published it in a beautiful, delicate little boxed book, printed in two colors, with line drawings by W. A. Dwiggins at the beginning of each chapter, all as suggestive as the text itself.

There is not much to say about the sources of *My Mortal Enemy.* There are significant references to Shakespeare, especially to the history plays and *King Lear.* Skaggs's suggestion that Myra may have been based on the actress Clara Morris seems sheer guesswork. Miss Cather said that Myra had an original who had died some fifteen years before the story was written, to which E. K. Brown added that Willa had known her in Lincoln. Woodress speculates that she may have been Myra Tyndale, the sister-in-law of the author's friend, Dr. Julius Tyndale; the daughter of an Irish immigrant, she died in Seattle in 1903. One other actual person appears under her own name among the minor characters. This is the great Polish actress, Helena Modjeska, whom Willa Cather tremendously admired and whom she had met. One of the unforgettable scenes in the book is that in which Modjeska sits regal in the moonlight while her unnamed fellow countrywoman sings the "Casta diva." At Christmastime, Myra sends Madame Modjeska a very expensive holly tree, which she can ill afford, and after the great actress has died, she has a mass for her soul's repose celebrated every year on the anniversary of her death. "My aunt often said," writes Nellie, "that Myra was incorrigibly extravagant, but I saw that her chief extravagance was in caring for so many people and in caring for them so much."

Who, then, is the "mortal enemy"? "Why must I die like this, alone with my mortal enemy?" There can be no doubt as to what Myra means. Her husband is her mortal enemy. At one point, her mind failing, she even blames him for the noise the "animals" are making overhead. "People can be lovers and enemies at the same time, you know. We were.... A man and woman draw back from that long embrace, and see what they have done to each other." "Perhaps I can't forgive him for the harm I did him."

But surely this is not the whole story. "We've destroyed each other." "It was money I needed." "I am a greedy, selfish worldly woman. I wanted success and a place in the world." But she is also a self-tormentor. A drive with Nellie through the park in a hansom cab is ruined for her when they pass an acquaintance who bows to her from her own carriage, and a matinee is embittered because she glimpses in a loge a man who, she thinks, failed her husband in friendship. "It's all very well to forgive our enemies; our enemies can never hurt us very much. But, oh, what about forgiving our friends? — that's where the rub comes!" And Nellie ponders how "violent natures like hers sometimes turn against themselves ... against themselves and all their idolatries."

But had Oswald failed her? The first thing Nellie noticed about him was a something "that suggested personal bravery, magnanimity, and a fine, sensitive way of doing things." Obviously he is very sensitive to the charm of women, and obviously Myra has been jealous of him; their quarrel over the keys and the incident of the topaz cuff links are enough to prove that. Aunt Lydia, "sick of Myra's dramatics," exclaims, "Man never *is* justified, but if ever a man was...." Even at the end, when he is both working and worrying himself to death over Myra, he obviously derives comfort from the crude little "newspaper girl" at the hotel who admires him and turns to him for counsel. But one can hardly believe that any such flirtations were very serious on his part. Even at the end, he still believes that he would rather have been "clawed" by Myra than "petted" by any other woman. Unlike his wife, who, in her bitterness, would wipe out their past as well as their present and future, he cherishes the memory of every happy hour they ever spent together, thinking of Myra in her youth as a "wild, lovely creature" the memory of whom nothing that came afterwards could ever take away from him. All in all, if Oswald ever wronged Myra, it was less by being attracted by other women than by marrying her himself under the circumstances in which they were placed. After all, a man must have more confidence in himself than most of us can justify to allow a woman to throw away what Myra does to place her whole reliance upon him.

Myra's devotion to her friends and her response to all the nobler qualities in human nature and in art are undoubtedly attractive. "How the great poets do shine on, Nellie! Into all the dark places of the world. They have no night." Yet I must confess I am less attracted by her charms than I am by Mrs. Forrester's, for example. When we first glimpse her, she is "a short, plump woman in a black velvet dress" with "a beautiful voice, bright and gay and carelessly kind," who holds her head haughtily high because she is beginning to develop a double chin and is sensitive about it, but her bantering manner suggests that she is more interested in indulging her own caprices than she is in the feelings of others. "Her sarcasm was so quick, so fine at the point — it was like being touched by a metal so cold that one doesn't know whether one is burned or chilled." As she came to know her better, Nellie would learn — and the reader with her — that Myra's gay and happy laugh could turn malicious and frightening ("she had an angry laugh, for instance, that I still shiver to remember") and that when she was scornful her mouth could seem "to curl and twist about like a little snake."

"Myra Henshawe's tragedy," writes Susan Rosowski, "is that she expected a lover to satisfy her every need; her triumph is that she turned from her idolatries to the truths of religion." The odor of sanctity in which she dies, having learned that religion differs from everything else in that here alone "seeking is finding," prompts the young priest who attends her to wonder "whether some of the saints of the early Church weren't a good deal like her," a statement that strikes some readers as sentimental or even naive. Myra's religion at the end seems without much ethical content; certainly it does not affect her treatment of Oswald, nor does it save her from bitterness and a sense of failure. "Yes, I broke with the Church when I ran away with a German freethinker; but I believe in holy words and holy rites all the same." This seems to be one of her complaints against her husband, yet there is no reason to doubt his complete sincerity when he says he never meant to separate her from her religion, nor is it easy to see why her marriage should necessarily have had this effect. Certainly many Catholic women who married outside the church have still remained faithful to it.[23]

But if many readers and critics of today are not ideally equipped to understand the religious emphasis at the end of *My Mortal Enemy*, they certainly need no help in attempting to read autobiographical significance into works of art. What, then, if anything, is *My Mortal Enemy* saying about Willa Cather and about life?

Certainly Miss Cather's other late books can leave no doubt in any intelligent reader's mind that she sympathized — and sympathized deeply — with Myra's religious devotion at the end. But does this mean that we must agree when Elizabeth Gates Whaley tells us that *My Mortal Enemy* presents "human relationships" as "a tragic necessity" which is never wholly satisfactory and that the book indicts "all that human beings hold most dear — friendship, love, growing old together with someone one loves"?[24] Or that Miss Cather meant just this when she indicated agreement with Fanny Butcher's statement, in her review of the book, that it expressed "the fundamental hatred of the sexes one for the other and their irresistible attraction one for the other"? Or even with Woodress, who says that the novel "apparently drained the last bit of gall from [Willa Cather's] system and cleared the way for the serene historical novels of the next decade"?

Woodress's statement recalls the Shakespearean commentators of other days, who used to talk about the dramatist recovering from the pessimism of his "tragic period" and moving into the serene atmosphere of his "reconciliation plays." That there is nothing in all this I am not prepared to asseverate of either writer, but when, upon hearing the fatally ill Myra lament that she must die alone with her mortal enemy, Nellie Birdseye says, "I had never heard a human voice utter such a terrible judgment upon all that one hopes for," it may be well to remember that Myra is expressing the judgment of a sick mind. This is certainly not Nellie's view, and there is no more necessity to make it Miss Cather's than there is for supposing that Macbeth was speaking for Shakespeare when he saw life as "a tale told by an idiot... signifying nothing."

7

Novels: The Lovely Past

1

Whether or not *The Professor's House* and *My Mortal Enemy* express Willa Cather's mood at the time she wrote them, it must have been clear to her that she could not long continue in this vein. During her last years, sickened by the horrors of World War II, she used to declare that though our present was ruined, we had had a lovely past. But when, in the later twenties, she sought fresh laurels in her two French Catholic novels — *Death Comes for the Archbishop* (1927) and *Shadows on the Rock* (1931) — it was not to the past of her own generation that she directed her search.

In her letter to the editor of the *Commonweal,* describing, at his request, "how I happened to write *Death Comes for the Archbishop,*[1] she tells how she came to feel "that the story of the Catholic Church" in the American Southwest "was the most interesting of all its stories" and that Archbishop Lamy, the first bishop of New Mexico, whose statue she had seen "under a locust tree before the Cathedral of Santa Fé," which he had built, had become almost a personal friend. But none of these impressions jelled for her until she came across a book by William Joseph Howlett, obscurely published in Pueblo, Colorado, *The Life of the Right Reverend Joseph P. Macheboeuf.* "Then, before morning, the story was in my mind. The way of it was on the white wall of that hotel room in Santa Fé, as if it were all in order and color there, projected by a sort of magic lantern."[2] In the book, Lamy became Jean, Father Latour, and Macheboeuf was his right-hand man, Joseph, Father Vaillant.

The novel was not written in "only a few months," as Miss Cather once claimed, but in 1925 and 1926. She stayed four months in the Southwest in 1925 to renew her impressions of the country and began writing upon her return to New York. But it is probably true that "the happy mood in which [she] began the book never paled," and she certainly felt lost after she had finished it. She told

Ida Tarbell that writing it had been the purest pleasure of her life, and to her chosen biographer, E. K. Brown, she expressed the opinion that it was her best book. When it had been completed, she felt so confident of its success that she asked Mr. Knopf for an increase in her royalty rate, which he granted. It was serialized in the *Forum* in advance of book publication.

Howlett's biography of Macheboeuf was then the principal source, but it was by no means the only one. She read diligently in local history and consulted local authorities, sacred and secular. It has been suggested that Chaucer influenced the characterization,[3] that both *The Divine Comedy* and the pattern of the Angelus may have been brought to bear upon the form,[4] and that the "December Night" episode may have been modeled upon Flaubert's "Le Legende de Saint-Julian-Hospitalier."[5]

There were also influences from art, outstandingly from the Puvis de Chavannes frescoes in the Pantheon:

> Since I first saw the Puvis de Chavannes[6] frescoes of the life of Sainte-Geneviève in my student days, I have wished that I could try something a little like that in prose; something without accent, with none of the artificial elements of composition. In the Golden Legend[7] the martyrdoms of the saints are no more dwelt upon than are the trivial incidents of their lives; it is as though all human experiences, measured against one supreme spiritual experience were of about the same importance. The essence of such writing is not to hold the note, not to use an incident for all there is in it — but to touch and pass on.

Another minor influence from visual art concerns the prologue, whose whole outer aspect is taken, feature by feature, from Jehan George Vibert's painting, "The Missionary's Return."[8] The *Commonweal* letter also mentions a much more important matter: "The title...was simply taken from Holbein's *Dance of Death*," in one of which series death comes for an archbishop, but I cannot help feeling that this is a kind of fake source. Miss Cather knew so little about these pictures that in the form in which her letter first appeared she called Holbein Dürer; this was corrected in later printings, in *Willa Cather on Writing* and elsewhere, but this is not the important point. She was not always fortunate in her titles. *Obscure Destinies* is a perfect title, and *The Troll Garden* and *Youth and the Bright Medusa* are at least clever, but, as we have seen, her publisher moved heaven and earth to persuade her not to call *One of Ours* "Claude," and nobody understood what she meant by *The Song of the Lark* until she had painfully explained it. But surely no other title is so glaringly inappropriate as *Death Comes for the Archbishop,* which attempts, for no discernible reason, to drag the charnel house into a book that is a triumphant affirmation of life. Death has no more to do with Latour than with any other human being, nor is any attempt made to make it more important; moreover Latour does not even become an archbishop until the very end of the book.[9]

The action of *Death Comes for the Archbishop* opens in 1851, where we find Father Latour, a "solitary horseman," on the way to his new diocese, and ends in 1889 when he dies, with the prologue in Rome set back in 1848, but most of the events take place between 1851 and 1861, when the cathedral is completed. The underlying theme is the establishment of order and the authority of Rome over the vast, half-civilized territory, but the book is episodic far beyond the author's wont, and the chronology is loose. There are nine "books," besides the prologue, and for the first and last time in Willa Cather's oeuvre not only the books but the chapters within the books have titles. There are separate stories, and there are stories within stories. Events are juxtaposed freely, and there are backward and forward glances where they are needed: "The Latours were an old family of scholars and professional men, while the Vaillants were people of much humbler station in the provincial world." And again: "Bishop Latour's premonition was right, Father Vaillant never returned to share his work in New Mexico." On the whole, scene is more important than sequence. Willa Cather believed that "picture making" was what she did best in fiction, and in no other book has she created anything like so many effective pictures as here. When necessary, historic fact yields to aesthetic arrangement. In life, Bishop Lamy did not live to see his cathedral completed, but he did outlive Macheboeuf, while in the novel the latter is the first to go.

Method too is as homely and comfortable as structure. Mention has already been made of the "solitary horseman," who sent the minds of all seasoned readers of Victorian fiction back to G. P. R. James, who had the habit of beginning his novels with just such a figure. "How, then, had Father Latour come to be here?" "On his arrival at Santa Fé, this was what had happened...." There are straight expository passages also: "In those days, even in European countries, death had a solemn social importance." Or take such comments as this on an Indian custom of which Miss Cather, the passionate conservationist, must have heartily approved: "It was the Indian's way to pass through a country, without disturbing

anything; to pass and leave no trace, like fish through the water, or birds through the air.... [Indians] seemed to have none of
the European's desire to 'master' nature, to arrange and recreate.
They spent their ingenuity in the other direction; in accommodating
themselves to the scene in which they found themselves.... When
they hunted, it was with the same discretion; an Indian hunt was
never a slaughter."

A very wide variety of tone appears in the episodes included.
There is humor in the account of how Father Vaillant persuaded
Manuel Lupon to give him the two white mules he needed and
craved and in the account of how Doña Isabella was pressed into
at last revealing her true age in order to save her daughter's inheri-
tance. There is horror in the account of the killing of Friar Baltazar
and in that of how Buck Scales, the professional killer, was at last
brought to justice, and, above all, in book 4, "Snake Root," which
takes us into the cave once used for snake worship and other ancient monstrosities. No reptile appears here, but the overwhelming
horror many people feel in the presence of reptiles is powerfully
evoked. And there is sweet, simple piety in the saint's legend explaining the origin of the shrine of Our Lady of Guadalupe, and the
touching episode of the poor Mexican woman Sada, whose bigoted,
unsympathetic Protestant American masters have long deprived her
of the consolations of her religion, and who is carried away by
her renewed contact with the holy things of the altar and by the
bishop's ministrations there when she is at last able to steal away
one December night.[10] Here is the same sacramental approach to
religion that Myra Henshawe cherishes in the last part of *My Mortal Enemy,* and even those whose attitude is very different must feel
that this one is in tune with the whole tone of the book as well as
with Miss Cather's own conviction that basically art and religion
are one. Skaggs, who notes that in each episode of the *Archbishop*
there is "some precious object or significant shape to which Latour
is sensitive," also notes that he thinks of his cathedral as "a physical body" that shall express his aspirations "after he has passed
from the scene." In other words, in this book material objects and
events are used to suggest spiritual values; the bishop even finds a
thousand years of history in Father Vaillant's soup. Man is not yet
all spirit; there must be a *means* through which spiritual values can
reach him. Even Calvin, who was certainly no sacramentalist, spoke
illuminatingly of "accommodation." The Bible itself cannot tell us
what God *is;* it can only suggest something of what God is *like* in
terms that our mortal minds can grasp.

The two priests are of course the most carefully drawn and shaded characters, and except that Father Vaillant is not, save fleetingly, as in the episode of the white mules, a comic character, their partnership almost suggests that of Don Quixote and Sancho Panza. Latour is an intellectual aristocrat, refined, aesthetic, and a trifle aloof, all qualities better calculated to endear him to Willa Cather than to the Indians of early New Mexico. Vaillant, on the other hand, is simply, as Woodress puts it "a man of great faith and energy, force of will, and practical know how," and Miss Cather herself tells us that a stranger meeting him for the first time was likely to feel first of all "that the Lord had made few uglier men." As a youth he had aspired "to lead a life of seclusion and solitary devotion: but the truth was, he could not be happy for long without human intercourse." "Doctrine is well enough for the wise, Jean," he tells his friend, "but the miracle is something we can hold in our hands and love." Each man is incomplete without the other, but they make a perfect partnership, and the church needs both.

These, as I say, are the outstanding characterizations, but there are other vivid sketches, some of persons whom we see only very fleetingly. It has been said that some are presented only as personifications of one or another of the seven deadly sins — Father Martínez of lust, Father Baltazar of gluttony, Doña Isabella of female vanity, and so on. The mouth of Father Martínez "was the very assertion of violent, uncurbed passion and tyrannical self-will, the full lips thrust out and taut, like the flesh of animals distended by fear or desire." Surely no medieval physiognomist — not even Chaucer — could have made a better job of describing a man's outer aspect as an index of his inner being. For all that, Miss Cather's characterization of Martínez is by no means unshaded. He is lustful, but he is not mere lust. He has made himself a dictator over the parishes in northern New Mexico, and the bishop knows that, "rightly guided, this Mexican might have been a great man." Latour had never heard the Mass sung more impressively than he sings it. "The man had a beautiful baritone voice, and he drew from some deep well of emotional power. Nothing in the service was slighted: every phrase and gesture had its full value...." Miss Cather daringly allows him to state the case against clerical celibacy in New Mexico with considerable power, and however she may have felt about this, she must certainly have recognized the force of his argument that if the church is to be firmly established in the Southwest, she cannot afford to ignore the native temperament and customs. So does the bishop himself, to such an extent indeed, that when

Martínez falls under ecclesiastical censure and organizes his own schismatic church, he temporizes until, unexpectedly, the padre's own death solves the problem for him.

Death Comes for the Archbishop may be, as its author told E. K. Brown, her finest book, but this does not mean it is the easiest to write about. Moreover, this fact may be the very badge of its greatness. Its materials are too richly varied to be fitted comfortably into any tight pattern of description or characterization. There are not many handles to catch hold of in approaching it, and certainly there is little or nothing to argue about. Speaking of Christina Rossetti's poetry, Sir Walter Raleigh, the Oxford don, once remarked that it came too close to being "pure poetry," with no extraneous elements in it, to make a good subject for discussion. "Sanded poetry," he said, made the best material for lectures; Christina made him wish to cry, not lecture. Something of this sort might, with modifications, be said of the *Archbishop*. It was made not to be discussed but to be read and loved, as it has been, ever since 1927, by a vast number of readers. Perhaps, after all, that is what literature is for.

2

Reference has already been made to the general impression that *My Ántonia* and *Death Comes for the Archbishop* are Willa Cather's most significant novels. The present writer concurs in these judgments, but if he is to be quite frank, he must add that the two he loves best are *Shadows on the Rock* (1931) and *Lucy Gayheart*. I was much pleased when I learned that Ferris Greenslet, whose literary judgment I respected, had said that the *Rock* was the Cather novel he reread most often.

Both books are French Catholic, and both, to use a portmanteau term, are historical novels, but there the resemblance between them ends. The *Rock* is set not in the American Southwest but in French Canada, in Quebec, at the very end of Count Frontenac's life and of the seventeenth century, and instead of being spread out over a large territory during a long stretch of years, as is the *Archbishop*, it all takes place during a twelvemonth. More important than any of this however is the difference between the tone of the two books. The *Archbishop* is vital, passionate, and ardent, the story of two priests who spend their lives in establishing an ecclesiastical kingdom in a pioneer territory, while the loveliness of *Shadows on the Rock* is the loveliness of pale moonlight; its beauty is refracted and reflected through old chronicles of the past. The piece is played steadily, perhaps a bit monotonously for some tastes, in a minor key. Here, indeed, and not in the *Archbishop,* is the real resemblance to Puvis de Chavannes.

Such a book might well have been expected to be caviar to the general, but to the surprise of both author and publisher, this was not the way it turned out. Willa Cather had been in love with the Southwest since 1912, but she never set eyes on Quebec until 1927. After three more visits there, the manuscript of the *Rock* was finished in 1930 and published the next year. It was a Book-of-the-Month Club selection and put its author on the cover of *Time,* and there were three more printings before the end of the year. "And indeed," wrote Alfred Knopf, "it turned out that *Shadows on the Rock* had the largest sale of any novel by Miss Cather published by us: over 183,000 copies through 1963."[11]

Francis Parkman was Willa Cather's favorite American historian, and she was probably familiar with his *Count Frontenac and New France* long before she ever thought of setting a novel in Quebec. E. K. Brown calls the *Jesuit Relations* her second principal source. She substantially accepted Parkman's view of Frontenac, but she rejected both his "rationalism" end his anti-clericalism. The main influence upon her view of the bishop himself must however have come from the Canadian Abbé Henri Arthur Scott, an authority on ecclesiastical history and a biographer of John Baptist Lamy, whom she met and consulted. Among her other sources Brown names Juchereau's history of the Hôtel Dieu at Quebec and the letters of Mother Marie de l'Incarnation, to which Miss Lewis adds Saint-Simon's *Memoirs* for the French background, for Miss Cather explored not only Quebec but also Frontenac's haunts across the sea, before he was swallowed up by his transatlantic exile. Both here and in the *Archbishop* her treatment of Catholicism was so sympathetic that in the thirties it was widely believed she had been converted and she finally felt compelled to set the record straight: "I'm an Episcopalian and a good one, I hope."

There was also one important manuscript source, the diary she found in the Louvre of an apothecary who served under Frontenac. This was important not only for what it contributed directly to the novel but also because it enabled her to refute a learned society that had accused her of permitting Euclide Auclair to use a drug that was unknown in his time.

The Bible speaks of the shadow of a great rock in a weary land, and Christ called Peter's faith the rock upon which he would build his church. In this novel the rock is both literal and symbolic, the actual, physical rock upon which Quebec is built and upon which so many men and events have cast their passing shadows and a symbol of man's longing for permanence and solidity, something upon whose resistance to time and change he may reasonably rest his hopes.[12]

The novel is divided into six books, with an epilogue set fifteen years later. The main action begins in October 1697 and ends in November 1698, being organized around the changing seasons (in which connection Woodress compares it to *Walden*) and the coming of the ships from France, which brings supplies and good or bad news, thus providing the only link between the colonists and the outside world. Cécile Auclair is twelve when the story begins; in the epilogue, set in 1713, she is a happy wife and mother, with Pierre Charron as her husband. There are flashbacks to events lying outside the main range of the story, as in the account of the apothecary's life in France before he came to Quebec as Frontenac's personal physician when the count was appointed governor-general of Canada, and there are rather loosely related episodes, like the saint's legend at the end of book 1, recounting that favorite medieval theme, the mercy of the Blessed Virgin to a repentant prostitute; the story of poor Bichet, helpless victim of French "justice"; and the appalling story of Jeanne Le Ber, the religious recluse.[13]

The action is centered in the apothecary's shop, situated between the Upper Town and the Lower Town and ministering to both, and the principal characters are Euclide Auclair and his daughter Cécile, quite the youngest and probably the most idealized of Miss Cather's heroines, a quite adorable girl. The author's characteristic glorification of the home and the domestic arts finds its ultimate expression in this book. Everything that is warm, comforting, and human is centered in the apothecary's kitchen. The interest in alien customs and culture that informs the *Archbishop* is quite absent from this book; the forest is there all right, but it exists only as a menace. The whole interest of the Auclairs — and, by implication, that of the other colonists — consists of transplanting a bit of French culture, which is the only culture they know or are apparently able to conceive of, into the new world. "Without order," the late Madame Auclair had instructed her little daughter, "our lives would be disgusting, like those of the poor savages. At home, in France, we have learned to do all these things in the best way, and we are conscientious, and that is why we are called the most civilized people in Europe and other nations envy us." But there were still times when "she would think fearfully how much she was entrusting to that little shingled head, something so precious, so intangible, a feeling about life that had come down to her through so many centuries and that she had brought with her across the wastes of obliterating, brutal ocean."

It is not surprising, then, that household ritual, even household utensils, should take on an almost sacramental quality in this book, so that when Cécile goes to visit the Hanois family, who are good, kind people, but slovenly and dirty, she should be so unhappy that she embraces her first opportunity to ask Pierre Charron to take her home. "They had kind ways, those poor Hanois, but that was not enough; one had to have kind things about one, too." That there was a certain narrowness, perhaps even intolerance, about all this Willa Cather realized as clearly as any of her readers. No doubt this is one of the things she had in mind when, in the letter to Governor Wilbur L. Cross reprinted in *Willa Cather on Writing,* which has already been referred to, she said that she had found in Quebec "a kind of feeling about life and human fate that I could not accept, wholly, but which I could not but admire." Narrow it might be, but it had integrity and reality. Or, as she generalizes in the novel itself: "When an adventurer carries his gods with him into a remote and savage country, the colony he founds will, from the beginning, have graces, traditions, riches of the mind and spirit."[14]

As has already been noted, Willa Cather was surprised by the sales her novel achieved and the wide acceptance it found. She had feared it was too static to appeal to many. She had been powerless to change this, for it was indispensable to the effect she sought. Its "curious endurance" was the essential, unchanging quality of the "kind of culture" the French emigrants brought to Quebec. "There another age persists." Picture therefore necessarily became more important than either movement or sequence in her presentation of this life, the effect sought being that of a "series of pictures remembered rather than experienced."

It is important to remember all this in reading *Shadows on the Rock,* but it is also important not to exaggerate it. As has already been noted, the drama, if it can be called that, is centered in the home; the characters turn their backs on the forest. Nevertheless, the forest is *there,* and, across the ocean, but remembered still, France and the French court are there too, in the unjust treatment that has been meted out to Count Frontenac, in the pathetic figure of poor Blinker, who was brought up to be a torturer in the king's prison at Rouen and must live now with the tortures of his own conscience. At that refined court, fine ladies drink viper's broth, and a little girl is torn to pieces by the carp in the king's fishpond. The apothecary's shop may be a closed entity, but these horrors not only lurk just outside the door but gain entrance through the minds and memories of those inside.

The names of the great French explorers echo through this book. La Salle is dead, says Noel Pommier, the shoemaker.

The people who say he will come back are fools. He was murdered a thousand miles from here. Tonti brought the word. Robert de la Salle has come into this shop many a time when I was a lad. He was a true man, mademoiselle, and nobody was true to him, except Monsieur Le Comte; not his own brother, not his nephew; not his King.

Coming closer, Frichette, the woodsman, still suffers from the rupture he sustained pursuing his trade in the woods, and closer still, there is Pierre Charron, "hero of the fur trade and the *coureurs du bois,*" whom Cécile is destined to marry when she grows up.

Willa Cather is never a sentimentalist, even in her most pastoral, most idyllic mood. You may shut the forest out from the rock, but you cannot shut out the basic problems of human nature. Poor, sweet, simple little Jacques Gaux, whom Cécile looks after and befriends, is the neglected child of a prostitute, but neither she nor her father shrink from contact with him on that account. Even the church itself must suffer from the weaknesses of human judgment and from human ambition and self-seeking. Old Bishop Laval stands opposed to the new Bishop de Saint-Vallier, who has supplanted him and brought in newfangled ideas. "Auclair had never liked de Saint-Vallier. He did not doubt the young Bishop's piety, but he very much doubted his judgment," and, all in all, the best thing that can be said of him is that he learns humility and self-doubt as he grows older. Yet the contrast between the two men is by no means that between black and white. Nobody has ever doubted that Laval was a faithful shepherd of his sheep, but "his manner was imperious, and his administration had been arrogant and despotic."

And, for that matter, even the saints.... "Let us not be afraid to surprise the human heart naked...even in the saints," counseled the wise Sainte-Beuve. When Willa Cather wrote that in Quebec she found "a kind of feeling about life and human fate that I could not accept wholly," was she thinking among other things of Jeanne le Ber, Pierre Charron's early love, daughter of the richest merchant in Montreal, whose desire "was for the absolute solitariness of the hermit's life, the solitude which Sainte Marie l'Egypttienne had gone into the desert of the Thébais to find," and who finally had herself immured in a cell from which she emerged only at midnight, to pray alone before the altar in the church? Is this saintliness or is it masochism? Does God expect such service from His children, and did He intend all the loveliness with which He had crowded His world only for the enjoyment of sinners? If so Saint Teresa must have known what she was talking about when she told Him that she wondered not that He had few friends in the world but that He had any at all, in view of the way He treated them.

So, even on the sure foundation of the rock, in Willa Cather's sober reading of life, human nature remains human nature, with its triumphs and its failures, its spiritual glories and its human despairs.

8

Last Novels and Tales

1

In 1932 Willa Cather published *Obscure Destinies,* her first collection of short stories since *Youth and the Bright Medusa* in 1920 and the last she would live to see in print. It comprised three items — "Neighbour Rosicky," "Old Mrs. Harris," and "Two Friends." The first had been written in 1928 and the other two in 1931. The first two were rather long and the third much shorter. All three are more pictures than stories, and all are vintage Cather. The book's title was taken from Thomas Gray's "Elegy Written in a Country Churchyard" ("destinies obscure"), and Randall has suggested that the collection may have been patterned after Flaubert's *Trois Contes.* "Rosicky" and "Two Friends" first appeared in the *Woman's Home Companion,* and "Mrs. Harris" appeared in the *Ladies' Home Journal* but not until after the publication of the book.[1]

With *Obscure Destinies* Willa Cather is back in the Middle West and in "Rosicky" with the Czechs of whom she had written so eloquently in *My Ántonia.* E. K. Brown was sure that Rosicky, the Bohemian farmer, had been inspired by Annie Pavelka's husband, not without influence (as to character, not circumstances) from Willa's own father, which would make Mrs. Rosicky, here called Mary, a pendant to the earlier full-length portrait of Ántonia. There is really only one incident, Rosicky's death; what one remembers the story for is the warm atmosphere created by the Rosicky family and their satisfying life together. We see them partly from Dr. Burleigh's point of view, but more from direct observation and the flashbacks to Rosicky's earlier life. "Old Mrs. Harris" too is partly from Mrs. Rosen's point of view, but there is no overt concern with technique; neither of these stories would be so satisfying as they are if there were. At the beginning, which is set in early spring, Dr. Burleigh tells Rosicky that he has a bad heart and must avoid strain. He dies the next spring, and "one soft, warm moonlight night in early summer" Dr. Burleigh stops by the country graveyard where he has been buried to think about him. In between there has been only one "scene," that in which Rosicky suffers a nearly fatal attack of angina while alone with his daughter-in-law, Polly. Such a summary must inevitably suggest the macabre, but the tale is anything but this. At the end it seemed to Dr. Burleigh at the cemetery that "nothing could be more undeathlike than this place.... Rosicky's life seemed to him complete and beautiful."

Rosicky's son, Rudolph, had married a town girl who was not a Czech, and Rosicky had been worried lest she might have difficulty in making the necessary adjustment to a new way of life. To prevent this he had done everything in his power to help her, even to the extent of insisting upon washing the dishes on Saturday night and sending her and Rudolph off to town in the family car to the "picture show." But it is not until he has his heart attack when there is nobody there but Polly to look after him that he fully realizes he has won his fight to save his son's marriage. Not only does Polly serve him devotedly but she tells him she is going to have a child even before she has told either her husband or her mother. "You'll be the first to know." For Polly too is learning. "She had a sudden feeling that nobody in the world...loved her as much as old Rosicky did.... It was as if Rosicky had a special gift for loving people, something that was like an ear for music or an eye for colour." And Rosicky himself dies in peace, knowing now that Polly "would make a fine woman after the foolishness wore off. Either a woman had that sweetness at her heart or she hadn't. You couldn't always tell by the look of them, but if they had that, everything came out right in the end."

Woodress calls "Old Mrs. Harris" "perhaps the best story Cather ever wrote." At least there is none better. It is also by all means her most autobiographical story. Mrs. Harris is Grandmother Boak. The Templetons are Charles and Jennie Cather, and Vickie is Willa herself on the eve of her departure for college. Though the scene of the story is ostensibly Colorado, to which the Templetons have moved from Tennessee, the Cather house in Red Cloud is re-created, even in detail, in the Templeton house, and Mr. and Mrs. Rosen are the Cathers' Jewish neighbors, Mr. and Mrs. Wiener. Mr. and Mrs. Rosen play much the same part in Vickie's life that the Wieners did in Willa's, except that Mr. Wiener did not have to supply the money to send Willa off to college as Mr. Rosen does for Vickie in the story. Where so much comes direct from life, it may seem foolish to look for literary sources, but "Old Mrs. Harris" seems to me so much like Katherine Mansfield's stories about the Burnells, "Prelude" and "At the Bay," that I cannot help wondering whether there was some influence here, especially since Willa Cather read and admired Katherine Mansfield and published an appreciative essay about her in her only collection of nonfiction writing, Not under Forty (1936).

At the beginning we see Mrs. Harris from Mrs. Rosen's point of view, as the family drudge who wears herself out looking after the Templeton children while her daughter, Victoria Templeton, plays the fine lady. At the outset, then, the reader is likely to dislike Mrs. Templeton; later, without ever finding Mrs. Rosen quite wrong, he will judge her more charitably. She had been a belle in Tennessee, and she had never quite adjusted herself to the ways of the little Western town to which her loving but ineffectual husband had dragged her, and where she is being worn out by constant childbearing in a crowded, cluttered house. Thus, though it is quite true that Mrs. Harris is being much imposed upon with looking after the little Templetons, whom she dearly loves, and who are well worth loving, her situation is quite what elderly women in her class accepted in her time and place; indeed she herself sums up the situation quite without malice: "Victoria had a good heart, but she was terribly proud and could not bear the least criticism." As for Vickie, she is at the moment too much concerned with being an eager adolescent, anxious to try the waters of life and to win the scholarship that will enable her to go to the university to have much time or energy left to be greatly concerned with anybody or anything else.

What may at first seem an infelicitous introduction of Victoria Templeton is therefore not a fault in this story. Mrs. Harris is a quite convincingly drawn portrait of a household saint, but the story is neither a brief for her defense nor an indictment of her daughter and her grandchildren. It is rather "a drama of the generations," in which both the satisfactions and the inevitable disappointments of family life are fairly presented, but since we know that the author herself was part of the picture, it is hard to read her last paragraph as anything but a cry of "peccavi" from her own heart. Mrs. Harris, she tells us, is now dead, but Victoria and Vickie — and what they stand for — must still go on.

When they are old, they will come closer and closer to Grandma Harris. They will think a great deal about her, and remember things they never noticed, and their lot will be more or less like hers. They will regret that they heeded her so little; but they, too, will look into the eager, unseeing eyes of young people and feel themselves alone. They will say to themselves: "I was heartless, because I was young and strong and wanted things so much. But now I know."

If Willa Cather had ever failed her mother, she would certainly seem to have tried to atone for it during the long period of disability that preceded Jennie's death. By the time she wrote "Old Mrs. Harris," it was too late to atone for anything with Grandma Boak except as an artist, but perhaps this is one of the things that art is for. In his introduction to *Ellen Terry and Bernard Shaw: A Correspondence,* Shaw wrote: "Let those who may complain that it was all on paper remember that only on paper has humanity ever achieved glory, beauty, truth, knowledge, virtue, and abiding love."

The last story, "Two Friends," though much slighter, is perfect in kind. Though not derived from Willa Cather's own family, it is drawn from the same deep well of memory as "Old Mrs. Harris." The two friends are R. E. Dillon, a banker, based on Mr. Miner, and J. H. Trueman, a livestock dealer, both of Red Cloud, here turned into worthies of a small Kansas town. Every summer night they sat together, their chairs on the sidewalk before Dillon's store, and talked, while the narrator, unheeded, drank in what they were saying. The only clue given to the listener's sex is that she plays jacks, but it seems clear that here, as in the epilogue to *Sapphira and the Slave Girl,* Miss Cather is painting a portrait of herself as a child. Nothing happens except that one night the friends quarrel and part over William Jennings Bryan, who has just delivered the famous "cross of gold" speech at the Democratic convention in Chicago, thus winning the presidential nomination for himself. Dillon, who had heard him, has returned home convinced that Bryan is the new messiah who will lead the West into the Promised Land, but to Trueman he is only a big windbag. The rift, which was permanent, left the listener with a real sense of loss and regret. Something had been broken "that could so easily have been mended"; "something delightful" had been "senselessly wasted"; and a truth had been "accidentally distorted." Thus the tale ends with the same emphasis on "the tears of things" as "Old Mrs. Harris."

Willa Cather said that "Two Friends" was not about two men, "but about a picture they conveyed to a child." The atmosphere is perfect. "I suppose there were moonless nights, and dark ones with but a silver shaving and pale stars in the sky.... But I remember them all as flooded by the rich indolence of a full moon, or a half-moon set in uncertain blue." But with Miss Cather life always kept close company with literature and art. Was the reference to the occultation of Venus suggested by Longfellow's poem, "The Occultation of Orion"? She herself told Alfred Knopf that she tried to make her story like a picture by Courbet. Moreover, steeped in memory though it is, the story is by no means a literal or accurate report on the author's own experience. She seems to have been incapable of accurate reporting in either her writing for publication or her letters. That she listened entranced in the moonlight to the talk of the two men I firmly believe. But it was not in 1896, and the conversation was not about Bryan. In 1896 Willa Cather was a busy young journalist of twenty-three, writing, among many other things, about the presidential campaign.

2

Willa Cather's work on her penultimate novel, *Lucy Gayheart* (1934) began in 1933, but progress was slowed by indifferent health and a serious disability of her right hand. After having been serialized in the *Woman's Home Companion,* the book appeared on August 1, 1934. The American Book Company ordered ten thousand copies in advance of publication, and the volume earned its author seventeen thousand dollars in royalties during its first year.

Three months after beginning to write, Miss Cather told Zoë Akins that Lucy was a silly young girl and that she was beginning to lose patience with her. After publication she told E. K. Brown that she didn't think much of the book but that she was glad Myra Hess and the Hambourgs did. The reviews were divided, some of them almost savage; at one time Mr. Knopf told her he hoped she would not read them. On the surface *Lucy Gayheart* was a sad, sweet love story that appeared at a time when some of the most influential critics had somehow been convinced that insensibility was a virtue in fiction. Worse still, the proletarian and sociological novelists had persuaded many that fiction no longer had anything to do with the private life and that without "social consciousness" it was worthless. This roughly is the point of view exemplified by Granville Hicks's notorious article, "The Case against Willa Cather,"[2] which J. Donald Adams justly described as very likely the most insensitive piece of writing he had ever read about any author. Miss Cather herself had disposed of such nonsense way back in 1895: "Perfect art is truth, truer than any science, even political economy. It is unfortunate that the economic sciences cannot keep to their place, but insist upon overrunning and coarsening everything else. We shall be hearing economic symphonies and sonatas next."[3] It was indeed fortunate for her that her guardian angel intervened in time to prevent her calling the novel "Blue Eyes on the Prairie," as she at one time planned. (As it turned out, Lucy's eyes happened to be brown.)

A number of recent critics have to be sure done their best to undo the injustice their predecessors may have done this book.[4] Maxwell Geismar called *Lucy* one of Willa Cather's "most convincing" novels; David Stouck considers it "her most complex novel philosophically"; while to Paul Comeau it is "possibly her most daring and certainly her most profound novel," "a philosophical work in which the author reflects on the artistic process and its relationship to life, death, and immortality from a long perspective and in such a way as to effect a perfect marriage of form and content — in the final analysis, the processes of art and life are shown to be the same creative process of memory."[5]

Lucy Gayheart is set in Nebraska (this time Red Cloud is called Haverford on the Platte) and Chicago, to which Lucy, like Thea Kronborg, repairs for the study of music. The main action begins around Christmastime in 1901 and ends with Lucy's death in January 1903; the epilogue of course takes place twenty-five years later. So far as she had an original, Lucy seems to have been derived from a Red Cloud girl named Sadie Becker, who, like Lucy, went away to study music and suffered misfortunes similar to though not identical with Lucy's, and from a Miss Gayhardt, whom Willa seems to have met only once but who impressed her as too fine, delicate, and sensitive for a country schoolteacher. Susan J. Rosowski sees an indebtedness to the English Gothic novels of the late eighteenth and early nineteenth centuries, but though Woodress seems to accept this, I do not find it very convincing.[6] (He, I think, makes a better case for it in connection with *Sapphira and the Slave Girl*.) Sebastian's world-weary melancholy may indeed suggest the Byronic hero, but Gothic and Byronic heroes had no monopoly on sadness, and I find no suggestion in Sebastian of the sinister aspects of Gothicism. Sebastian, to be sure, dies, but this is an accident, quite unconnected with either his melancholy or his love affair with Lucy.

The action is simplicity itself. Lucy goes to Chicago in pursuit of her musical aspirations, falls adoringly and romantically in love with the great singer for whom she plays accompaniments, is crushed by his death, and has just begun her recovery and readjustment when she goes skating on the Platte, where she breaks through the thin spring ice and is drowned.

Lucy Gayheart is a lovely, volatile, quicksilverish kind of girl, more like Marie Tovesky than any other Cather heroine, and, as has been noted by others, even more like the heroine of another (1911) story, "The Joy of Nelly Deane." When the good people of Haverford remembered her after her death, it was as "a slight figure always in motion: dancing or skating, or walking swiftly with intense direction, like a bird flying home," and after Sebastian's death, Mrs. Ramsay, without knowing the cause, still observes the difference. "It used to be as if she were hurrying toward something delightful. . . . Now it was as if she were running away from something, or walking merely to tire herself out." Before her departure for Chicago, she had been courted assiduously by the town banker, Harry Gordon, rich, fashionable, a self-satisfied, genial young man, who feels and projects a sense of control. Even a slight contact with him usually set Lucy up. She does not break with him until he comes to Chicago to share a week of opera with her, when he tries to pressure her into setting an early date for their marriage and she heads him off by telling him she is in love with Sebastian, and upon his grandly asking her how far this nonsense has gone, angrily replies, "All the way; all the way."

This is the most controversial passage in the novel, and many have found it a false note, hopelessly out of character for Lucy. I myself formerly shared this view and expressed it in *Cavalcade of the American Novel*. Now I am not so sure. This does not mean that Lucy's lie is not out of character. It is, but it is not therefore necessarily unbelievable. People, and especially such impulsive people as Lucy, often act out of character, especially when they are angry or have been backed into a corner. A week of Harry's smug self-satisfaction, insensitiveness, and careless assumption of knowing what is good for Lucy better than she knows herself have proved more than she can take. For the time being, she wants to hurt him and get rid of him, and there was nothing else that could have done this more effectively than what she says. Certainly her lie is no more out of character than his brutality toward her after their return to Haverford, when he repulses her every advance, even to the extent of leaving her standing on a wintry road, where she has asked him for a lift home. During all the rest of his life he realizes that this has left a "dark place in his mind," and once, when driving with his wife, the wealthy, worthy, but unlovely Harriet Arkwright, whom he had married in spite after losing Lucy, he forgets himself to the extent of bursting out with "Well, it's a life sentence." In the last chapter we find him going through the Gayheart house, following the death of Lucy's father, twenty-five years after her own, and brooding over the place in the sidewalk where he had seen her as a child leaving the print of her bare foot in the cement then being laid. For Harry too had his sensitive side, and though the author is clearly in Lucy's corner, she is scrupulously fair to everyone — to Harry, to Lucy's stolid, unimaginative, but not unworthy sister, Pauline, and to Harry's unloved wife. Only the nauseous James Mockford and the flippant Fairy Blair are left out in the cold.

The craftsmanship of *Lucy Gayheart* is nearly perfect.[7] It has been objected that we get almost nothing of Chicago during Lucy's stay there. It seems to me on the contrary that the novel is steeped in Chicago, though it is possible that I supply some of this from my own knowledge of the city. Just the right note of nostalgic melancholy is struck at the very beginning by having Lucy already dead and the whole action thus thrust back into the past: "In Haverford on the Platte the townspeople still talk of Lucy Gayheart." Clement Sebastian seems a rather startling anticipation, as artist though not as a personality, of the great German baritone, Dietrich Fischer-Dieskau, the outstanding Lieder singer of these latter days. When Lucy first hears him sing what seems to be mainly a Schubert program, she thinks she had "never heard anything sung with such elevation of style. In its calmness and serenity there was a kind of large enlightenment, like daybreak." And when, after they know they love each other, he leaves for Europe on the trip from which he never returns, she feels sure she shall never see him again. "The night he sang 'When We Two Parted' . . . she knew he had done something to her life." "From the very beginning there had been the shadow of some sorrow over her love for this man."

After Lucy's return to Haverford, nobody knew what had happened in Chicago, but the more sensitive could not but be aware that she had not only been changed but profoundly saddened. When she was drowned, consequently, there was some suspicion of suicide, but this was completely without foundation. In this life, even spiritual insight and victory are, on the material plane, pitifully subject to the vicissitudes of time and space and nature, and it was a cruel piece of irony that Lucy's body should have been destroyed just after she had learned the secret and achieved her reconciliation with life. Her victory was considerably more impressive than that of the much more intellectual and sophisticated St. Peter in *The Professor's House,* for he, after all, never gets much beyond the realization that it is possible to live "without delight."

"As Lucy had been lost by a song, so she was nearly saved by one." Willa Cather's skill and daring are very impressive at this point. The last Christmas of her life, her father takes his two daughters to hear Balfe's opera, *The Bohemian Girl,* which a second-rate traveling company gives in Haverford at a one-night stand on their way to Denver. It was neither a great opera nor a great performance. The soprano was past her prime and her voice was worn, but what she had lost had been replaced by "sympathy" and "tolerant understanding." She "sang so well Lucy wanted to be up there with her, helping her do it. A wild kind of enthusiasm flared up in her. She felt that she must run away tonight, by any train, back to a world that strove after excellence — the world out of which this woman must have fallen." So, once more, the Lord used the humble things of this world to confound the mighty. And so, too, Lucy makes her great discovery.

What if — what if Life itself were the sweetheart? It was like a lover waiting for her in distant cities — across the sea; drawing her, enticing her, weaving a spell over her.... Oh, now she knew! She must have it, she couldn't run away from it.... She must go back into the world and get all she could of everything that had made him what he was. These splendours were still on earth, to be sought after and fought for. In them she would find him. *If with all your heart you truly seek Him, you shall ever surely find Him.* He had sung that for her in the beginning when she first went to him. Now she knew what it meant.

Myra Henshawe too had learned in the end that religion differed from everything else because in religion seeking is finding, and with Willa Cather religion and art were one. *Elijah* has replaced Byron ("When We Two Parted"). Was it intentionally or accidentally that Willa Cather in the plenitude of her maturity and her powers should here have atoned so handsomely to Mendelssohn for her brash disparagement of him in the days of her youth?[8]

3

Willa Cather began writing *Sapphira*[9] *and the Slave Girl* (1940), her last published novel, in the autumn of 1937, but it was only completed on Grand Manan Island in September 1940. She had been saddened by the death of her brother Douglass and by that of Isabelle McClung Hambourg and, since 1939, by the horrors of World War II, and her health was far from what it had been. In both 1938 and 1939, she had remained in New York, in variation from her usual custom, until the end of July, because she did not wish to break into what she was writing, and in the spring of

1938 she went back to Virginia to refresh her memories of her first years. She had said that her usable materials for fiction had all been accumulated between the ages of nine and fifteen, thus excluding her pre-Nebraska period, but as she grew older, she found herself reaching still further back. Perhaps she was thinking of herself when she made Myra Henshawe say that we grow more and more like our forebears as time goes on. Knopf's advance printing order for *Sapphira* was for fifty thousand copies, and the Book-of-the-Month Club took care of two hundred thousand more.

Opening in the Shenendoah Valley in 1856, *Sapphira,* then, was Willa Cather's only Virginia novel, but this is not the only way in which it differs from her earlier works. Its central character, Sapphira Dodderidge Colbert, is a woman in her late fifties, invalided by a revolting disease, dropsy, "difficult," inscrutable, and in some aspects evil, and there is a more elaborate presentation of social customs, manners, and environment than Miss Cather attempted elsewhere; obviously much of the material eliminated in revision must have been of this character. In addition to all this, the whole tone of the narrative seems "different," but just wherein the difference consists is hard to define. For some time the best word I could think of was *pale,* by which I do not mean that anything presented was not made altogether clear. I now think that Edith Lewis found words better than mine when she wrote that the novel was written "austerely, with very little of that warmth and generous expansion of feeling so many of [Willa Cather's] readers delight in." David Stouck strikes the same note when he calls the book "A Winter's Tale."

To this I must add at once that the larger amount of background material included in *Sapphira* does not at all mean that for once Miss Cather had written a sociological novel. Since we are dealing with pre–Civil War Virginia, slavery is of course an established fact. It would be an exaggeration to say that the novel is morally neutral on this issue (only a fool could suppose that the author did not approve of Mrs. Blake's deliverance of Nancy Till by way of the Underground Railroad), but there is certainly no discussion of the rights and wrongs of the "peculiar institution." It is simply there, like fires and floods and colds in the head. The author does not treat her heroine one whit less respectfully because she is a "yaller girl" and a slave: "The girl had a natural delicacy of feeling. Ugly sights and ugly words sickened her." Yet she can still permit herself, in one passage, to refer to "the foolish, dreamy, nigger side of her nature."

Except that they were even looser than before, seasoned Catherites did not find their favorite novelist's structure or method of story telling notably different in *Sapphira* from what they had known before. The story is a third-person narrative, developed chronologically for the most part except for a very free use of digressions. Book 3 ("Old Jezebel") carries the story of Nancy's grandmother clear back to the slave ships, and book 4 ("Sapphira's Daughter") deals with Mrs. Blake's early life and marriage. Finally, there is book 9 ("Nancy's Return"), which takes place a quarter of a century after the rest of the book — a Cather epilogue to end all epilogues, as the saying goes. Here Willa writes unabashedly in the first person — "I was something over five years old" — as if she were inditing a memoir rather than a novel.

The sources were almost wholly family lore and Back Creek Valley tradition; the author said she could hardly tell what she herself had added. In the last section she writes:

> In summer Till used to take me across the meadow to the Colbert graveyard, to put flowers on the graves. Each time she talked to me about the people buried there, she was sure to remember something she had not happened to tell me before. Her stories about the Master and Mistress were never mere repetitions, but grew more and more into a complete picture of these two persons.

Rachel Blake was drawn from Grandmother Boak at a much earlier stage in her life than that depicted in "Old Mrs. Harris," and there may have been something from Charles and Jennie Cather in the miller and his wife, but if so, much less, I think, than in the Templetons. Nancy Till seems to have become a legend in the region by the time Willa came along, and the romantic story of her flight had been imprinted into the child's mind even before Nancy's return to her mother after an apparently happy and successful stay in the North.

Sapphira had been born into the slaveholding aristocracy of Loudon County and had taken her slaves with her when, for some reason never explained or perhaps understood, she had married "beneath" her and moved into Franklin County, which had been settled largely from Pennsylvania and where the "peculiar institution" was regarded with much less favor. She had been an imperious, self-willed girl, and when we meet her in her fifties, invalided by disease, she still rules her domain with an oddly padded rod of iron. "She bore her disablement with courage, seldom referred to it, sat in her crude invalid's chair as if it were a seat of privilege."

She and her husband, Henry Colbert, the miller, have apparently had only one child, the now-widowed Rachel Blake, who has abolitionist leanings and has never seen eye to eye with her mother. When we see the Colberts together at the breakfast table, they seem friendly but too polite to each other to suggest real intimacy or rapport, and we are not surprised to learn that Colbert spends much of his time at the mill and often even sleeps there. Reared a Lutheran but now a Baptist, Colbert is devoted to the Bible and Bunyan's *Holy War*. He searches the Scriptures diligently, marking with a large *S* all the passages that seem to have any bearing on slavery, and is disappointed that he can find no outright condemnation thereof. He regards the slaves as his wife's property, not his, and except for his refusal to give up his right, under Virginia law, to prevent her from selling a slave without his consent, he has no disposition to interfere with her management of them or, for that matter, of any other household matter. Indeed on one occasion he tells her frankly that she is the master and that he is the miller.

Sapphira's treatment of her slaves is both efficient and comparatively easygoing. She can be indulgent, as with old Jezebel and Tansy Dave or, when it pleases her, cruel, and she treats all her other subordinates in much the same way. "When the old broom-pedlar or the wandering tinsmith happened along, they were always given a place at the dinner-table, and she knew just how to talk to them. But with [the schoolmaster] Fairhead, she took on a mocking condescension as if she were all the while ridiculing his simplicity." When she was angry, there was no heat in her anger but only "a cold sneering contempt." All her life Rachel had actually hated the sound of her mother's voice in "sarcastic reprimand" and even more in "contemptuous indulgence." Susan Rosowski has stressed the significance of her "shallow" eyes, which she thinks suggests "the inner blankness of a woman from whom the moral sense is missing." But, as elsewhere, Miss Cather is always fair. As she carefully indicates the weaknesses in both Henry Colbert and his daughter, so the ambiguous, "capricious, cold, even malevolent" Sapphira is "heroic" in her "courage, fortitude, and independence." When Rachel angers her by engineering Nancy's escape, she sends her the following note:

Mistress Blake is kindly requested to make no further visits at the Mill House.
                              SAPPHIRA DODDERIDGE COLBERT

But when, during the diphtheria epidemic of the "dark autumn" that follows, one of her grandchildren dies, she invites Rachel and her one surviving child to come and stay with her. She dies sitting upright in her chair, watching the evening light fading "over the white fields and the spruce trees across the creek," with her unrung bell beside her.

Nevertheless Sapphira's behavior in the central situation of the novel puts her in a position where she must stand beyond the possibility of forgiveness from anything short of the Infinite Mercy. Nancy Till had once been a favorite with Sapphira, but now that she has conceived a suspicion, fed and fostered by two worthless slaves, that the innocent girl was having sexual relations with the miller, she has turned against her. Nancy "does" for Colbert at the mill, and he is fond of her in a gentle, fatherly kind of way. "She came in and out of the mill like a soft spring breeze; a shy, devoted creature who touched everything so lightly. Never before had anyone divined all his little whims and preferences, and been eager to gratify them."

Sapphira's first impulse is to sell the girl, but she cannot do this without her husband's consent, which he refuses to give, and it is at this point that she descends into hell. She invites her husband's nephew, Martin Colbert, the worst rake in the county, and throws Nancy in his way, even forcing her to sleep unprotected outside Sapphira's own bedroom door. When Rachel realized what she was doing, she "closed her eyes and leaned her arms and head forward on the dresser top. She had known her mother to show great kindness to her servants, and, sometimes, cold cruelty. But she had never known her to do anything quite so ugly as this."

Willa Cather is nowhere more subtle in her reading of the complexities of human character or more skillful in her handling of its vagaries than in her account of Henry Colbert's share in Nancy's escape. His daughter makes all the arrangements, but her plan cannot be activated without his providing the money. The miller knows what his legal rights are, but about his moral rights he is not so clear. Nor is he by any means at peace in his own mind. His wife's suspicions have spoiled his relations with Nancy along with everything else, and her presence at the mill is no longer the comforting thing it had been." He knew that the Colberts had bad blood where women were concerned, and he had fought and conquered sensuality in himself all his life. Now that his wife had turned Nancy into a sexual object, he did not desire her, but neither did he wish to have her about. It "would not be the same as yesterday. Something had come between them since then."

There is nothing more pathetic in Willa Cather's oeuvre than the miller's solution of the moral dilemma in which he finds himself when asked to make Nancy's escape possible. As weak humanity, when driven to the wall by conflicting considerations so often does, he attempts to solve his problem by evading it and in a sense succeeds in doing so. He will not *give* Rachel the money she needs, but he leaves it in his coat and tells her where the coat will be, which, in a world that often quite successfully evades both law and logic, somehow manages to work just as well!

David Stouck, as we have seen, calls *Sapphira* "A Winter's Tale," thus invoking Shakespeare's play, which not only also ends on a note of reconciliation, but in the long run sees good coming out of evil, for Nancy, in the long run, lived a much happier life in the North than she could have had, had she remained in Franklin County. In our imperfect — and profoundly illogical — world, good does sometimes come out of evil, even as, unfortunately, the best intentions can produce the worst results. For good or ill, much of the world's good work has been performed, out of mixed motives, by very imperfect men and women. Otherwise much of it must have remained undone.[10]

4

In the autumn of 1948 came one more collection of stories, *The Old Beauty and Others.* Willa Cather did not live to see it in print, but since she seems to have planned it and put it together, it must be considered here and not in the appendix with the uncollected tales.

Though it is considerably shorter than *Obscure Destinies,* like its predecessor, it comprises three stories, and again the first two are comparatively long and the third, "Before Breakfast," much shorter but considerably more significant than might at first appear. "The Old Beauty" has never interested anybody very deeply, but the second story, "The Best Years," is a not-unworthy successor to "Old Mrs. Harris," being more like that treasured tale than anything else the author ever wrote.

"The Old Beauty" deals with Henry Seabury's reencounter, at Aix-le-Bains, in 1922, with a once-famed Victorian beauty, Gabrielle Longstreet, whom he had known slightly many years before, and to whom he had once rendered a great service, but it was so long ago, and she is now so much changed that at first he does not recognize her. They become friends in these days of her obscurity and decline, and on the way back from an excursion to the Grande Chartreuse, they collide with a car driven by two vulgar, cigarette-smoking young American women — "bobbed, hatless, clad in dirty white knickers and sweaters," and though nobody has been injured, the shock to the frail old beauty is so great that she dies in her hotel that night.

There is nothing much wrong with "The Old Beauty" except that the emotional importance of the central character is never established. Even in her heyday, "she was not witty or especially clever. ...She said nothing memorable.... She was beautiful, that was all." Now that she is hopelessly out of touch with her time, modern dancing reminds her of "reptiles coupling." She dislikes smoking by women because it was not done in her prime. "Yes, you and Chetty may smoke. I will take a liqueur." But there does not seem to me much to choose between poison contra poison, and except that her manners are much better, there is no more reason for holding Gabrielle as something precious than those she condemns. Chetty, incidentally, is Gabrielle's companion, Chetty Beamish, an ex–music hall star, probably suggested by Vesta Tilley.[11]

"The Best Years" takes us back to 1899 in Nebraska. Evangeline Knightly, the county superintendent of schools, is a portrait of Willa's old teacher, Eva King Chase, whom she described as the first person she had ever loved outside her own family. I have suggested that there is a close affinity between this story and "Old Mrs. Harris," yet there is also one significant difference between them. Both are preoccupied with family life and love, but in "Old Mrs. Harris" there is tension as well as trust; there is nothing of this in "The Best Years." It is Willa Cather's purest exercise in the pastoral mode, yet the characterizations are quite convincing, and the tale does not cloy.

Perhaps the reason for this is that not even perfect love is proof against the vicissitudes of mortality. There is nothing in "Old Mrs. Harris" that has anything like the unbearable poignancy in kind of the death of the teenaged schoolteacher-daughter of the Ferguesson family in "The Best Years." Yet even here there is a stalwart, bittersweet compensation. Lesley perishes of the pneumonia she contracts when she is trapped in the country schoolhouse with her little pupils by a blizzard that drops four feet of snow in an hour, but her behavior during the ordeal vindicates human nature as well as herself. And since this is a Cather story, the last section must be a kind of epilogue, in which Miss Knightly, now Mrs. Thorndike, visits Lesley's mother, twenty years after her daughter's death. The Ferguessons are much more prosperous now than they were then but they are still looking back nostalgically to the old days when they were young and Lesley was alive. To the end of the line, in what may be the last story Willa Cather ever wrote, it was still "optima dies...prima fugit."[12]

There is affirmation again, though once more of a rather sombre sort, in "Before Breakfast," which is almost an interior monologue by Henry Grenfell, the senior partner of Grenfell & Saunders, who reads Shakespeare, Fielding, Scott, and Dickens, and likes John McCormack more than Serge Koussevitzky, especially when his superior wife and son discuss how the conductor "would take the slow movement of the Brahms Second" and whether or not his reading would be preferable to Karl Muck's. Grenfell is one of Miss Cather's very few sympathetic portrayals of an American businessman. His professorial sons would seem to have reduced the arts to sciences; perhaps Miss Cather, at the end of her career, was still fighting Professor Sherman, who, in her undergraduate days, had wanted her to "diagram" poems.

The scene of "Before Breakfast" is a tiny island off Nova Scotia, and Miss Cather surely could never have written it if she had not discovered Grand Manan. Disillusioned and oppressed by the thought of man's insignificance in the universe on an island whose age is placed by a geologist at about 136 million years, Grenfell has his equilibrium restored by the sight of the geologist's daughter, in a pink bathing suit, taking a morning dip in freezing water ("Crazy kid!"). A hundred and thirty six million years or twenty, the human will, human courage, even human foolhardiness could still count for something, still accomplish something beyond the scope of the rocks. This, like the end of *Lucy Gayheart,* is a positive note that goes beyond Godfrey St. Peter's acceptance of a life without delight. It was not a bad testimonial for a distinguished writer to leave behind at the end of her career.

Part 3

9

Character and Personality

1

Willa Cather was about five feet, six inches tall, with a figure neither stocky nor sylphlike. Her eyes have been described as every possible shade of blue or gray; Edith Lewis calls them dark blue, with a look "transparently clear" and a "level, unshrinking gaze." The lashes were dark. Her hair was a reddish brown or bronze, straight and simply arranged. In 1924 Burton Rascoe found her mouth "ample, with full flexible lips," and the voice that came out of it has been spoken of as deep and resonant, suggesting energy, strength, and forcefulness.

For business she wore plain, workaday clothes, with skirts somewhat shorter than fashion prescribed in her early years, and low shoes. She liked shirts and shirtwaists, as in Edward Steichen's middy blouse photograph that many have found quite the most attractive picture ever made of her. Grant Reynard[1] says that the design on the cuffs and pockets of the "mannish short coat" she wore at the MacDowell colony made him think of Annie Oakley and Buffalo Bill's Wild West show, and, as previously noted, as a very young girl she was fond of wearing men's or boys' clothes. Before she reached Pittsburgh however she had got this out of her system and for festive occasions, then and thereafter, she was quite capable of turning herself into a bird of paradise. She favored brilliant colors and marked patterns, often affecting color combinations that many persons would have considered inharmonious. We hear of a "Pasha-like turreted turban, so heavy with gold lace, velvet and aigrettes." Norman Foerster speaks of her wearing blue stockings with white polka dots as a high school teacher, and Burton Rascoe says she was one of the few women who could wear salmon pink and green together.

When she applied for library privileges at the New York Society Library ("I'd like to subscribe if I may. My name is Cather. I'm by way of being a writer"), the librarian saw "a rather short, stocky lady in an apple-green coat and matching pork-pie felt hat," with a husky voice. She was not always so deferential as this however. *Downright* was the word Eleanor Hinman associated with her first of all. "She spoke with her whole body, and her conversation was more stimulating than captivating." Another calls it "staccato." "Whatever she does is done with every fibre." All this of course was when she was in her prime. The principal witness to change in after years is Hamlin Garland, who, meeting her again in 1930, found her greatly altered — "a plain, short, ungraceful, elderly woman," who "spoke without force or grace, with awkward gestures." Though Garland does not sound like a very friendly observer, some of Miss Cather's last photographs do give some suggestion of what he meant.

We are told that in early life Willa Cather suffered an illness that left her "supposed" to use a crutch for a time. It has been conjectured that this was a mild attack of polio, but nothing is really known about it. Nor do we know much more about the "typhoid pneumonia" she is supposed to have brought back to Lincoln with her from her trip to Chicago for a week of the visiting Metropolitan Opera Company. Generally speaking, she gives the impression of vigor and vitality through all her early maturity. We never think of her as a sportswoman, yet there are references to tennis and target practice as well as six-mile hikes. In Pittsburgh she rode a bicycle to work; once she speaks of using it to race a streetcar. She was lost for several hours during the Mesa Verde trip in 1915 and even after having been rescued experienced hardship and exercised athletic prowess in getting back to civilization. When she went home for Christmas in 1922 she got out her skates, and in 1927 she made a trip on horseback with her brother Roscoe through the Big Horn Mountains in Wyoming. Yet she would seem to have had more than her share of painful illnesses: mastoiditis in 1911; blood poisoning from an infected wound, caused by having pricked her scalp with a hatpin, which entailed hospitalization, a shaved head, and much depression caused by the drugs given to her to relieve her pain; neuritis and a difficult tonsillectomy in the early 1920s; and a gallbladder operation in 1942; at least two attacks of appendicitis, both of which yielded to treatment without an operation; to say nothing of recurrent bouts of influenza. Edith Lewis thought she was never really well again after 1942, and according to at least one report, her weight finally went down to a hundred pounds.

For a writer however what happened to her in 1932, when she

tore a tendon in her left wrist and had to have her hand strapped to a board may well have been the most painful and exasperating of all these difficulties. As if this were not enough, she injured her hand in 1938 and then ran into further difficulties with a tendon in her *right* wrist when at work on *Sapphira and the Slave Girl.* When this novel was published, she had her arm in a sling and her hand bandaged in a splint, and before she was through, she was compelled to wear a steel and leather brace for eight months. More than any other cause, these mishaps were responsible for her having written so little during her last years. Since Willa Cather lived only to write, perhaps only another writer can have any idea of what this must have meant to her.

2

She was a very intense woman. She herself said that she always wanted to hang garlands on people or else put them to torture, and this tendency was so strong in her that it evidently rubbed off on those whose paths crossed hers, for all her life people seem either to have liked her greatly or else felt repelled by her. She made Thea Kronborg say that there was such a thing as "creative hate"; a good example of this in her own writing is her review of D'Annunzio's *Il Fuoco,*[2] which she resented for its treatment of Eleonora Duse.

Her temperament affected her critical judgments. It influenced her love for Stevenson and her enthusiasm, especially in the early days, for books like *The Prisoner of Zenda* and plays like *Cyrano de Bergerac,* and it links up with matters with which literature as such has nothing to do. When she praises Frank Norris because he is "big and warm and sometimes brutal," we understand why she loved stormy weather at sea, why in her college days, she seems to praise football less in spite of its brutality than because of it, why she regretted having missed her chance to see a bullfight on her first trip to Europe, and why, in praising Fridtjof Nansen, she must step aside to praise "the power of the strong arm" that was "the glory of Caesar and Napoleon." Nansen may be honored by a few universities because of his scientific discoveries, but to the people at large he is a hero because he reached the eighty-sixth parallel."

Her intensity appears in its least-attractive aspect in her writings about the theater. Even more than book-reviewing, music and drama criticism seems to bring out the worst in its practitioners, probably because it is harder to resist the temptation to be cruel to what you dislike when the creator presents himself and not simply his product for your dissection. In her reviewing days, Willa Cather was called "the meat-ax young girl," and Gustave Frohman himself said that fear of her pen caused actors to tremble as they approached Lincoln, Nebraska. Thus:

Frederic Warde had no talent at all and his costar Louis James very little. That "most brazen sham," Lillie Langtry, not only could not act but could not even read her lines properly. Lewis Morrison stopped just where elocution ends and acting begins. In *Nathan Hale,* Maxine Elliott was "rather elephantine in the kittenish pranks of a schoolgirl." Miss Cather trembled all through one season for fear Maggie Mitchell might come again, "old and shrunken and 'wrinkled deep in time,'" and the announcement that Lillian Lewis, "with her nose and her emotion," was to play Imogen made her hope that "they dug Shakespeare's grave very deep." Beatrice Cameron presented a Portia "totally without dignity and quite without charm." Anna Held, Julie Opp, and Maude Adams are lumped together as representative of the "brazen incompetence and china playfulness" that have taken over the theater. "Besides her unfortunate habit of imbibing strong intoxicants," Sybil Johnson is a woman "entirely without intelligence or refinement." Margaret Mather, once lauded for her Juliet, had now been ruined by "much Milwaukee beer and all the other things that go to make up the pace that kills." Lillian Russell can neither sing nor act, and even Henry Irving and Ellen Terry are "a cold, intelligent man and a nervous, flighty woman."

I am not saying that none of these judgments are correct; I am sure some of them are. But they are cruel nevertheless, and those that pass beyond the performer to the private person are indecent. Moreover it is difficult to believe that they were not written with relish.

Moreover, it would not be accurate to say that this kind of thing never appears in Miss Cather's book reviews. Oscar Wilde does not "apotheosize filth," but he "plays with it because he likes it when it is pretty." A book by Richard Le Gallienne is "a promissory note written with violet ink on scented paper, signed by a bankrupt genius whose paper is at a discount on the market." Edgar Saltus is "a little man physically, and it is a fact that small men are often both cynical and sensational." Even those she has admired can feel the lash when they displease her, as did Stephen Crane with *War Is Kind:* "Either Mr. Crane is insulting the public or insulting himself, or he has developed a case of atavism and is chattering the primeval nonsense of the apes." Even the great Mark Twain is a "blackguard," a "provincial," and "an all-around tough" after his attack on Paul Bourget, and she condemned his book about Joan of Arc, which he considered his masterpiece, as "thoroughly stupid." (Incidentally, why was she invited to his seventieth birthday dinner in 1905, long before she was a celebrity?) She condemned Hardy for his *Jude the Obscure* when, as "Hearts Insurgent," it was running serially in *Harper's Magazine*. Once she got herself into very hot water by seizing the occasion of a Mendelssohn concert to attack that composer as "pitiably weak and childish" and appealing "especially to effeminate minds just as the graceful lyrics of Tennyson do." Well, if you are out for scalps, you may as well go in for big game.

Public appearances played a small part in Willa Cather's own literary career. It was her opinion that public speaking was undesirable for writers because it interfered with their work and was bad for their characters. Yet she did make a brief tour in 1921 and another, even briefer, in 1925, during which a student of mine, who heard her in Chicago, told me that she spoke so softly that nobody in back of the first few rows could hear what she said. In her youth, however, before she had found her definitive outlet, she "spouted" freely. Little Marie Tovesky's exhibition in one of the early chapters of *O Pioneers!* may well have been based upon a memory of one of Willa's own; we know that the merchant, Mr. Miner, called her "a young curiosity shop" after a performance in his store. Later a recitation of *Hiawatha* in Indian costume, with bow and arrow, was one of her war-horses, and she astonished the good clubwomen of Pittsburgh, shortly after her arrival in that city, by virtually reciting her early essay on Carlyle when he happened to be the topic of discussion at one of their meetings. She also appeared in amateur productions of plays, often in male roles, from childhood into college years. Clearly, then, the public performing instinct was there. Her last offense of this kind occurred on May 4, 1933, when her remarks at a Princeton banquet at the Plaza Hotel were broadcast on NBC.

3

In any reasonable consideration of Willa Cather's temperament, such nonsense as "meat-ax" judgments are only the tip of the iceberg however. We have already heard her called "downright." *Foursquare* would be another good word. She had her feet firmly planted on the good red earth, and she faced life unafraid. In *O Pi-*

oneers! the land is the central character to which all the others must adjust themselves or perish. She regarded cooking as quite as important an art as writing. When she went back to Nebraska, she did the cooking for her family and took pride in her ability to do it well, and even in New York, where she employed a cook, she enjoyed going to the public markets kept by the immigrants in Greenwich Village to buy the food herself. She was passionately fond of flowers (as Michel Gervaud has remarked, "she invested gardens with a biblical, almost sacred character"), and Elizabeth Sergeant has testified that going into her apartment was like entering a greenhouse.

Though there is one photograph of Miss Cather in the Autograph Edition that shows her caressing a dog, I do not get the impression that animals were very important to her, at least as pets, but it is clear that she had observed both dog and cat behavior pretty carefully. In a childish composition on "Dogs" that is the earliest piece of her writing that has survived,[3] she contrasts the "kind, noble and generous dog" with the "snarling, spitting, cruel cat," but her canonical writing does not reinforce this. In one trip west she traveled with the canine film star, Rin-Tin-Tin, who, she said, interested her more than any other celebrity she had met. Though it is true that Don Hedger's dog, Caesar, in "Coming, Aphrodite!" is more elaborately characterized than any cat in her fiction,[4] cats seem to turn up more often than dogs in her stories. Carl Linstrum's rescue of little Emil Bergson's kitten, which has run up a telegraph pole on a windy day to get away from a dog is the earliest incident in *O Pioneers!* Jim Burden's grandmother keeps a cat in *My Ántonia,* as do the Shimerdas, poor as they are. Claude Wheeler has a lovely scene with a cat in *One of Ours* (book 3, section 5), and there are less-significant passages in *Alexander's Bridge, Death Comes for the Archbishop,* and "Uncle Valentine." But the cat of cats in Willa Cather's writing is unquestionably Blue Boy in "Old Mrs. Harris," the account of whose dying wrings the heart.[5] Feline imagery is used suggestively in *The Song of the Lark,* where Dr. Archie sees the marks of approaching age around Thea's eyes as "mere kitten scratches which playfully hinted where one day the cat would scratch," but the only heartless or horrible passage is in "The Way of the World," where Mary Ellen Jenkins boasts that she can skin a cat as well as Spreckle, and this was probably not meant to be taken seriously.

Mules, horses, and goats all play their part in the *Archbishop,* to which one might well add *One of Ours* (book 3, section 11), and Miss Knightly's old mare, Molly, is an individual in "The Best

Years." Snakes are associated more than once with "the Ancient Evil," as in Jim Burden's killing of the giant rattlesnake. The murderer Buck Scales in the *Archbishop* has a head that "played from side to side exactly like a snake's," and when Myra Henshawe is in her bitterest mood, her lips curl like a snake.

Young Willa was of course exploiting her shock value when she wrote in a friend's autograph album that "slicing toads" was her favorite summer occupation and "amputating limbs" her idea of "perfect happiness." Yet the fact remains that she was at this time intending to pursue a scientific career and that she championed vivisection, even for amateurs, in her high school graduation address. About all that seems to have survived her shift away from science to the humanities was her love for the stars, as shown, for example, in "Before Breakfast," and her interest in Henri Bergson,[6] yet even those who find her scientific period hardest to understand must admit that it does link up with her characteristic tendency to blink nothing.

This same tendency of course harmonizes with her admiration for pioneers. She liked what was "real," honest, straightforward, clean by the standards of common, decent humanity. As early as her first trip to Europe in 1902, she turned with relief from Monte Carlo, where she felt that the artificial activities carried on corrupted even nature. In the *Archbishop* she would deplore the replacement in the churches of the Southwest of the original, crude, handmade art created by the people themselves with cheap purchased images, factory-made, and imported from the East. Even in Nebraska, once the generation of the pioneers had passed, a new breed came in that was more interested in driving into town in an automobile to buy something instead of staying on the farm and making it.

All this may even connect with the many instances of brutality and violence in Willa Cather's writings that have led Leon Edel and others to find in her work "a disagreeable vein of sadism."[7] In the short story, "The Profile," which deals with a woman one side of whose face has been distorted by a hideous scar and of the effects of this misfortune on her mind and her marriage, the "old painter" declares that "the only effects of horror within the province of the artist are psychological. Everything else is a mere matter of the abattoir." This does not always seem to have been Miss Cather's practice however. In *O Pioneers!* we have not only the murder of Emil and Marie by her jealous husband but the reference, probably suggested by Hawthorne's "Egotism; or, The Bosom Serpent," to the man who had swallowed a snake and was thereafter compelled to feed it and be tormented by it. In *The Song of the Lark* there is the filthy, diseased tramp who revenges himself upon Moonstone by drowning himself in the standpipe and poisoning the town's water supply. *My Ántonia* is well supplied with horrors: Pavel's story of the bride thrown to the wolves; Shimerda's suicide, with the horrible details of the finding of his body in the barn, frozen into its own blood; the tramp who killed himself by jumping into the threshing machine; and the gruesome murder and suicide perpetrated by Wick Cutter. In *One of Ours*, Claude Wheeler sees rotting bodies in the trenches. In *A Lost Lady* Ivy Peters's blinding of the woodpecker is wanton, calculated sadism. In *Sapphira and the Slave Girl*, old Till as a child had seen her mother burned to death, and even in the dreamlike *Shadows on the Rock*, the rock itself is only a refuge in an evil world; in the background hover the terrors of the forest.

This list is not complete; it could be considerably enlarged by reference to the short stories. In "Consequences" the whole story is devoted to suicide as a problem. In "The Clemency of the Court" there are two suicides on one page. Miss Cather's very first published tale, "Peter," was later reworked as Mr. Shimerda's suicide in *My Ántonia*. "Paul's Case" too ends with a suicide, and the brutal story of the Aztec princess in "Coming, Aphrodite!" was no tale to tell to Eden Bower or any other girl. "It is at once surprising and painful," wrote Curtis Bradford, "to find a girl of twenty-two publishing a story ["On the Divide"] involving alcohol, delirium tremens and rape, and making it clear by her handling that these were all a part of the general experience of life in a pioneer community."[8]

Mildred Bennett[9] was probably the first to note that Willa Cather was almost obsessed with mutilation, especially of the hand. I certainly do not mean to suggest that everything I have chronicled here is used as it might have been by the Fat Boy in *Pickwick*, "to make your flesh crawl." The death of the tramp in *The Song of the Lark*, for example, is used, quite legitimately, to bring Thea face-to-face with the fact of evil and to help her to fortify herself against it.[10] But I think one can still wonder whether the detailed description of the young hero's death in "The Namesake" was quite necessary, or the hand of the corpse that would not stay buried in *One of Ours*, or that of the singer Graziana, "snapped off at the wrist as clearly as if it had been taken off by a cutlass," found on a window ledge after the hotel fire in "Behind the Singer Tower."

I leave the detailed explanation of all this to the Freudians. It is clear however that the obsession with mutilation was a genuine complex, springing from Willa's early encounter with a demented youth who wanted to cut off her hand, and it may well be that some of the other incidents also derived from haunting memories that she consciously or unconsciously tried to exorcise. Elizabeth Sergeant, who knew her well, leaves the impression that she was even wary of orthodontics because she tended to feel that mouths "were as individual as ears and should be left as nature made them."

4

In dealing with so definite and forthright a personality as Willa Cather's, it would seem safe to assume that its possessor — or possessed — had considerable confidence in herself. This, however, seems to have been true with Miss Cather only up to a point.

Her publisher, Alfred A. Knopf, was a fine, kind, generous man, but he was also a strong personality, not easily overawed, and he has testified that though she called him "Alfred," he always addressed her as "Miss Cather" and would have felt it unnatural to call her anything else. Yet Edith Lewis felt that whether it showed or not, there was an underlying strain of melancholy in Willa Cather's makeup. Whether *melancholy* is the right word or not, it is certainly safe to say that she was not free of self-doubt. If Knopf was overawed by her, she herself was overawed at first by Olive Fremstad and refused an invitation to the singer's summer place in Maine because she did not think she could risk such close contact with a dominating personality. It was not unreasonable that in 1896 she should have written a friend that she did not think she would ever accomplish much, but that so late as 1933 she should permit herself to be troubled about such lightweight critics as Granville Hicks and describe herself as a bundle of sensations and enthusiasms who had been running away from herself all her life is more suggestive. Though she lived to write, she seems to have found it necessary to break away from her work and give herself a change of scene at frequent intervals.

She also obviously enjoyed being looked after to an extent that seems unusual in a self-confident person. The star example of course is her allowing Isabelle McClung to move her into the family mansion in her Pittsburgh days. It has been said that this was done over the objections of Isabelle's parents and that she had threatened to leave home if they did not give her her way, but this does not seem to have been substantiated. Nevertheless Willa must have known that in moving into the McClung house, where she paid no board, she was incurring an obligation that many sensitive persons would find it difficult to assume. She once told Dorothy Canfield that Isabelle "babied" her. So did Dorothy herself when Willa, sick with the grippe, went to her in Columbus, where she was taken care of for a week. Once, when she was living alone, she appeared one night at the dressing room of Lizzie Hudson Collier, and the actress took her to her hotel and looked after her for several days. It was the same with Olive Fremstad after she and Willa had established friendly relations. When Miss Cather had blood poisoning, Madame Fremstad visited her at the hospital, brought her flowers, and showed her how to do her hair so that her shaved scalp would be covered over, and after another illness, the singer sent her motor car for her every evening to bring her to dinner. Willa also used her publisher almost as freely as Hawthorne did in the nineteenth century, accepted gifts and invitations from him and his wife, at one time had her mail handled through his office, and when she was at Grand Manan did not even hesitate to order food through him.

But since writing was the most important thing in her life, I am most of all impressed by her attitude toward herself in this connection. With most writers, I am persuaded, writing is their supreme form of self-expression. Probably the classical statement of this point of view is Middleton Murry's "To know a piece of literature is to know the soul of the man who created it, and who created it in order that his soul should be known." Miss Cather, on the other hand, speaks of wishing to present her materials by juxtaposition with each other, without comment or interpretation by her, and of her writing as a means of forgetting herself for a few hours each day. When she was at Breadloaf she said of the writer that he must "be so in love with his subject that he forgets 'self' in his passion." Elsewhere, more mystically, she speaks of him as fading away into his work and dying of love only to be born again. I do not mean that I believe these statements are to be taken quite literally; indeed she herself says that the great satisfaction of having written a book is that it is "all yours." Nevertheless, I believe that the contrast between her emphasis and Murry's is significant. Surely the inscription on her tombstone was not chosen idly: "At any rate, that is happiness: to be dissolved into something complete and great."

5

A human being's attitude toward himself is generally very closely connected with how he treats other people. During her later years,

Willa Cather guarded her privacy to such an extent that she gained the general reputation of being unapproachable. According to Marion Marsh Brown and Ruth Cone, who have covered her New England sojourns in a quite undocumented but obviously honest, able, and fair-minded book, *Only One Point of the Compass,* she could go to almost fantastic lengths to achieve this. She gave careful directions to a woman who had lost her way in the woods, but kept her face averted to such an extent that the questioner thought she had a stiff neck! She refused to go to the microphone when she received a degree at Princeton, and when she went to the hospital for her gallbladder operation, she registered under Edith Lewis's name rather than her own.

There were legitimate reasons for some of these apparent idiosyncrasies. After she had achieved celebrity, her time was cruelly broken into, which was the more serious in view of her declining health. She was quite accurate when she told Fanny Butcher that "everyone who professed to like one's writing did all in his or her power to prevent the writer from having one untroubled day in which to write again." Her intensity made casual contacts very difficult for her; she could love or loathe on sight. Sometimes there was a rational reason for the latter, but there were also times when she seems to have loathed people for no apparent reason but that they did not seem to be on her wavelength. Perhaps she came closest to being a social lion during her early days in Pittsburgh; she had always taken a very dim view of women's clubs, but after she had been drawn into the social current there, she found herself belonging to six! Later she had a flurry of being lionized in the Middle West, just after Sinclair Lewis had lauded her, and she seems to have enjoyed it thoroughly, even writing Greenslet, rather naively, of how proud she was that on one occasion a thousand people had paid five dollars a plate for dinner merely to see and hear her. But at Peterboro we are told that she spent most of her time trying to be alone and that she never stayed after dinner for talk or games. It is true that in her Bank Street days, there was a period when she was "at home" on Friday afternoons, but even here, according to Elizabeth Sergeant, she had no "light touch" in conversation, and no gift for "amalgamating disparate human elements." Neither did she care to discuss a subject on which she had already made up her mind. According to Edith Lewis, "her voice always took on the colour of what she was saying. It could be harsh, hard when she felt scornful of something. But when anything moved her deeply, it often had a low, muted, very musical quality." Surely she understood herself well when she wrote in her essay on

Katherine Mansfield "that human relationships are the tragic necessity of human life; that they can never be wholly satisfactory; that
every ego is half the time greedily seeking them, and half the time
pulling away from them."

6

For her, then, human beings were individuals, not members of
groups. She is said to have been liberal in sharing her bounty with
others, after she had won it, but she did not give to organizations
but rather to individuals whom she knew and liked, and her gifts are
said to have enabled old friends in Nebraska, including "my Ántonia" and her husband, to save their farms and weather the Great
Depression. She took endless trouble to get a poor scrubwoman
who had been consigned to an insane asylum by unsympathetic relatives put back into circulation. But one did not need to be in pain
or trouble to awaken her interest. She once sent an expensive set of
Spode to Mrs. Ralph Beal, who, with her husband, had served her
on Grand Manan, because she had heard that she liked fine china.
"Miss Cather was always pleasant," said Ralph. "If she made a
mistake, she would admit it."

It is this intense individualism of Willa Cather's that makes it hard
for me to take too seriously the charges of racism and, more specifically of anti-Semitism that some have seen fit to bring against her.
There are hideous, disgusting Jews in "The Diamond Mine" and
in "Scandal" — Miletus Poppas, who victimizes Cressida Garnet,
and Sigmund Stein, who manufactures a scandal about Kitty Ayrshire — and the Australian art dealer in "The Marriage of Phaedra"
is not endearing. I say nothing of Louis Marsellus in *The Professor's House* because I do not believe the view that he is a portrait of
Jan Hambourg can be sustained, and, in any case, Marsellus is not
an evil character. As for Poppas and Stein, as Woodress says, Willa
Cather has "a good many villains...who are white, Anglo-Saxon
Protestants." I admit frankly however that there can be no excuse
for such a statement as this about Poppas: "He was a vulture of the
vulture race, and he had the beak of one."

It is not fair to cite these instances however without also mentioning Mr. and Mrs. Rosen in "Old Mrs. Harris," directly derived
from the Wieners, who were so kind to Willa Cather in Red Cloud,
nor Becky Tietelbaum in "Ardessa" (1918), a little charmer under
many handicaps, whom Miss Cather's readers have noticed much
less than she deserves. Rena Kalski, in the same story, "a slender

young Hebrew, handsome in an impudent, Tenderloin sort of way,"
is a bird of another sort, but she too shows an attractive humanity at the end. Moreover what we know of Willa Cather's personal
life squares with all this much better than it does with "The Diamond Mine" and "Scandal." There is no hint of anti-Semitism in
her early review of Richard Mansfield's production of *The Merchant of Venice*, which was designed as an apology for Shylock, nor
yet in her review of a lecture by Israel Zangwill.[11] Nor can any be
found in her relations with Mr. and Mrs. Louis Brandeis or Mr. and
Mrs. Knopf nor in the very close and affectionate relationship with
the Menuhin family that gave her so much satisfaction in her later
years, and in which Yehudi said that she was "a tower of strength
and sweetness."

In closing this subject, I must admit however that there is one passage in Willa Cather's later writing that shocks me quite as much as
the reference to the "vulture race." Americans in general do not
nearly often enough remember the frightening wave of intolerance
that swept this country during and after World War I when the
Alien and Sedition Acts were passed and Wagner's operas had to
be sung in English. This crusade left Miss Cather cold and led her
to remark sarcastically that our lawmakers labored under a rooted
conviction that a boy must be a better American if he knew only
one language than if he knew two. Yet in her essay on Sarah Orne
Jewett in *Not under Forty* (1936) we find her referring to a "hypothetical young man ... perhaps of foreign descent: German, Jewish,
Scandinavian," to whom English is without "emotional roots" and
"merely a means of making himself understood." From the writer
who had glorified the immigrants on the Divide, condemned the
WASPish youths in Nebraska who had thought the foreign "hired
girls" not worth marrying, and dared to present Ántonia in her final
phase as having almost forgotten her English through the general
use of Bohemian in her home, I think we must agree that this is a
bit much.

Slighting references to Asians all seem to be early. In 1893 the
Chinese are "an unearthly people." In 1894 she calls Japanese children "little Japs," and sees war between China and Japan as a
"mutual extermination of barbarians." On the other hand, she was
well aware of the existence of an ancient civilization in China and
did not think that the Chinese needed American missionaries to
tamper with it.[12]

There are suggestions of an old-fashioned condescending Southern attitude toward blacks in her 1897 review of Frank Mayo's

Pudd'nhead Wilson play but not in the much later *Sapphira and the Slave Girl.* Indians too are treated with respect in the *Archbishop,* but in "The Dance at Chevalier's" (1900), "dull submission" derived from "red squaw ancestors" wars with the French love of pleasure in men of mixed ancestry. In "A Singer's Romance" (1900) a slight suggestion of effeminacy is attributed to Latins, which is somewhat surprising in view of the author's own passionate admiration of French art and culture. Certainly she was never Anglophilish even in youth; when she saw Olga Nethersole, she was surprised that an English girl could act so well! In 1901 she praised the Russian minister of Transportation, Prince Michael Hilkoff, for not "aping French manners and French vices" and for seeming "more American than Russian."

Certainly any race or class prejudices that Willa Cather may have cherished were aberrations, totally out of tune with her intense individualism, which shows up even, I believe, in her comparative indifference to all mass movements and activities, including politics. In view of the hardships the depression of the 1890s brought to her family, one might have expected her to sympathize with the Populists and their outstanding spokesman, William Jennings Bryan. In her 1900 essay on him, she tries to do him justice, finding him synthesizing "the entire Middle West; all its newness and vigor, magnitude and monotony, its richness and lack of variety, its inflammability and volubility, its strength and its crudeness, its high seriousness and self-confidence, its egotism and its nobility." She found "the almighty force of the man" driving one "to distraction" and his "everlasting seriousness" making one "want to play marbles."[13] All in all, she preferred McKinley.

In later days Willa Cather hated the New Deal for its bureaucracy and what she saw as its tendency to undercut or destroy the heroic individualism she had always admired; along with her indifference to "causes" and the whole *New Republic* attitude toward social issues this placed a strain on her friendship with Elizabeth Shepley Sergeant. She opposed government subsidies even for artists, who ought to stand on their own feet and make their way as she had made hers. This does not mean however that she should be set down as indifferent to social issues. It is true that the campaign to save the cottonwoods that she refers to so feelingly in *One of Ours,* was the only public crusade in which she was ever involved, but no muckraker could have painted a more devastating picture of official Washington than she does in *The Professor's House.* Above all, as we have already seen in connection with

the Indians and elsewhere, she was a passionate conservationist;
her Republicanism would have been badly strained had she lived
to witness the indifference of recent Republican presidents to this
vital issue.[14]

Willa Cather owned no car and refused to ride in a plane. She
liked boardwalks and kerosene lamps. She believed that a house
could not be beautiful until it had been lived in for a considerable
time and that it was inadvisable for an actress to wear a new gown
on the stage until she had worn it at home long enough to make it
look as though it belonged to her. The real Archbishop Lamy had
welcomed "progress" in the development of the West, but in the
Archbishop his fictional counterpart deplores it.

Her love for old friends and old familiar ways naturally grew
upon her as she herself grew older. But however much one's own
temperament may incline one to sympathize with her, I do not see
how one can reasonably deny that at times her love for "the precious, incommunicable past" was carried to an untenable extreme,
as in such statements that "an old house built in miserable taste
is more beautiful than a new house built and furnished in correct taste." Even modern Shakespearean scholarship seems to fall
under suspicion, for she had an idea that the Temple Edition of
Shakespeare's plays was the only one worth having. The classical
statement of this point of view is in the preface to *Not under Forty,*
discreetly omitted when the book was republished in the Autograph
Edition as *Literary Encounters.* This is where she declares that the
world broke in two about 1922 and resolutely took her place on the
thither side of the break. "It is for the backward, and by one of their
number that these sketches were written."

What must be remembered however is that all this was primarily a matter of temperament, not something determined primarily
by Willa Cather's attitude toward any political or social issue. Even
if the world had been wagging more to her liking than it did during her later years, she would still have been looking backward.
She is the novelist of memory; all her best stories are recollections.
In his pioneering study of her uncollected tales, Curtis Bradford
wrote: "Apparently Miss Cather could discern positive values only
after the passage of a great deal of time. Hers was a temperament which could long nostalgically for the [eighteen] eighties and
nineties, times which she had disliked when she was living through
them," and the Nebraska she glorified in her early novels was a
remembered, not a present Nebraska.[15]

7

But if, then, Willa Cather's world was composed not of groups but of individuals, and if she was inclined to react strongly to such of these individuals as crossed her part, what shall be said as to her relationship with the closest and most passionate of such ties? In writing of most unmarried ladies among writers — say Jane Austen or Mary Johnston — it would be impertinent even to ask such a question. But since a number of recent writers have seen fit to speak of Miss Cather as a lesbian, it would seem that the time has come to look at the record, so far as there is one and insofar as it may bear, directly or indirectly, upon this point, even though this operation may require more time and space than its importance warrants.

Those who see Miss Cather as a lesbian usually begin by adducing her youthful fondness for wearing men's clothing, her playfully signing her name "William Cather, M.D.," when she aspired to a medical career, and her tendency to prefer to tell her stories from a man's point of view (all of which is undeniable), from which they go on to allege that heterosexual love does not play an important part in her fiction, which is much more doubtful. It is true of course that she does not pop the boy and girl into bed together, often with little or no preparation, as many of her successors do, almost as casually as if they had gone out together for a cup of coffee, but this was not the custom in her time, and we know she believed that "a novel crowded with physical sensations" was as inartistic as one crowded with furniture. Nevertheless it is quite clear that she knew, as Heine reminded the prudish lady, that people are naked under their clothes.

The first and best-known poem in *April Twilights* is "Grandmither, Think Not I Forget," which is the lament of a sex-starved woman for her frustrated or forbidden love, and there are a number of other poems in this collection in which sex is important. The first novel brings us Bartley Alexander, torn between his wife and the love of his youth who has come back into his life. In *O Pioneers!* it may well be true, as has been said, that the love between Alexandra and Carl Linstrum is as mild as the loves of the plants (Alexandra's real love is the land), but whatever her fantasy-dream of the mysterious figure who picks her up and carries her off may mean, it is certainly not sexless, and the passion that flares up between her favorite brother, Emil, and Marie Shabata has been clearly though tastefully indicated before her husband kills them both under the white mulberry tree, where, for the first and last time, they have been joined in the act of love. In *The Song of the Lark* we are not told whether or not Thea Kronborg and Fred Ottenburg had sex in Panther Canyon, but Susie Thomas is not unreasonable when she calls this episode "one of the most open-air portrayals of passion in literature," and Loretta Wassermann goes even further when she finds a suggestion here that "an affair of sexual passion" is important in the development of an artist.[16] In *My Ántonia*, Jim Burden's affection for Ántonia seems rather strangely sexless, but Ántonia is betrayed by a promise of marriage from another man and returns home with a baby to support, of which we are told she was never ashamed and she herself says she would not have married Cuzak if his attitude toward the child had not matched hers. Sex is ugliest in this novel in Wick Cutter's frustrated attempt to rape Ántonia and most amusing in the hired man, Otto Fuchs, who had "undraped female figures" on his chaps, which "he solemnly explained, were angels," and for that matter, there is also humor of another sort in the Wick Cutter incident, which is rather suggestive of some of the passages in Chaucer's fabliau tales. The most alluring creature sexually in *My Ántonia* is, however, the "rosy semi-naked beauty," Lena Lingard, whom E. K. Brown called "the most beautiful, the most innocently sensuous of all the women in Willa Cather's works." Jim's dream at the end of chapter 12 of her coming to him across the fields with a sickle in her hand and rejoicing that now she can kiss him as much as she likes and Alexandra's dream of being carried are both uncommonly generous gifts to the Freudians from a writer who hated Freud. Though Lena does not desire a husband, it is hard to believe that she led a celibate life.

There is an abundance of sexual data in *One of Ours*. Even in Nebraska, the high-minded Claude Wheeler had "strong impulses" though with no idea of "trifling with them." He dropped Peachy Williams because her interest in "petting" disgusted him, but he loved the frigid Enid Royce with a man's passion at the same time he was looking up to her as if she were semidivine; once he was frightened by a dream in which she saw him naked. There is an amusing passage in which the black servant Mahailey watches the marriage ceremony intently to see if she can find out what it is the preacher does "to make the wrongest thing in the world the rightest thing in the world," but there is less humor than plain, downright honesty in the frank admission of the German singer Madame Schroeder-Schatz, that it is her cross in life to be tied to a sick man.

This, more seriously presented, is also a large part of Marian Forrester's tragedy in *A Lost Lady*. She takes the best possible care of

Captain Forrester after he has been incapacitated, but it is clear both to her and to her creator that she needs something more than he is now capable of giving her, even when no better alternative is available than such scum as Ivy Peters, whose appearance is made to suggest both an erect penis and a snake. She still feels "such a power to live in me," which has only grown "by being held back." Godfrey St. Peter in *The Professor's House* was "not an unpleasant sight" in his pajamas; "for looks, the fewer clothes he had on, the better. Anything that clung to his body showed it to be built upon extremely good bones, with the slender hips and springy shoulders of an experienced swimmer," and that his wife was perfectly capable of appreciating this is obvious from her remark about one of her husband's colleagues: "I believe he thinks it's wicked to live with even so plain a woman as Mrs. Crane." Once, we are told, the St. Peterses had been very much in love, but their relationship had now grown stale. So has that of the Henshawes in *My Mortal Enemy*, which had begun on the high romantic note of "all for love and the world well lost," but this time rather on her side than on his. As she sees it, a man and a woman can draw back "from that long embrace" and see what they have done to each other.

In *Death Comes for the Archbishop*, sexual irregularity among both clergy and laymen is not the least of the problems Father Latour has to deal with in his new diocese. In *Shadows on the Rock* Pierre Charron's record before his marriage to Cécile Auclair has been far from spotless, and it is even whispered that Madame de Montespan had been Count Frontenac's mistress before she took up with the king. In a fit of temper, Lucy Gayheart tells Harry Gordon falsely, when she wishes to get rid of him, that her affair with Sebastian has gone "the whole way." In *Sapphira and the Slave Girl*, both Mrs. Ringer's daughters have been "fooled," and the whole plot revolves around Martin Colbert's attempt to rape Nancy.

This record could easily be enlarged by reference to the short stories; I will give only a few examples. In "Old Mrs. Harris" there is a washwoman every one of whose children is said to have had a different father. Mary Trask in "Two Friends" is a "madame," and Seabury's most vivid memory of the Old Beauty is of the time when in their youth, he was the means of saving her from threatened rape. In "The Bohemian Girl" Nils Ericson runs off with his brother's wife, and so far as we know, they live happily ever after. In "Coming, Aphrodite!" Don Hedger, whose past relations with women have been "casual," spies on Eden Bower while she exercises in the nude, after which they have a brief, passionate affair.

Uncle Valentine deserted his wife for a "bad woman"; only he does not see it that way:

"A woman's behavior may be irreproachable and she herself may be gross — just gross. She may do her duty and defile everything she touches. And another woman may be erratic, imprudent, self-indulgent if you like, and all the while be — what is it the Bible says? Pure in heart."

To pass now from literature to life, we know of two proposals of marriage to Willa Cather, one from Preston Farrar, a teacher of English in Allegheny High School, the other from a doctor whom she evidently considered seriously enough to introduce him to Dorothy Canfield and ask her opinion (she approved). She must also have felt some lasting tenderness for Charles Moore, the son of a business associate of her father's, for he gave her a gold snake ring that Helen Cather Southwick says she wore all the rest of her life on the little finger of her right hand. In Lincoln she created some comment by going about with Dr. Julius Tyndale, a fifty-year-old bachelor who also wrote dramatic criticism and who has been given the credit for arranging for her 1895 trip to Chicago for a week of opera, and later, in London for McClure, she seems to have seen a good deal of the critic William Archer.

But if Willa Cather ever felt a strong sexual attraction to a man, it must have been the young Mexican we know only as Julio whom she met on her first trip to the Southwest and who reminded her of a statue of Antinous she had seen in Naples. She describes him as the most beautiful human being she ever saw, and the impression he gave of masculine force and strength matched his beauty. He took her to the Painted Desert and to a Mexican dance at which she was the only Caucasian present (the original of the Mexican dance attended by Thea Kronborg in *The Song of the Lark*), and it was he who told her the story of the forty lovers of the Aztec queen that she used in "Coming, Aphrodite!" The unpublished letters she wrote about him after her return East show that she kept him on her mind for some time; she even speculated, probably not too seriously, about the possibility of bringing him to New York, where she thought he could easily make his way as an artist's model.[17] Later she seems to have felt, less intensely, some of the same qualities in Tony Luhan, Mabel Dodge's husband, for when somebody asked her how Mabel came to marry an Indian, she asked, "How could she help it?"

If Julio and Tony appealed to Willa Cather sexually, there was another man whom she knew much better and who appealed to her strongly on a more spiritual and intellectual plane. This was the composer Ethelbert Nevin, whose artistic achievement she glorified,[18] whom she called lovable and noble of soul, and whose untimely death in 1901 was a great grief to her. Nevin obviously suggested the composer in "Uncle Valentine." Taking off from the fact that Miss Cather gives Valentine an unhappy marriage, Woodress, who seldom indulges in such speculations, calls her portrait of Valentine's estranged wife "rather nasty," and hints that it may have been colored by dislike of Mrs. Nevin. If one wished to carry this one step further, one might wonder whether Willa would have married Nevin if she had had the chance.

Whatever else may be argued about Willa Cather's sexual orientation, however, two things are certain: the number of unhappy marriages in her stories is abnormally high,[19] and she believed it next to impossible for a woman to combine a successful career with a successful marriage. She is, to be sure, not entirely consistent on the second point; in 1921 she even told an interviewer that she saw no reason why a woman could not have both a home and a career. She praised the great French actress, Gabrielle Réjane, for having achieved this; one wonders why she did not also mention that shining example among American opera singers, Louise Homer, about whom she wrote in "Three American Singers." Her usual view, however, seems to have been that a woman's art takes so much out of her that she has no room for anything else, and Fanny Butcher is probably right when she says "that nothing mattered to her but writing books and living the kind of life that makes it possible to write them."

Interestingly enough, all this coexisted in Willa Cather with an intense appreciation of domesticity and family life. She confessed frankly that she cared more for *The Mill on the Floss* than for any other of George Eliot's novels not because it was better fiction but because "no other piece of fiction ever treated of family life so truly, so justly, so beautifully." In *The Song of the Lark* she has Thea Kronborg fail to go to her dying mother because it would have handicapped her advancement as a singer, but she herself broke into *Shadows on the Rock* in order to visit her own mother after she had been stricken in California. Moreover, her domestic feelings grew stronger with time, and she once made a special trip to Washington to comfort a cousin who had lost his wife. It is not surprising then that the late "Neighbour Rosicky," "Old Mrs. Harris," and "The Best Years" should have been richer in domestic feeling than anything else she ever wrote. In the last named, there is an incident, trifling in itself, of the kind generally treated bawdily or humorously when admitted into literature at all, that is made significant by the way she handles it. A nervous, sensitive little boy, called upon unexpectedly to recite before the county superintendent, wets his pants. The tenderness with which he is treated by his young teacher and the way the other children help her to pass over an embarrassing situation are beyond praise and, until we remember how much Willa Cather did for her younger brothers and sisters, somewhat surprising as coming from a writer who never had a child of her own.

Sharon O'Brien refused to call Willa Cather a lesbian until after she had read her unpublished letters to Louise Pound, in which she found the "jealousy, worshipful insecurity, self-condemnation [and] depression" characteristic of a "turbulent, passionate attachment." Louise Pound, later a distinguished philologist and folklorist (and, as noted, the first woman president of the Modern Language Association), was at this time a fellow student at the University of Nebraska, somewhat older than Willa Cather and a more distinguished figure on campus. As we have already seen, Miss Cather's likes and dislikes were always very keen, and she herself told Dorothy Canfield that her years in college were years of frenzy. Whatever the relationship between the two young women may have been, it ended in 1894, when Willa published her outrageous "character" of Louise's brother, Roscoe Pound, future dean of the Harvard Law School, in a campus publication, the *Hesperian*. They were later reconciled after a fashion, but their old intimacy was never renewed. Willa's motivation for her attack on Roscoe Pound is still a mystery, but Phyllis Robinson's statement that "the openness with which Willa talked about her feelings for Louise suggests that most people did not regard their friendship as perverse or anything but a not-uncommon college crush is interesting. Can it be possible that Roscoe was an exception and that Willa, outraged, struck back at him on this account?[20]

Willa Cather met Isabelle McClung in Pittsburgh in 1898 or 1899 in the dressing room of the actress Lizzie Hudson Collier. Isabelle, the daughter of Judge and Mrs. Samuel McClung, was considered by her contemporaries to be a far more beautiful woman than her surviving photographs show. Born in affluence, she was more interested in art and in creative people than in "society," though she had no talent of her own. The two young women took to each other immediately, and their friendship developed rapidly until Isabelle invited Willa to make her home in the McClung mansion, where she fitted up a private study for her in the attic. Miss Cather was very happy on Murray Hill Avenue, and she returned there from time to time even after she had deserted Pittsburgh for New York. She and Isabelle made several trips together, and when Willa finally left *McClure's*, it was Isabelle who found a house for her in Cherry Valley.

There can be no doubt that Isabelle McClung was the dearest friend Willa Cather ever made. She was also the person Willa loved best outside her own family, and it may even be that this exception need not be taken. Though *The Song of the Lark* is the only book she ever dedicated to her friend (in the original edition with a poem containing a veiled reference to the hospitality she had enjoyed), she also said that Isabelle was the person for whom all her books had been written, and when Isabelle died in 1938, Willa told Zoë Akins that she was comatose and unable to feel anything.

In the winter of 1915–16, when she was thirty-eight, Isabelle, whose parents had by this time died, decided to sell the house on Murray Hill Avenue and to marry the Canadian-Jewish violinist, Jan Hambourg, and Elizabeth Shepley Sergeant's account of the trauma this caused Willa Cather, whose face, she says, was "bleak" and her eyes "vacant," has obviously had considerable influence upon subsequent hypothetical speculative accounts of the relationship between the two women, but Woodress has now shown that there is good reason to suspect that Miss Sergeant's account is somewhat over-colored. Willa Cather always found change very difficult, and this one not only promised to effect a radical alteration in her relationship with her dearest friend but also deprived her of the place that had been more of a home to her than any other she had found since leaving Red Cloud. In any event, "bleak" though she may have been, she does not seem to have been too "vacant" to have a share in arranging for Isabelle's wedding, which was performed by John Haynes Holmes, in April 1916, at the Church of the Messiah in New York, and for the reception that followed.

Isabelle's marriage did not end her friendship with Willa Cather. When the Hambourgs were living at the Villa d'Avray near Paris they fitted up a study for her and hoped that she would live with them at least part of the year, but for some reason she did not find this a congenial place to work. Later she did stay with them for two months or more in Toronto. The testimony as to how she felt about Jan Hambourg personally is somewhat mixed. She dedicated two of her books to him, though for some unknown reason, both dedications were dropped from later editions, but there are no indications of a quarrel, and he seems to have been very kind to her when she was sick in France while working on *One of Ours*. In the spring of 1934 the Hambourgs came back to New York from Europe, Isabelle sick with what turned out to be an incurable kidney ailment. The depression had sapped her fortune, and Jan went back to concertizing to earn the money they now needed. During his absence Willa went to the hospital every day, virtually giving up her own work. After Jan returned in June, all three persons went together to Chicago, where Jan had a summer teaching appointment and from there to Europe. When Willa returned home alone, she knew she had said goodbye to her friend for the last time. Isabelle McClung Hambourg died in October 1938.

This, so far as I know, is an honest record of what is known about the Cather-McClung friendship. Anyone who thinks it indicates a lesbian relationship is welcome to his conjectures. Next he might try his hand at squaring the circle.

Willa Cather met Edith Lewis, whose family lived in Lincoln, Nebraska, in 1903 as an admirer of her work. Edith visited her while she was living with the McClungs and in New York the following summer. When Miss Cather moved to New York in 1906, she also moved into the apartment house that Edith inhabited, and from 1908 on they shared an apartment. Phyllis Robinson, who is so sensible about Willa's relationship with Louise Pound, becomes as ridiculous as most people do when they assume omniscience when she writes of Willa and Edith that "their life together was undoubtedly a marriage in every sense."

The two women were undoubtedly very close. Miss Lewis is "Darling Edith" in one surviving specimen of Willa's letters to her, and she chose to be buried near her friend in Jaffrey, New Hampshire. But I do not mean to denigrate Miss Lewis when I write that I do not believe they were ever quite equals. *One Point of the Compass* is not the only source that suggests that Edith was almost as much Willa's Girl Friday as her friend. Miss Cather always had to have people doing things for her; when Edith was not at hand to make her travel reservations for her, she would call on Irene Miner or somebody else; to do such things herself seems to have occurred to her only as a last resort. We are told too that when the Knopfs invited Miss Cather to share their box at the Metropolitan Opera House, she came alone. Edith was not included in the invitation. This hardly suggests "a marriage in every sense."

In taking leave of this inconclusive subject, it seems natural to ask whether Willa Cather ever took up any attitude toward homosexuality as a phenomenon. But there are many more questions in the world than answers, and I have found little or nothing except for her comments on the Oscar Wilde case in the 1890s, which are little short of savage. Wilde was "deservedly" imprisoned. Once, in referring to his poem "Helas," she hesitated to mention the author, since his conduct had made "even his name impossible." All his works seemed tainted to her; *Lady Windermere's Fan* was "a malicious lie upon human nature," stamped with insincerity, "the sin which insults the dignity of man, and of God in whose image he was made." In 1895 she told the readers of the *Nebraska State Journal* that "the eternal fact of sex seems to be at the bottom of everything. But after people have ceased to seek for love there is one thing that they seem to go on seeking for, and that is sympathy." All this is of course too early to be quoted as expressing her attitude during her whole lifetime. Let us hope at least that whatever she believed, there was some advance in the direction of Christian charity.

8

Many Cather scholars have viewed their subject as essentially a religious writer, but a reader who confined himself to her early work would probably not get this impression. There was a variety of churches in Red Cloud that she could attend in her youth and sometimes did, though not always for the reasons their founders intended. The dominant atmosphere of the Baptist church with which Willa's parents were affiliated was probably that of the Midwestern Protestant fundamentalism characteristic of the place and time. When she reached Pittsburgh, she found the Presbyterian version of the same as ubiquitous as smoke and greed; even Frederic Archer's Sunday organ recitals were frowned upon by many. To Willa Cather it must have seemed as if religion in Pittsburgh were something very much like what she imputed to Marshall McKann in "A Gold Slipper," "not very spiritual, certainly, but ... substantial and concrete, made up of good, hard convictions and opinions. It had something to do with citizenship, with whom one ought to marry, with the coal business (in which his own name was powerful), with the Republican Party, and with all majorities and established precedents."[21]

In "The Joy of Nelly Deane" (1911), the description of that young lady's immersion upon being received into the Baptist church is fairly sympathetic, but the minister who calls on Katherine Gaylord in " 'A Death in the Desert' " is a fool. The hero of "Lou the Prophet" goes crazy over the Book of Revelation, and Eric Hermannson would have been spared much agony if the ridiculous exhorter, Asa Skinner, had not convinced him that the violin he loved so well was a snare of the devil's. In "The Conversion of Sum Loo," the whole conflict between the Taoist priest and the Mission of the Heavenly Rest is presented satirically.

The minister most fully presented in Miss Cather's early fiction is Thea's father in *The Song of the Lark,* the Reverend Peter Kronborg. Brother Weldon in *One of Ours* is far more repellent, but we see nothing of him save through his effect upon Claude. As for Peter, though he is far from being an Elmer Gantry type, his portrait could hardly be more devastating. He is ignorant, lazy, and what Shakespeare calls "a huge feeder," cut off much the same piece of cloth as the Reverend Lars Larson, whom Thea encounters in Chicago, who chose the ministry "because it seemed to him the least laborious of all callings." As if this were not enough for one novel, Thea's Aunt Tillie, who had been converted in a revival meeting, is also presented contemptuously, and her suspicions not only of the Mexicans with whom Thea associates musically but even of Dr. Archie are not only uncharitable but prurient besides. Is Dr. Archie speaking for the author when he tries to comfort Thea, who is worrying herself sick over whether Moonstone has violated the teachings of the Gospel in its treatment of the tramp who drowned himself? Dr. Archie thinks all religions are good and that they are all pretty much alike, but he does not see how people can live up to them in the sense Thea suggests. While we are in the world, we must live for the good things of the world. If we keep the Commandments and lend a helping hand when we can, that is all that can be asked of us.[22]

Some of Willa's classmates have been quoted as calling her an unbeliever in her college days, but I have found no real evidence for this. That she is supposed to have expressed admiration for Robert Ingersoll does not get us far, for Ingersoll was an agnostic, not an atheist, and he might well be shocked by some of the things that are being taught about the Bible in perfectly orthodox theological seminaries today. In her daring high school commencement oration, she declared that "superstition has been the curse of the church, and that since her principles are true, no scientific truth can contradict them." But quite as sound evidence as this to prove that Willa Cather lived against an essentially religious frame of reference, even in her earlier life, may be found again and again in contexts not essentially religious in themselves. "The world was made by an

Artist." Jean Valjean is "the most Christlike character ever put in
a novel." Shakespeare "is ours, as Christ is ours," and all novels
about Christ fail because "the Christ ideal is higher than it has yet
been given any writer of fiction to reach." Watching a great actor is
"watching a man give back what God put into him," and to watch
Mrs. Fiske at her best was to feel that "somewhere, sometime there
is a resurrection and a life, that nothing can destroy."

Later on of course there is much more. Catholicism fares better
than Protestantism in Miss Cather's books, the kind of Protestantism that she knew in her youth at any rate, and I am sure
Edith Lewis is right in tracing her interest in Catholicism back to
her childhood. It was not until 1922, when, together with her parents, she was received into the Episcopal church, that Miss Cather
regularized and institutionalized her religious feelings and convictions. Why, then, she chose the Episcopal rather than the Roman
Catholic church I am unable to say, but at least it is significant that
the choice she made was in harmony with her respect for tradition
and historical continuity. In *O Pioneers!* Marie Shabata is "truly
a devout [Catholic] girl." Count Frontenac, dying in *Shadows on
the Rock,* believes that he faces judgment because that is what his
church has taught him, but he also believes "because he knew there
was something in himself and in other men that this world did not
explain." And when Jim Burden's Protestant grandfather prays in
perfect charity by Mr. Shimerda's grave, it seems that all Christians
have become one at last.

Willa Cather's essay on Thomas Mann's *Joseph and His Brothers*
in *Not under Forty* may be the best single testimonial we have to
what the Bible meant to her, but the most precious word of all for
her as an artist was Godfrey St. Peter's view that art and religion
are one and are themselves responsible for the only real happiness
man has ever had. In the Parable of the Talents, the faithful servants
who had worked their talents to their utmost limits were praised
while the one that hid his in the earth was condemned. Willa Cather
worked her talents to their utmost limits if anybody ever did. It was
good that in doing this she was permitted also to realize that she
was serving the Best and Highest she knew.

Appendix

Willa Cather's Uncollected Stories

In this section, arranged alphabetically for easy reference, are brief descriptions and evaluations of all the short stories not reprinted by Willa Cather from the periodicals in which they appeared. Each title is followed by a notation indicating (1) its place of original publication and (2) abbreviations indicating the book or books in which it has since been reprinted by Cather scholars. These are:

Writings from Willa Cather's Campus Years, edited by James R. Shively. University of Nebraska Press, 1950; cited as Shively.

Early Stories of Willa Cather, selected and with commentary by Mildred R. Bennett. Dodd, Mead & Company, 1957; cited as *ESWC.*

Willa Cather's Collected Short Fiction, 1892-1912, introduction by Mildred R. Bennett. University of Nebraska Press, 1965; cited as *CSF.*

Uncle Valentine and Other Stories, Willa Cather's Uncollected Short Fiction, 1915–1929, edited by Bernice R. Slote. University of Nebraska Press, 1973; cited as *UV.*

It will be noted that a few of the stories listed hereafter were published pseudonymously. It is entirely possible that Willa Cather may have published thus other stories that have not yet been identified.

Finally, James R. Shively's book contains samples of a few other types of Willa Cather's early writings, including some dialogues from the *Hesperian,* a University of Nebraska campus publication, which, so far as I know, have not elsewhere been reprinted.

THE AFFAIR AT GROVER STATION (*Library,* June 16, 1906; *ESWC; CSF*) is Willa Cather's first story with a railroad background, and the important characters are railroad men. Grover Station is not precisely located, but there are also scenes in Omaha and Cheyenne, where the author's brother Douglass had worked for the Burlington and where she had visited him. It is a well-told murder mystery, spiked by a touch of the supernatural, but the return of the victim's ghost to chalk on the blackboard the clue that leads to the solution of the mystery is not adequately prepared for.

ARDESSA (*Century,* May 1918; *UV*) is a light, amusing, only mildly satirical tale, which takes on special interest as the story most clearly derived from the author's journalistic experiences. Though the details differ, the editor O'Mally has obviously been based on S.S. McClure. Young Becky Tietelbaum — crude, unformed, generous, ambitious, and a glutton for work — is a jewel of a girl, who steals the show from the lazy, arrogant, self-centered title character who has been almost O'Mally's second in command. But this is not a fault in construction, for the way in which it almost inevitably occurs is essentially what the story is about.

BEHIND THE SINGER TOWER (*Collier's*, May 1912; *CSF*) is Willa Cather's most emphatic contribution to the social protest fiction of her time. Its theme is the cost in lives and suffering of our urban, skyscraper-ridden civilization and the indifference of corporations and career men to human values. Probably deriving from the Windsor Hotel fire of 1899, it may also have been influenced, as Sharon O'Brien has suggested, by Allan Updegraff's poem, "From a Skyscraper," in *McClure's*, February 1911. In the story the hotel is called the Mont Blanc, and its destruction occasions the reporter Hallet's telling of the accident that killed his little Italian friend Caesarino and how, for once, the corporation that intended to call it quits with half a night's pay after the fatal accident was taken to court and forced to pay damages.

THE BOHEMIAN GIRL (*McClure's*, August 1912; *CSF*) was written in the fall of 1911, before *O Pioneers!* It is the longest of Willa Cather's uncollected tales and by all means her most ambitious picture of life in early Nebraska before *O Pioneers!*, but neither Clara Vavrika, the Bohemian girl, who marries Nils Ericson's stolid but ambitious brother Olaf after Nils has gone away, nor Nils himself, who, after his return, persuades her to run off to Norway with him, is an especially sympathetic character, though both Clara and old Mrs. Ericson are interesting because of their complications of character. The best scene is that of the barn party, which E. K. Brown compared to the wedding chapter in *Madame Bovary*, and especially memorable is the behavior of the old women who officiate there. There are some suggestions of the feeling for the land that was to be better developed in *O Pioneers!* and *My Ántonia*, and there is the characteristic Cather time lapse before the last section. The most emphatic position in the story is rather oddly given at the end to the attempted flight of Nils's younger brother, Eric, to Norway, upon an invitation from Nils and Clara, and his return to his mother.

THE BOOKKEEPER'S WIFE (*Century*, May 1916; *UV*) is the poorest story written by Willa Cather after she had begun publishing novels; it seems surprising indeed that so distinguished a magazine as the *Century* should have accepted it. Percy Bixby, upon whom the focus rests steadily until just before the end, and his predicament, are convincingly presented. He "borrows" one thousand dollars from company funds on which to get married. When the day of reckoning comes, his employer lets him off by withholding ten dollars a week from his check until the debt shall have been paid. Though this may seem somewhat surprising, it will pass. But the scene in which Percy's wife Stella reveals her heartlessness not only by leaving him but by cruelly telling him off is as hopelessly theatrical, artificial, and cliché-ridden as anything in the old melodramas; it could not have been accepted even if it had been prepared for by a much fuller revelation of her character than had previously been made.

THE BURGLAR'S CHRISTMAS (*Home Monthly*, December 1896, under pseudonym of Elizabeth A. Seymour; *CSF*) is Exhibit A in the endeavor to show that Willa Cather, on the threshold of her career, could turn out sentimental bathos for the women's magazines on demand. A young man who has lived by his wits and failed finds himself on Christmas eve starving on Prairie Avenue in Chicago, to which his parents have recently moved. Attempting to burgle their house, he finds himself safe at home. The account of his mental processes before he goes into the house is rather well done.

THE CLEMENCY OF THE COURT (*Hesperian*, October 28, 1893; Shively; *ESWC; CSF*) tells the painful story of Serge Pavolinsky, who slays a man who has brutally and wantonly killed his dog, the only living being who has ever shown him any affection. Through "the clemency of the court," his death sentence is commuted to life imprisonment, which is no improvement, for he is tortured in prison because he cannot learn how to hoop barrels. The powerful social criticism involved is implied, not stated, and only the somewhat sentimental final sentence is out of harmony with the tone of this brief, biting tale. Mildred Bennett (*Early Stories of WC*, p. 32) finds sources in Victor Hugo, Guy de Maupassant, and "possibly" in Turgenev. See L. Brent Bohlke, "Beginnings: WC and 'The Clemency of the Court,'" *PS*, 48 (1974), 134–44.

CONSEQUENCES (*McClure's*, November 1912; *UV*) is the only story by Willa Cather that could be called obscure. Bernice Slote's two guesses — that it was derivative of "The Jolly Corner," by Henry James, and that the loathsome old creature who haunts Cavenaugh is a projection of what he will become if he continues in his present way of life — both seem reasonable; there may also have been some influence from *The Picture of Dorian Gray*, by Oscar Wilde. The long discussion in the first part between Cavenaugh and the lawyer, Henry Eastman, about whether suicides are sometimes simply inexplicable or whether, if we could know all about the suicide's life and mind, the mystery would be resolved (in the course of which a number of chilling instances are briefly cited) is organically related to the outcome when Cavenaugh's own death supports his argument in behalf of the latter view.

THE CONVERSION OF SUM LOO (*Library*, August 12, 1900; *ESWC; CSF*) is a brief, light, satirical tale about a prosperous Chinese merchant in San Francisco who tries to straddle Taoism and Christianity but turns against the latter when his son dies shortly after having been baptized.

Though competent, entertaining magazine fiction, it has nothing about it that suggests Willa Cather's individual gift.

THE COUNT OF CROW'S NEST (*Home Monthly,* September–October 1896; *CSWC; CSF*) is a somewhat rambling, unfocused tale, set in a cheap Chicago boardinghouse, inhabited mainly by artists and journalists, just before the World's Columbian Exposition. The honorable, improvident Count de Koch has a florid, vulgar daughter, Helena, who is a showy, incompetent singer, and a collection of letters from European notables whose publication could cause an immense scandal. After having vainly tried to persuade Harold Buchanan to edit and publish these letters, Helena makes a futile attempt to steal them. Both she and the count are rather vividly realized characters, and Woodress thinks this Willa Cather's best story to date. *Cosmopolitan* wanted it, but the author was compelled to keep it for the *Home Monthly,* on which she was employed at the time. The influence of "The Aspern Papers," by Henry James, is pretty obvious, and Mildred Bennett suggested Turgenev's "Old Portraits" as another possible source.

THE DANCE AT CHEVALIER's (*Library,* April 28, 1900, under pseudonym Henry Nickelmann, derived from Hauptmann's *The Sunken Bell; ESWC; CSF*) is an unconvincing piece of sensational melodrama, set in the cattle country of Oklahoma and crowded with racial stereotypes. Both the "greaser" known as the Signor, and the Irish "ladies' man," Davis, are employed by Chevalier, and both are in love with his daughter Severine, who favors Davis. On the night of the dance, the Signor kills his rival with poisoned wine and flees. Peter Sadelack, who kills himself in the author's first published story ("Peter") is one of the fiddlers at the dance.

DOUBLE BIRTHDAY (*Forum,* February 1929; *UV*) is a fairly long short story, with very little plot but rich in the reminiscential quality that went along with the author's tenderness for the past, especially in her later phase (for the sources in Willa Cather's life in Pittsburgh, see Bernice Slote's introduction to *Uncle Valentine and Other Stories,* especially pp. xxviii–xxix). The double birthday is that of Dr. Albert Engelhardt, eighty, and his nephew and namesake, forty-five. The family, once wealthy, has come down in the world. Both the Engelhardts are devoted to music. The doctor, now retired, lives in his memories and his relish of music now largely fallen out of fashion (as Mrs. Parmenter tells him, he has the last ten years of the nineteenth century and the first ten of the twentieth shut up in his house). He was a throat specialist, with a special interest in singers. His great adventure and his great heartbreak came with his discovery of a phenomenal voice in Marguerite Thiesinger, a conventionally minded German girl who died of cancer before she was able fully to realize, much less exploit, her potential. Bernice Slote derives Dr. Engelhardt from Dr. Julius Tyndale of Lincoln and Margaret Parmenter and her father from Isabelle McClung and her father the judge.

EL DORADO: A KANSAS RECESSIONAL (*New England Magazine,* June 1901; *CSF*), one of the most ambitious of the early stories, gives us the nether side of Midwestern pioneering — nature in her most unamiable aspects and crooked promoters luring gullible Easterners west with the promise of glittering rewards to be reaped in boomtowns that exist only on paper. Colonel Josiah Bywaters, a Virginian, a Civil War veteran, and a "Christian gentleman" ("Dry Goods, Groceries, and Notions") is the last survivor at El Dorado, in the Solomon Valley of western Kansas, living alone with his cat and too kind to take money from the few stragglers that pass by once in a coon's age. The story is more successful in its parts than as a whole. There is much good writing, but the narrative as such is not satisfactorily handled, and the way one of the promoters is brought back at the end to die of rattlesnake bite is forced and artificial.

ELEANOR'S HOUSE (*McClure's,* October 1907; CSF) is perhaps Willa Cather's most Jamesian story, but though she is able to handle all James's complications, she does not come within hailing distance of his ease; she was right, I believe, when she decided that his method was not for her. Harold Forsythe, virtually destroyed by grief after the death of his wife, marries another woman — "to talk about Eleanor," says their friend, Harriet Westfield — and naturally Ethel is very unhappy. He faces up to his responsibilities and achieves maturity only after Ethel has dared to force the issue by going to Fortuney, where he had lived with Eleanor, and there telling him that she is to have a child. The story is told by the omniscient author with a good deal of guidance from Mrs. Westfield. See Marilyn Arnold, *WC's Short Fiction* for a somewhat different interpretation from mine.

THE ELOPEMENT OF ALLAN POOLE (*Hesperian,* April 15, 1893, unsigned; reprinted in *The Kingdom of Art,* edited by Bernice Slote, pp. 437–51) is a brief, tragic, objectively told tale about a young Southern moonshiner, who is shot by a revenue officer on his way to elope with his sweetheart and dies in her arms. The dialogue is good, and the characters are as vividly realized as the limited space permits. The nature background is vivid, and the story gains added significance from being the earliest, so far as is presently known, in which Willa Cather made use of her childhood memories of Virginia. See *The Kingdom of Art,* pp. 104–6.

THE ENCHANTED BLUFF (*Harper's Magazine,* April 1909; *CSF*), more than any other tale, forecasts the mature Willa Cather (see David Stouck, *WC's Imagination,* p. 69, n. 9). A simple, plotless, but magnificently written account of six boys on a sandbar in the Republican River of the author's own youth, it is rich in motifs later developed elaborately in "Tom Outland's Story" in *The Professor's House* and elsewhere. It has a melancholy ending: nobody ever reaches the bluff.

ERIC HERMANNSON'S SOUL (*Cosmopolitan*, April 1900; *ESWC; CSF*) is one of the most ambitious of Willa Cather's early stories and contains many suggestions of even better work to come. It is a study of religious fanaticism as it manifests itself on the Divide. By nature, Eric Hermannson, a big Norwegian, is a slave to beauty, but all he knows of it has been derived from his violin, which the Free Gospellers, who have already been responsible for a few suicides and who have sent "a good-sized delegation to the state insane asylum," regard as a snare of Satan. Their preacher, Asa Skinner, is "a man made for the extremes of life," a converted river gambler, who had been "one of the most debauched of men" and was now "one of the most ascetic." He converts Eric in a revival meeting, where, having starved all the other passions, he falls victim to "the basest of them all, fear." He backslides when he encounters Margaret Elliot, "a beautiful, talented, critical, unsatisfied" girl from the East, who is already "tired of the world at twenty-four," for he believes that when he accepted her invitation to a dance, "he delivered his soul to hell." The story suggests Willa Cather's own appreciation of and attraction toward both primitivism and civilization. Symbolism is used effectively, and the significance of the action is reinforced by mythological and allegorical references. There is also more generalizing, even moralizing, than is characteristic of our author.

THE FEAR THAT WALKS BY NOONDAY (*Sombrero* [University of Nebraska publication], III, 1894; *ESWC; CSF*) is a combination ghost story and football story, about the most uncharacteristic piece Willa Cather ever wrote. The plot was Dorothy Canfield's, but all the writing is by Willa Cather. A dead football player comes back to the playing field to win the day for his school, with intense cold and depression testifying to his presence. The technique is pretty sophisticated for a twenty-year-old, and there is no suggestion that the writer is a female.

HER BOSS (*Smart Set*, October 1919; *UV*) is a powerful story that, despite its blackness and irony, manages also to be very tender and moving. Paul Wanning is a disillusioned, middle-aged lawyer with an unsympathetic family (cf. *The Professor's House*). He has just received his death sentence from his doctor, but the family refuses to take the matter seriously or to allow it to interfere with their plans for the summer. Left alone, he finds comfort in dictating his autobiography to a little stenographer employed in his office, who generously gives him her companionship. There is nothing remarkable about Annie Wooley except her kindness of heart, and she and Wanning have no romantic interest whatever in each other. He intends — and voluntarily promises to reward her for services upon which no monetary value could be placed by making her a sharer in his will, but after he is gone, his scandal-snooping partner conspires with his greedy family to frustrate his intention, and the girl, now without a job, and her honorable, poor family, are left believing that Wanning has not kept his word.

JACK-A-BOY (*Saturday Evening Post,* March 30, 1901; *CSF*) is the story of an enchanting six-year-old, who moves into Windsor Terrace, where they did not care much for children, and wins all hearts, especially those of the Professor who cared only for Greek roots; the "Woman Nobody Called On"; and the music teacher, Miss Harris, who tells the tale. It is pleasantly told, but so drenched in sentiment that many readers will find its pathos turned to bathos. Moreover, though the child was based upon Miss Cather's youngest brother, whom she nursed through a dangerous illness in 1895 and dearly loved, his talk is far from creating the illusion of reality. Of course he dies (of scarlet fever) in the best nineteenth-century fictional tradition, leaving everybody better and kinder for having known him.

THE JOY OF NELLY DEANE (*Century,* 1911; *CSF*) is a real tear-jerker. The title suggests a Mary Miles Minter film of the days of the movie's innocence (e.g., *The Eyes of Julia Deep* or *The Ghost of Rosy Taylor*). Nelly, a charming, carefree girl, meets a sad fate. Having been secretly engaged to a traveling salesman, who jilts her, she teaches school, which she does not enjoy, and marries a prosperous, dour village youth, who becomes indirectly responsible for her death after the birth of her second child. The story is told in retrospect by a close friend. It ends on an upbeat note, with the focus on Nelly's daughter. Several critics have found in it an anticipation of *Lucy Gayheart.* This is best developed by Susan J. Rosowski (*Voyage Perilous,* pp. 220–22), who also finds the three fates in Mrs. Dow, Mrs. Freeze, and Mrs. Phinney.

LOU, THE PROPHET (*Hesperian,* October 14, 1892; Shively; *ESWC; CSF*) is the story of a young Danish farmer on a homestead in the West (obviously Nebraska), who, in a time of drought, goes crazy over the Book of Revelation and proclaims the imminent end of the world. His only converts are a group of Danish boys, who shelter him in a cave, and who, when he disappears at the end, are sure that, like Enoch, he has been "translated," without passing through the ordeal of bodily death. The story is told not unsympathetically but dryly without any commentary upon or interpretation of Lou's state.

THE NAMESAKE (*McClure's,* March 1907; *CSF*) is a well-written tale, perhaps most interesting for the varied interests it touches. A great sculptor relates to his young admirers in Paris how all his work has been inspired by what he knows of his uncle-namesake, who was killed in the Civil War while still in his teens. One passage, relating how, on one occasion, he felt he had made a vital contact with his uncle, skirts the supernatural. Social consciousness is revealed in the passage describing the pollution introduced into a Pennsylvania city (obviously Pittsburgh) by industrialism. "The Namesake," may also deserve to be taken into consideration in connection with Willa Cather's own attitude toward family solidarity (cf. her identically entitled poem on her Civil War uncle, in *April Twilights*) and perhaps also her attitude toward war itself, which became a subject of some public interest when she published *One of Ours*.

NANETTE: AN ASIDE (*Lincoln Courier,* July 21, 1897; *ESWC; CSF*) is Willa Cather's earliest treatment of an opera singer. The characters are Madame Tradutti, who is not happy in her private life, and the devoted maid who has taken care of her for years. In New York, Nanette falls desperately in love with a head waiter, and Madame generously lets her go. "Nanette" is hardly more than an anecdote, but Willa Cather was always interesting on the psychology of singers, and the dialogue is amusing.

A NIGHT AT GREENWAY COURT (*Nebraska Literary Magazine,* June 1896, reprinted in the *Library,* April 21, 1900; Shively; *ESWC; CSF*) shows Willa Cather capable, had she had a mind to it, of turning out popular historical fiction of the kind esteemed in the 1890s and early 1900s. The place is Virginia, the date 1752, and the central incident is a duel in which Thomas, Lord Fairfax, wreaks vengeance upon a disreputable Frenchman who has proclaimed himself both antimonarchist and atheist. The story is told in the first person, in a manuscript supposed to have been written by one Richard Norman, a fellow guest at the scene of the duel. The variations between the two serial versions of the duel are noted by Mildred Bennett in *ESWC*.

ON THE DIVIDE (*Overland Monthly,* January 1896; *CSF*) marked Willa Cather's first appearance as a fictionist in a magazine of anything approaching national circulation, and its hostile picture of life on the plains contrasts sharply with the nostalgic mood of her later works. Canute Canuteson is a barbarian out of the sagas who drinks raw alcohol, and his story threatens to degenerate into movie or comic-book farce when he picks up the girl he wishes to marry (it is hard to see why, for she is the nastiest young woman in the whole Cather oeuvre, and she has treated him worse than a dog) and carries her off to his shack and, on top of that, forces a frail and ailing clergyman to come out into the cold and marry them without a license! "Crazy Lou" (see "Lou, the Prophet" above) is mentioned toward the end.

ON THE GULLS' ROAD: THE AMBASSADOR'S STORY (*McClure's,* December 1908; *CSF*) is a first-person narrative, occasioned by a visitor's interest in the ambassador's drawing of Alexandra Ebbling, a beautiful woman from Finmark, whom he had met on shipboard, twenty years before, when she was already dying. Her husband, the engineer of the boat, was an insensitive, loathsome philanderer, totally incapable of appreciating her. Though the love that she and the ambassador feel for each other is only a flower blooming at the gates of death and thus quite incapable of fulfillment, the reader is left with the feeling that it was the most precious thing in both their lives and its own justification.

PETER (*Mahogany Tree*, May 1892, reprinted with variants in the *Hesperian*, November 24, 1892, and in the *Library*, July 21, 1900; Shively; *ESWC; CSF*), apparently Willa Cather's first published story, is significant primarily because it was reworked for Shimerda's suicide in *My Ántonia*. Peter Sadelack, who lives with a mean, parsimonious son, who tyrannizes over him, on a farm in southwestern Nebraska, is a very different man from Shimerda however. He had been second violin in a theater in Prague, where he had seen Rachel and Liszt and Bernhardt, but though he is handled most sympathetically, he is pretty much of a wreck by the time we meet him, with not much interest in anything except his whiskey, when he can get it. The contrast between him and his son forecasts that between the Nebraska pioneers and their descendants of which so much was to be made in *One of Ours*. There is glamour in the theater scenes in Prague. *ESWC* records the variants between the three magazine texts.

THE PRINCESS BALADINA — HER ADVENTURE (*Home Monthly*, August 1896, under the pseudonym Charles Douglass; *CSF*) is a mildly amusing, slightly wry story about a spoiled princess who, to punish her family, starts out one morning to find a wizard to enchant her and a prince to rescue her. She finds the quest so unrewarding that she is just about to settle for the miller's son in place of the prince when the king her father overtakes them and carries her home.

THE PRODIGIES (*Home Monthly*, July 1897; *ESWC; CSF*) has a foolish, almost hysterical, mother who forces and exploits the genuine musical gifts of her two children until the girl collapses, after which the delicate boy is told to remember that he now has two destinies in his throat instead of one. Both the satire and the implied condemnation are laid on with a heavy hand. The story is written in the third person, but toward the end the situation is seen mainly from Dr. Mackenzie's point of view. "The Prodigies" may have been suggested by the Dovey Sisters; see *The Kingdom of Art*, pp. 145–48, and of course it gains interest from Miss Cather's association with the Menuhin family in later life. It reminds Woodress of Hawthorne, especially in "The Birthmark" in subject matter and of James in technique.

THE PROFESSOR'S COMMENCEMENT (*New England Magazine*, June 1902; *CSF*) probably interests the author's admirers most for its many references to artists and writers, old and new, familiar to her and to cultivated Americans generally at the time of its composition. The "professor," a teacher of English in a high school located in a city, obviously Pittsburgh, being rapidly defaced and polluted by industrialism, has labored all his life as a conserver of culture and human values in an unfriendly environment. At a dinner given in his honor at his retirement, he tries to recite a poem he had failed to remember at his own graduation and breaks down again at exactly the same point.

THE PROFILE (*McClure's*, June 1907; *CSF*) is an ambitious psychological study, rather remarkably successful for this early stage in its writer's career, except perhaps in its too-pat ending, where Dunlap takes as his second wife the cousin of his first, whose beauty, like her predecessor's, had been ruined by a burn. The story begins when Dunlap is engaged to paint a portrait of the daughter of a very wealthy man whose face had been thus ravaged. Neither she nor her parents give any indication that they are aware of her disfigurement, and the girl promptly sets her cap for the artist and succeeds. He loves her at first despite her scar, later almost because of it. But he soon comes to feel that her failure to recognize her misfortune or to take him into her confidence concerning it constitutes a barrier between them, and he is further antagonized by her avidity for social display and her tasteless, extravagant clothes, as well as later by her indifference toward their sickly, plain daughter. Finally, when, after having been pushed beyond endurance, he almost inadvertently refers to the scar, she leaves him and their child and afterwards divorces him. The title has a double meaning. Dunlap paints his wife in profile, and it is only a profile she presents not only to the world but even to him. Marilyn Arnold (*WC's Shorter Fiction*) accuses Dunlap of neurotic, perverse, abnormal fixation on the scar and on himself as a chivalrous healer or messiah, but this interpretation seems to me foreign to the tone of the story.

A RESURRECTION (*Home Monthly*, April 1897; *ESWC; CSF*) is set in Brownville, Nebraska, after a change in the course of the Missouri River had robbed the town of its onetime prosperity. Insofar as it deals with the history of the town and the fascination it held for its sons, the piece is successful, but as a story the less said about it the better. It deals with a rather hapless man who is lured away from his rightful mate by a worthless girl and who, after his wife's death, takes their child to the other woman to care for, and it has a forced, sentimental ending. Margie's helplessly self-revealing outburst, when she believes him about to take Bobbie, whom she has come to love, away from her, is especially artificial.

THE SENTIMENTALITY OF WILLIAM TAVENER (*Library*, May 12, 1900; *ESWC; CSF*), as Mildred Bennett pointed out, is the only story in which Willa Cather draws upon both her Virginia and her Nebraska background. Hester Tavener is a managing woman with a henpecked Nebraska farmer-husband, but the coming of the circus that their two sons passionately wish to attend softens them both and brings them closer together when Hester learns for the first time that her husband-to-be had also been present at a performance that both have fondly remembered from their Virginia youth. One minor character, Tap, reappears in *Sapphira and the Slave Girl*.

A SINGER'S ROMANCE (*Library*, July 28, 1900; *ESWC; CSF*), which Mildred Bennett calls a rewrite of "Nanette," is an amusing, slightly cynical tale with an O. Henry surprise ending, about a "competent" German singer at the Metropolitan with a spendthrift husband in Monte Carlo, who has never had a real romance and is beginning to be distressed by symptoms of aging. Shadowed by a young man who dogs her footsteps in New York, always on hand to do her a courtesy, but who never speaks in response to her overtures, she is tempted for once in her life to behave as some people believe all singers do, but is rudely disillusioned when she learns that the young man is fascinated not by her but by her pretty little maid.

A SON OF THE CELESTIAL: A CHARACTER (*Hesperian,* January 14, 1893; Shively; *ESWC; CSF*) is primarily concerned with Yung Le Ho, a Chinese of learned background, who occupies himself in San Francisco by carving ivory objects d'art and other Oriental beauties. His only friend is an American, Ponter, a former professor of Sanskrit, whom unwise habits have brought down in the world; both men have been seduced by the treacherous illusions of the opium pipe. Though Yung Le Ho dies at the end, the piece is more character sketch than narrative as the subtitle warns. There are a number of observations, both favorable and unfavorable, on Chinese character.

THE STRATEGY OF THE WERE-WOLF DOG (*Home Monthly,* December 1896; *CSF*) is a children's Christmas story about Santa Claus, his helper the White Bear, and the Were-Wolf Dog, who hates Santa and the innocent little World-Children, and everything that is good, and who lures Santa's reindeer out the night before they are to start on their annual journey and gets them drowned in the Polar Sea. Dunder survives, and White Bear saves the day by recruiting fresh reindeer at the Christmas festival gathering of the Animals of the North. This story was written for and told to the author's young siblings. The drowning of the reindeer seems a sadistic touch in a story for young children.

A TALE OF THE WHITE PYRAMID (*Hesperian,* December 22, 1892; Shively; *ESWC; CSF*), as Woodress points out, marks Miss Cather's earliest use of the first-person narrator. It is the work of a priest of Phtahah in the great temple at Memphis, describing the entombment of "Senefrau the first, Lord of the Light and Ruler of the Upper and Lower Kingdoms," and it describes a marvelous feat of strength and courage performed by a gifted youth, a favorite of the new pharaoh, who is disliked by the people because he belongs to the alien Shepherd race of the north. The ceremonial and the feat are both described in a stately, formal manner well suited to the material. For an ingenious Freudian analysis of an inconsequential tale probably intended only as a literary exercise, see Sharon O'Brien in *WC: The Emerging Voice,* pp. 198–203.

TOMMY THE UNSENTIMENTAL (*Home Monthly,* August 1896; *ESWC; CSF*) is rated by Woodress as marking the first sympathetic treatment of Nebraska in Willa Cather's fiction. It centers on Theodosia Shirley, the feckless banker's daughter in the town of Southdown. She not only runs her father's business for him but even takes on Jay Ellington Harper, the son of a friend of her father's, who is equally inefficient. Tommy fully realizes both Jay's and her father's shortcomings but loves them both, believing that one likes people or not, without much regard to whether they deserve it. But when Jay and a dainty, languid Eastern girl whom Tommy has brought back home with her after a year at school, fall in love, Tommy generously aids and abets their romance, though not without an underlying touch of malice. The interest of the story centers mainly in Tommy herself, who seems much the same kind of girl as her creator was in her teens, but it culminates in an exciting race against time by bicycle undertaken in Jay's behalf (Jessica goes along but falls by the wayside), which is a startling anticipation of the chase films that were just around the corner in the movies.

THE TREASURE OF FAR ISLAND (*New England Magazine,* October 1902; *CSF*), like the vastly superior "Enchanted Bluff," is obviously based on the author's own memories of her early delight in an island on the Republican River. The narrative is a sentimental and rather labored account of a successful playwright's return to the scenes of his youth and to the only girl he should have known he wanted long ago. The playwright, Daniel Burnham, had been Spreckle Burnham in "The Way of the World" (1898).

UNCLE VALENTINE (*Woman's Home Companion,* February–March 1925; *UV*) is, like "Double Birthday," "The Professor's Commencement," "Paul's Case, and "The Namesake," a Pittsburgh story. Its tone is not unlike that of "Double Birthday," and it is equally loosely woven. It is long on character and short on plot, and the reader must be alert if he wishes to keep the various uncles clear in his mind. Valentine Ramsay, an accomplished, though as yet largely unrecognized composer of songs, is the best of the lot and has obviously been suggested by Willa Cather's friendship with Ethelbert Nevin, whose family owned the *Pittsburgh Leader,* on which she was employed, though the characters of the two, the circumstances of their lives, and, except that they both die young, their fates are very different. Except for a brief introduction, "Uncle Valentine" is a firstperson narrative, told in retrospect by a friend of the composer. There is a rather full study of this story in Marilyn Arnold's *WC'S Short Fiction,* pp. 119–26.

THE WAY OF THE WORLD (*Home Monthly,* April 1898; *CSF*) presents Willa Cather as Penrod. Spreckle Burnham and his friends create a town out of packing boxes in Spreckle's backyard, somewhere in the country "beyond the Missouri," each boy presiding over an establishment derived from his father's. Mary Ellen Jenkins bribes her way in with real "goodies" and soon replaces Spreckle himself as the dominating figure. But when a "New Boy" from Chicago arrives in town with real money instead of pins, and is shown marked favor by her, the town breaks up. "The Way of the World" will never rob *Tom Sawyer* of its primacy in this area, but the children seem real; both the dialogue and the action are convincing; and the use of a narrator introduces both commentary and irony. Willa Cather as a child had herself had a playtown similar to the one in the story.

WEE WINKIE'S WANDERINGS (*National Stockman and Farmer,* December 24, 1896; reprinted in *Vogue,* June 1972) was identified as Willa Cather's work by Bernice Slote, who pointed out the resemblances between its background and the locale described in *Sapphira and the Slave Girl;* see the discussion in John J. Murphy, *Five Essays on WC,* pp. 5–8. It is a pleasant story about a little girl who decided to run away from home. Her mother helps her pack and sees her off. At night she returns, worn out. Her mother washes and feeds her and puts her to bed, and nothing more is said about her adventure.

THE WESTBOUND TRAIN: A THIRTY-MINUTE SKETCH FOR TWO PEOPLE (*Lincoln Courier,* September 10, 1899; *CSF*) is set in the waiting room of the Union Pacific depot at Cheyenne. There are four people in it, not two, but most of it consists of a soliloquy by one character. The subject is marital jealousy and misunderstanding. It is such an unbelievably amateurish piece of work that it is hard to believe Willa Cather could have been responsible for it at any period. Clearly the drama was not her form. For other examples of her experiments with dialogue, see Shively, pp. 93–108.

THE WILLING MUSE (*Century,* August 1907; *CSF*), a first person narrative, set mainly in New York City, but with Olympia, Ohio, as a background, strongly suggests the influence of Henry James's most-subtle and least-popular novel, *The Sacred Fount.* Kenneth Gray, a gifted but wholly impractical writer, quite incapable of making terms with the conditions of literary production, marries Bertha Torrence, a superbly efficient writing machine, who turns out two books of quite decent quality every year and enjoys a tremendous vogue. Inevitably absorbed into her orbit, he finds himself reading her proofs, handling her tremendous correspondence, etc. When the pressure gets past the bearing point, he simply disappears. The narrator is a friend of Gray's, who is keeping his secret.

Notes

Part 1

Chapter 1: A Writer's Life

1. She was christened "Willella," after an aunt who had died, not, as she liked to believe or to pretend, after her Civil War soldier-uncle, William Sibert Boak, whom she commemorated in the poem and story both called "The Namesake." She herself changed "Willella" to "Willa" in the family Bible and at home was often called "Willie." In youth she liked to call herself "William Love Cather" after a favorite Dr. Love and even "William Cather, M.D." "Sibert" or "Seibert" was a family name on the mother's side, and Willa Cather's early books were published as by "Willa Sibert Cather." This was discontinued about 1920, but "Willa Sibert Cather" remained her legal name to the end, and "W. S. C." was engraved on her stationery.

2. For reasons best known to himself, S. S. McClure advised Willa Cather to "knock a year or two" off her age. From 1909 to 1919 her birthdate appeared in *Who's Who in America* as 1875 and thereafter as 1876, which still stands on Miss Cather's tombstone. See Leon Edel's amusing and authoritative account of how the correct date was discovered in Bernice Slote and Virginia Faulkner, eds., *The Art of WC*, UNP, 1974, pp. 191–98.

3. Willa Cather's most considered nonfictional expression of her attitude toward Nebraska is in her article, "Nebraska: The End of the First Cycle," *Nation*, 117 (1923): 237–38, but this is far more systematically formulated than anything she could have written while still living in the state.

4. *On Native Grounds,* Reynal and Hitchcock, 1941, p. 230.

5. In 1956 her travel letters to the *Nebraska State Journal,* descriptive of this expedition, were published in *WC in Europe;* in 1970 a better text appeared in *The World and the Parish,* vol. 2, pp. 889ff.

6. S. S. McClure, *My Autobiography,* Frederick A. Stokes, 1914.

7. See L. Brant Bohlke, "WC and *The Life of Mary Baker G. Eddy,*" *AL,* 54 (1988): 288–94.

8. See "148 Charles Street," in *Not under Forty.*

9. "WC and the Indian Heritage," *Twentieth Century Literature,* 22 (1976): 433–43.

10. See "My First Novels (There Were Two)" in the *Colophon,* part 6 (1931), reprinted in *WC on Writing.* There seems to have been one earlier novel, submitted to the McClure outfit and rejected, but it has vanished without leaving a trace, and nothing further is known about it.

11. The references to this edition in a number of books about Willa Cather are inaccurate and misleading. The leading publishers of collected editions of standard authors, sold by subscription, during the early twentieth century were Houghton Mifflin Company and Charles Scribner's Sons. The idea for such an edition of Willa Cather originated with Scribners, but since Houghton Mifflin were not willing to release the four novels they controlled, it fell to them to publish the set. (Knopf did not publish subscription books.) Several writers have spoken of this matter as if two editions were planned — a limited, signed Autograph Edition and an unlimited Library Edition. The fact is however that only the Autograph Edition was announced in 1937, limited to 970 signed and numbered copies, of which 950 were for sale. By 1937 however subscription publishing was no longer greatly in vogue, and the edition did not sell out. The publishers therefore took out the signature page, bound the remaining copies in boards, and sold them at a lower price, under the name "Library Edition."

12. In obedience to her friends' wishes, but to the regret of all lovers of Miss Cather's writings, Edith Lewis destroyed the manuscript of "Hard Punishments," and little is known about it except what Miss Lewis herself recorded in *WC Living;* George Kates's chapter in the Viking paperback, *Five Stories by WC,* adds nothing of importance. Four pages of the manuscript are now in the University of Virginia library. See Woodress, *Willa Cather: A Literary Life,* p. 493.

Chapter 2: Storing the Well

1. See L. P. Jacks, "The Classics and WC," *PS,* 35 (1961), 289–96, and Donald Sutherland, "WC: The Classic Voice," in Slote and Faulkner, eds., *The Art of WC.*

2. See Michel Gervaud, "WC and France," in *The Art of WC.*

3. "A Chance Encounter," in *Not under Forty.*

4. "He liked Scott's women. Constance de Beverley and the minstrel girl in 'The Fair Maid of Perth' ... were his heroines." Who Constance de

Beverley may be I have no idea, for I cannot find her among Scott's characters. Willa Cather thought Robert Burns a "glorious voice" who gave new life to English verse in a day when it had become "stiff and stilted."

5. Daiches, *WC,* p. 187.

6. Reprinted in Bernice Slote, ed., *The Kingdom of Art,* pp. 421–25.

7. Her review of *Plays Pleasant and Unpleasant,* in William M. Curtin, ed., *The World and the Parish,* pp. 594–97, is probably as good a statement of this view of Shaw as has anywhere been made.

8. Is her dismissal of *Uncle Tom's Cabin* as "exaggerated, overdrawn, abounding in facts but lacking in truth" to be ascribed to her birth in Virginia? Perhaps not, for it was very much in tune with the judgment of the period in which she wrote. Only of late years have critics swung round to a fairer evaluation, freed of sectional and political prejudices, of that far from faultless but nevertheless powerful book.

9. See book 1, chapter 17, and; book 4, chapter 2.

10. Bernice Slote has an admirable summary of what Willa Cather had to say about Whitman in the introduction to her UNP edition of *April Twilights;* for Willa Cather's judgment of a number of later American poets see "Poets of the Younger Generation," reprinted in *The World and the Parish,* pp. 879–88. Her tenderness toward Eugene Field is an interesting expression of her softer side.

11. See F. B. Adams, in the *Colophon,* New Graphic Series, vol. 1, no. 3 (1939): 89–100.

12. *The World and the Parish,* pp. 955–58.

13. Ten pages of *The World and the Parish,* pp. 443–52, are devoted to what Miss Cather thought of this production.

14. See, for example, "Bernhardt and Maude Adams," in *The World and the Parish,* pp. 813–21, written when both actresses were appearing in *L'Aiglon.* (Maude Adams was one of Miss Cather's pet "hates"; she was blind to the charm that so endeared her to most of the theatergoers of her generation.) In passing mention may be made of her careful consideration of another Rostand play, *Cyrano de Bergerac* (*The World and the Parish,* pp. 497–502), an article notable for its combination of rapturous appreciation with clear-sighted ability to distinguish between various kinds of theatrical values and qualities.

15. David Stouck, *WC's Imagination,* p. 110n., is important in this connection; see also Willa Cather's preface to Gertrude Hall's *The Wagnerian Romances* (Knopf, 1925), reprinted in *WC on Writing.*

16. See *The World and the Parish*, pp. 178–82, and *The Kingdom of Art*, pp. 214–15.

17. As to the "caprices," there is a spirited description of her behavior at a recital in *The World and the Parish*, pp. 409–11, and I am sure it is accurate, for she was still at it when I heard her in the twilight of her career in the early 1920s.

Chapter 3: How to Write Fiction

1. Ferris Greenslet, *Under the Bridge*, HM, 1943.

2. Despite all her disgust at Oscar Wilde's sins as a man, Willa Cather did, in the last analysis, do justice to him as an artist and to his art as the product of a divine gift. See Stouck, *WC's Imagination*, p. 172, and cf. Slote, *The Kingdom of Art*, pp. 393–98.

3. Bernice Slote saw her as "torn between the Dionysian and the Appollonian forms of rapture and repose, release and containment."

4. I may add that she sometimes includes details whose significance, if any, is not always made clear; one suspects that these are remembered from people she has seen. Thus in *The Professor's House* Professor Crane's "lips had no modeling; they were as thick at the corners as in the middle, and he spoke through them rather than with them." Sometimes the name of a character suggests his personality, but the significance of this has been forced by some critics. On the general subject, see Mildred R. Bennett, "How WC Chose Her Names," *Names*, 10 (1962): 29–37.

5. "WSC," *Bookman*, 52 (1921): 212–16.

6. See Sergeant, *WC: A Memoir*, pp. 203–4.

7. Some recent critics have found considerable symbolism in Willa Cather. Obviously this is a field in which it is easy to force the note, reading "in" rather than reading, as when the dressmaker's models in *The Professor's House* become "deceptive comfort and heartless femininity" or the singing of the "Casta diva" in *My Mortal Enemy* is made to suggest resemblances between Norma and Myra Henshawe. Elsewhere, however, new and valuable insights are suggested, and I have little doubt that more work of value will be done in this field. Incidentally I may note that Miss Cather often quotes inaccurately, especially when referring to verses, and that her spelling is not infrequently unreliable. Christina Rossetti becomes "Christine," and Woodress notes that in different printings of "A Wagner Matinee" we find "Beireth," "Beyruth," and "Beyreuth" (all incorrect) for what Mark Twain dubbed "the shrine of St. Wagner."

Chapter 4: The First Books

1. *April Twilights* here shares vol. 3 with *Alexander's Bridge,* both of course out of chronological order. *O Pioneers!* as vol. 1 had the honor of opening the series, probably because it was the only one of the early books that Miss Cather continued really to like. The original "Dedicatory" of *April Twilights,* to "R. C. C." and "C. D. C." that is to Roscoe and Douglass Cather, was replaced in 1923 by "To My Father for a Valentine," but this too was dropped from the Autograph Edition. The definitive edition of *April Twilights* is now that edited by Bernice Slote for UNP in 1962 and revised in 1968, whose introduction is the fullest historical and critical study of Miss Cather's poems. See also F. B. Adams in *Colophon,* New Graphic Series, vol. 1, no. 3 (1939): 79–100.

2. The full text of the passage is reprinted in Slote, *The Kingdom of Art,* appendix 3; also in Susan J. Rosowski, *Voyage Perilous,* pp. 18–23; cf. her note p. 251. See also Marilyn Arnold, *WC's Short Fiction,* pp. 43–46.

3. See E. K. Brown, *WC: A Critical Biography,* pp. 113–18; Stouck, *WC's Imagination,* pp. 178–81; James Woodress, in the introduction to his edition of *The Troll Garden,* UNP, 1983.

4. Willa Cather afterwards called the reception of *The Troll Garden* "a bitter disappointment," and if one reads the hysterical outburst it inspired in *The Bookman,* one can see why — "a collection of freak stories that are either lurid, hysterical, or unwholesome, and that remind one of nothing so much as the coloured supplement to the Sunday papers." Most of the characters are "mere dummies, with fancy names on which to hang epigrams." All in all, the stories came from "the ash-heap of the human mind."

5. By all means the best appreciation of " 'A Death in the Desert' " that I have encountered is that of David Daiches, in his *WC,* pp. 140–42. See especially his comparisons between it and *The Master of Ballantrae* and *The Doctor's Dilemma.*

6. *The Landscape and the Looking Glass,* pp. 32–33. In "The Homosexual Motif in 'Paul's Case,' " *SSF,* 12 (1975): 127–31, Larry Rubin argues that Paul was homosexual. The argument is very ably handled, but since I find no evidence in the tale itself that sex, either normal or abnormal, enters into the problem of Paul's alienation, it does not seem to me to contribute much to the understanding of the story. See an excellent article by David R. Carpenter, "Why WC Revised 'Paul's Case': The Work in Art and Those Sunday Afternoons," *AL,* 59 (1987): 590–608.

7. The *Smart Set* version may be read in Bernice Slote, ed., *Uncle Valentine and Other Stories: WC's Uncollected Short Fiction, 1915–1929.* There is a long analysis of "Coming, Aphrodite!," not all of which I accept, in Marilyn Arnold's *WC's Short Fiction.*

8. See Cather, "My First Novels (There Were Two)," the *Colophon,* part 6, 1931, reprinted in *WC on Writing.*

9. John P. Hinz, "The Real Alexander's Bridge," *AL,* 21 (1950), 473–76.

10. L. Brent Bohlke, ed., *WC in Person,* p. 6.

11. There is a succinct account of the Thaw-White case, one of the great scandals of early twentieth-century America in the present writer's *American Profile, 1900–1909,* University of Massachusetts Press, 1982, pp. 29–36. Gerald Langford's *The Murder of Stanford White,* Bobbs-Merrill, 1962, gives a detailed account of Thaw's two trials, and Michael Macdonald Mooney's *Evelyn Nesbit and Stanford White: Love and Death in the Gilded Age,* Morrow, 1976, is a thoughtful, sensitive study.

12. Rosowski, *Voyage Perilous,* p. 263, n. 11.

13. See the latter's long and valuable introduction to the paperback edition of *Alexander's Bridge* published by UNP in 1977 in the "Bison Book" series. Note especially her consideration of symbolism in this novel and her mythological references.

14. There is a much stronger statement of what I have argued here in Raymond Thornberg's "WC: From *Alexander's Bridge* to *My Ántonia,*" *Twentieth Century Literature,* 7 (1962), 147–58: "A matter developed within the consciousness of the protagonist is settled by forces operating outside of it. . . . Alexander is reduced to insignificance and powerlessness, and meets doom as the victim of external forces, rather than being given punishment or reward upon a moral testing." There may be some overstatement of a strong case in this article. If he had not been with Hilda, his assistant's first telegram would probably not have missed Bartley, and while this would not have prevented the collapse of the bridge, it might have saved his life and the lives of those who perished with him. But this fact alone will hardly bear the weight that the adherents of the man-bridge parallelism in this novel seek to impose upon it.

Part 2

Chapter 5: Novels: Studies in Fulfillment

1. One of the first was Curtis Bradford, *AL,* 26 (1955): 537–51. For a very emphatic recent statement, see Sharon O'Brien, *WC: The Emerging Voice,* pp. 297ff.

2. For the revision *O Pioneers!* underwent for the Autograph Edition, see F. B. Adams, *Colophon,* New Graphic Series, vol. 1, no. 4 (1940): 103–8.

3. See Rosowski, *Voyage Perilous,* pp. 55ff., on this and other classical matters. Her attempt to make a case for "The Eve of St. Agnes" seems to me less convincing.

4. The author cut out a long section dealing with Thea's student days in Germany before sending the manuscript to the publisher, but even so, it ran to about two hundred thousand words. It was cut for the 1932 edition, but UNP has since reprinted the first edition in paperback. The *Lark* runs 581 pages in the Autograph Edition as against 514 for *One of Ours,* 372 for *My Ántonia,* and 348 for *Death Comes for the Archbishop.* For details of the revision, consult Robin Heyeck and James Woodress, "WC's Cuts and Revisions in *The Song of the Lark,*" *Modern Fiction Studies,* 25 (1979): 651–58.

5. Bernice Slote's comments in *The Kingdom of Art,* pp. 86–89, on this point and other aspects of Thea's early experiences merit careful reading. See also p. 95 on moon imagery in the *Lark.*

6. *McClure's Magazine,* vol. 42: 33–38.

7. When Miss Farrar mentioned her ambition to sing Wagner to her great teacher, Lilli Lehmann, that imperial lady exclaimed, "Ach Gott, Kind, du hast ja doch keine Brust!"

8. Both Miss Garden and Miss Farrar left autobiographies. *Mary Garden's Story,* written with Louis Biancolli, was published by Simon and Schuster in 1951. Miss Farrar wrote two books: *Geraldine Farrar, The Story of an American Singer,* by herself, HM, 1916, a brief account, came early in her career, while *Such Sweet Compulsion, The Autobiography of Geraldine Farrar,* Greystone Press, 1938, is much longer and more thoughtful. She also sanctioned the present writer's *Geraldine Farrar: An Authorized Record of Her Career,* which was published in 1929 by the University of Washington Book Store in a limited edition, which she autographed.

9. "WC" in *The Borzoi, 1925,* Knopf, 1925.

10. *My Ántonia* was illustrated with line drawings by W. T. Benda. In "The Benda Illustrations to *My Ántonia:* Cather's 'Silent' Supplement to Jim Burden's Narrative," *PMLA,* 100 (1985), 51–67, Jean Schwind shows how the author "closely" and "autocratically" supervised the making and the placing of these pictures and how in 1937 she succeeded in aborting Houghton Mifflin's plan to publish a deluxe edition of the novel, illustrated with paintings by Grant Wood. Ms. Schwind's article is valuable for the light it sheds on Miss Cather's relations with her publishers both before and after she became famous, and it also gives a fine account of the changes made in the introduction between the 1918 and the 1926 editions. But I cannot help wondering why if the Benda illustrations were as important to

her as Ms. Schwind thinks, she consented to omitting all but one of them from the Autograph Edition.

11. "The Drama of Memory in *My Ántonia*," *PMLA*, 84 (1969), 309–11.

12. When Grandmother Burden hears of the suicide, she exclaims, "I don't see how he could do it," whereupon her informant, thinking she means she does not understand how the fatal act was performed, thoughtfully explains the modus operandi to her. What she means however is that she cannot understand how a man "always considerate and unwishful to give trouble" and a Catholic could so "forget himself and bring this on us!" and I have always shared her perplexity. Shimerda had married his wife having fathered a child upon a girl inferior to himself in both character and standing, even though he could have paid her off, and I have never been quite convinced that he could have brought himself to leave his family without resources in this new, cruel, bleak land. But Ántonia's (i.e., Annie Sadilek's) real-life father did commit suicide before the Cathers moved to Nebraska.

13. Mildred R. Bennett's *The World of WC* is the authoritative pioneering book on the novelist's early years. See also Bernice Slote, *WC: A Pictorial Memoir*. Annie Sadilek Pavelka died in 1955 in her mideighties.

14. *The World of WC*, pp. 82–85.

15. Curtis Dahl's "An American Georgic: WC's *My Ántonia, Comparative Literature*, 7 (1955), 43–51, is the fullest study. Though Dahl believed that Miss Cather read into Virgil's lines "a romantic, almost sentimental romanticism and an emotional concern with the passing emotions of youth and primitive ages that the lines themselves... do not explicitly state and probably do not imply," he still thought that though she might at times have "seen Virgil too much in her own image, she [had] well represented in her novel his depth, spirit, and artistry." Susie Thomas's suggestion is in her *WC*, pp. 89ff. She is particularly good on Shimerda's association with the Virginian concepts of pietàs and *lacrimae rerum*.

16. For the wolf story, see Paul Schach, "Russian Wolves in Folktales and Literature of the Plains: A Question of Origins," *Great Plains Quarterly*, vol. 3, no. 2 (1983), 67–78.

17. See Blanche H. Gelfant, "The Forgotten Reaping Hook: Sex in *My Ántonia*," *AL*, 43 (1971), 60–82. Like-minded in spirit, though very different in subject matter, is Deborah H. Lambert's "The Defeat of a Hero: Autonomy and Sexuality in *My Ántonia*," *AL*, 58 (1982), 676–90. These articles certainly show that sex is much more of a factor in *My Ántonia* than had previously been realized, but the inferences drawn from this

will be completely convincing only to readers as much committed as their authors to the Gospel according to Sigmund.

18. Cf. Stouck, *WC's Imagination*, pp. 2–3.

19. Harold Bloom, ed., *My Ántonia*, Chelsea House, 1987, reprints a good selection from the critical studies of the novel published before the date indicated. James Woodress, "WC Seen Clear," *Papers on Language and Literature*, 7 (1971), 96–109, is a helpful review of the Nebraska books.

Chapter 6: Novels: Studies in Frustration

1. Fanny Butcher, *Many Lives — One Love*, Harper & Row, 1972, ch. 17. I remember hearing Miss Butcher say that her review of *One of Ours* was the most difficult for her of any she had ever written.

2. Which, though it has been parroted by others, was nonsense. Both the master and his apes describe the Griffith film so inaccurately as to make it clear that either they never saw it or else had almost entirely forgotten it.

3. David Hochstein, a violinist and a relative of Emma Goldman, whom Willa Cather had met, became David Gerhardt in the novel. See Bohlke, *WC in Person*, pp. 43–57, and Sergeant, *WC: A Memoir*, pp. 73–79. He was killed in the Argonne, likewise in 1918. He would seem to have come considerably closer to Miss Cather's interests than her cousin did, and it is a wonder he did not crowd Claude in the novel more than he does. Book 4, "The Voyage of the Anchises," was based on the diary of Dr. Frederick Sweeney, who had served on a troopship.

4. Stouck, *WC's Imagination*, p. 84.

5. Literary sources are not very important in *One of Ours*. In *The Voyage Perilous* Susan J. Rosowski calls her chapter on this novel "An American Arthurian Legend," but the parallels she points out between the novel and *The Idylls of the King* seem forced, and one wonders whether she would have thought of them if both writers had not used the name "Enid." As for the alleged resemblances to *Parsifal*, it is true that Miss Cather thought of calling book 5, "The Blameless Fool by Pity Enlightened," but the fact that she changed her mind about this would seem to indicate that she thought it less important than Ms. Rosowski seems to believe.

6. *Nation*, 117 (1923), 237–38.

7. "The 'Beautiful War,' in *One of Ours*," *Modern Fiction Studies*, 30 (1984), 53–72.

8. A number of critics have compared *A Lost Lady* to *Madame Bovary*, but though Miss Cather, who was devoted to Flaubert, must surely have considered this a compliment, there is no close resemblance. Recently Susie Thomas has argued that a better case could be made for *L'Education Sentimentale*. In his "Euripides' *Hippolytus* and Cather's *A Lost Lady*," *AL*, 53 (1981), 72–86, John J. Murphy offers a careful, detailed, and convincing comparison of the two works.

9. For more about Mrs. Garber, see Bennett, *The World of WC*, pp. 67–76.

10. See *WC on Writing*, pp. 30–32.

11. *WC's Gift of Sympathy*, pp. 159–61. For other views see Joseph X. Brennan, "WC and Music," *University Review*, 31 (1965), 175–83, 757–64, and Richard Giannone, *Music in WC's Fiction*, pp. 152–60. On pp. 162–68, Giannone shows how Willa Cather used Thomas's opera, *Mignon*, and *Ein Deutsches Requiem*, by Johannes Brahms, to point up and reinforce the novel's theme.

12. See Susan J. Rosowski and Bernice Slote, "WC's 1916 Mesa Verde Essay: The Genesis of *The Professor's House*," *PS*, vol. 58, no. 4 (1984), 81–92.

13. Such passages in Willa Cather's writings as the Washington scenes in *The Professor's House* and such stories as "Behind the Singer Tower" and "The Clemency of the Court" (see appendix) show clearly that her failure to consider social problems in her fiction was due neither to ignorance nor indifference but rather to her literary theory (see chapter 3).

14. Book 3, chapter 4.

15. See Elliot G. Fay, "Borrowings from Anatole France by WC and Robert Nathan," *Modern Language Notes*, 56 (1941), 377, and Wolfgang Bernard Fleischmann, "WC's *The Professor's House* and Anatole France's Le Mannequin d'Osier," *Romance Notes*, 1 (1960), 92–93. Susie Thomas reads *The Professor's House* as a reply to France's story, which she calls "cowardly, spiteful and stupid."

16. Olive Hart's "*The Professor's House*: A Shapely Story," *Modern Language Review*, 67 (1972), 271–81, from which I have quoted here, is an effective detailed attempt to defend the author's structure and the unity of the novel.

17. Because they are both Jews, some writers have been carried away by the idea that Marsellus is a malicious, satirical portrait of Isabelle McClung's husband, the violinist Jan Hambourg, to whom the novel was dedicated, but I find no evidence to support this idea.

18. "Strategies of Self-Deception in WC's *The Professor's House*," *SN,* 16 (1984), 72–85.

19. For "The Jolly Corner" see Edward Wagenknecht, *The Tales of Henry James* (Continuum, 1984), especially pp. 155–60.

20. For other interpretations see E. K. Brown, *Rhythm in the Novel,* University of Toronto Press, 1931, pp. 71–79; also Leon Edel, "WC's *The Professor's House*: An Inquiry into the Use of Psychology in Literary Criticism," *Literature and Psychology,* 4 (1954), 66–79, and WC *and the Paradox of Success,* 1960. See David Stouck's criticism of these items in *WC's Imagination,* pp. 98–100.

21. If there is a loose end in the novel, it must be sought in the scene in which Professor Crane's wife comes to St. Peter to ask him to support her husband's claim to a share in the profits of Tom's invention. Nothing comes of this, nor do we ever hear of it again.

22. Actually only Henshawe's mother was German; his father was an "Ulster Protestant."

23. Myra dies alone on a headland overlooking the sea, apparently soon after dawn. "Light and silence; they heal all one's wounds." Dawn, she feels, "is always such a forgiving time. When that first cold, bright streak comes over the water, it's as if all our sins were pardoned; as if the sky leaned over the earth and kissed it and gave it absolution." Some readers may feel that there is more nature than God here, but perhaps Christianity has never quite settled where nature ends and grace begins. Myra at least seems to be thinking of nature, in the aspect in which it functions here, as sacramental, and perhaps Willa Cather agreed with her.

24. "Cather's *My Mortal Enemy,*" *PS,* 48 (1974), 124–33.

Chapter 7: Novels: The Lovely Past

1. Reprinted in *WC on Writing,* pp. 3–13. On the general subject of WC's treatment of the past, see two articles by Robert L. Gale: "WC and the Past," *Studi Americana,* 4 (1958), 209–22, and "WC and the Usable Past," *Nebraska History,* 42 (1961), 181–90.

2. Bohlke, *WC in Person,* p. 109.

3. M. A. Stouck, "Chaucer's Pilgrims and Cather's Priests," *Colby Library Quarterly,* 9 (1972), 531–37.

4. Robert L. Gale, "Cather's *Death Comes for the Archbishop,*" *Explicator,* 21 (May 1963): item 76. D. H. Stewart in *Queen's Quarterly,* 73 (1966), 244–59, compares the novel to *The Divine Comedy.*

5. John H. Randall III, *The Landscape and the Looking Glass*, p. 407 n. 117. In the novel there are references to St. Augustine, Pascal, and Madame de Sevigné as among Latour's favorite authors. For a full study of sources see Edward A. and Lillian D. Bloom, *WC's Gift of Sympathy*, ch. 6.

6. Pierre Puvis de Chavannes (1824–98), French painter, noted for his murals in muted colors. Best known to Americans are the frescoes over the main staircase in the Boston Public Library.

7. A collection of saints' lives in Latin, put together by Jacobus de Voragine between 1243 and 1273, translated into English by William Caxton in 1482.

8. James Woodress, "The Genesis of the Prologue of *Death Comes for the Archbishop*," *AL*, 50 (1978), 473–78.

9. The cathedral in Sante Fé, which Miss Cather knew, might also be cited as a source for her novel. Cf. Mary Austin, *Earth Horizon: Autobiography*, HM, 1932, p. 350: "When it [the *Archbishop*] was finished, I was very much distressed to find that she had given her allegiance to the French blood of the Archbishop; she had sympathized with his desire to build a French cathedral in a Spanish town. It was a calamity to the local culture. We have never got over it." Miss Cather's readers have sometimes wondered how a writer who had always depended so much upon her memories of her own experiences and who believed that only that which had been held in the mind for years could produce literature should at last have drawn such a good book from a seemingly alien time, place, and culture. But to Willa Cather the Southwest not only had a strong affinity to the interest in pioneers that stemmed from her memories of Nebraska but had itself been an important part of her own experience since her first visit there. She did not, like so many writers of historical fiction, look up the Southwest for the purpose of writing about it; indeed, she herself said that writing the book was like a return to childhood and early memories. She was also, of course, a devoted Francophile, which paid off for her both in this book and in *Shadows on the Rock*. Hans Holbein (1497?–1543) was a German portrait painter and wood engraver, who was also a court painter to King Henry VIII. The *Dance of Death* series was published in 1538.

10. As *December Night* this episode was published separately by Knopf in 1933 as a Christmas gift book, printed by Elmer Adler and designed and illustrated by Harold von Schmidt.

11. Slote and Faulkner, eds., *The Art of WC*, p. 213. See the author's own discussion of *Shadows on the Rock* in *WC on Writing*, pp. 14–17.

12. For an interesting study of Willa Cather's rock symbolism, see Philip L. Gerber, "WC and the Big Red Rock," *College English,* 19 (1958), 152–57.

13. There is a careful, detailed study of the structure of this novel in John J. Murphy's "The Art of *Shadows on the Rock,*" *PS,* 50 (1976), 37–51. "The more one reads it, the more one encounters events, inner narratives, and images linked to others; a fabric emerges, a tapestry depicting in borders and scenes a medieval world of severe order."

14. See Ann Romines, "After the Christmas Trees: WC and Domestic Ritual," *AL,* 60 (1988), 61–81, who finds in the *Rock* a "sustained attempt to portray the achieved ritual of a place...and an attempt to examine the stages and levels of a spirited female child's immersion in that life."

Chapter 8: Last Novels and Tales

1. See Michael Leddy, "Observation and Narration in WC's *Obscure Destinies,*" *Studies in American Fiction,* 16 (1988), 141–53.

2. *English Journal,* 22 (1933), 703–10; reprinted in James Schroeter, *WC and Her Critics.*

3. *The Kingdom of Art,* p. 219.

4. A conspicuous exception is Merrill Skaggs, whose treatment of *Lucy Gayheart* in her otherwise generally satisfactory book, *After the World Broke in Two,* is one of the curiosities of Cather criticism. Ms. Skaggs takes a very dim view of both Lucy and Sebastian. She apparently cannot forgive Lucy for not being Thea Kronborg; for her there seems to be no room in art for anything but the very great talent. Her contempt for Sebastian is so great that it even leads her to downgrade Schubert's great song cycle, *Winterreise,* which Sebastian sings. Harry Gordon is the only character in the novel she really admires ("It is Harry Gordon's predicament that justifies the effort of writing — or reading — the book"), but she even has a good word for the nauseous James Mockford, whom she sees as victim rather than victimizer.

5. "WC's *Lucy Gayheart:* A Long Perspective," *PS,* 55 (1981), 199–209. This article is also interesting on the use of symbolism in *Lucy Gayheart.*

6. My own feeling is that Marilyn Callander makes a considerably better job of establishing her thesis in *Willa Cather and the Fairy Tale.* "My contention is that Cather was often aware of her use of fairy tales and used them for specific reasons, and that this usage developed into a steadily elaborating technique." For Ms. Callander the *Lark* is Willa Cather's "Cinderella story" (it is interesting that this had been previously suggested by

H. L. Mencken); "The Sleeping Beauty" and "Snow White" are each an "integral part of the structure of 'My Mortal Enemy' "; the *Archbishop* is "remarkably close to the age-old motif called 'Two Brothers' "; and *Shadows on the Rock* "shows how Cather gathered all her knowledge of fairy tales together and used it to create a novel which is in itself a fairy tale." I am far from accepting all Ms. Callander's specific interpretations, but at the very least she must be credited with having given us our clearest demonstration of Willa Cather's intimate knowledge of the classic fairy tales and made it seem likely that she used them consciously.

7. There are only two touches, both in the treatment of backgrounds, that seem to me awkwardly handled. When Mr. Gayheart plans to take his daughters to *The Bohemian Girl*, we read: "He liked to reach the opera house early and watch the people come in. (The theatre in every little Western town was then called an opera house.)" And at Mr. Gayheart's funeral: "The coffin was taken from the express car to the Lutheran church in an automobile hearse (these were modern times, 1927), and after a short service it was brought to the graveyard."

8. *The World and the Parish*, vol. 2, pp. 176–78.

9. According to Alfred Knopf, Miss Cather pronounced the second syllable as if it were "fear."

10. See Richard Giannone, "WC and the Unfinished Drama of Deliverance," *PS*, 52 (1978), 25–46.

11. Critics in general have tended to identify Gabrielle's disparagement of everything modern with that of Willa Cather herself, a conspicuous dissenter being Marilyn Arnold, who, in *WC's Short Fiction*, sees the author as undercutting the reader's sympathy with the old beauty and rejecting her extreme views. See also Loretta Wasserman, "WC's 'The Old Beauty' Reconsidered," *SSF*, 16 (1988): 217–27.

12. See Sargent Bush, Jr., " 'The Best Years': WC's Last Story and Its Relation to Her Canon," *SSF*, 5 (1968): 267–74.

Part 3

Chapter 9: Character and Personality

1. "WC's Advice to a Young Artist," *PS*, 46 (1972): 111–24.

2. See *The World and the Parish*, vol. 2, pp. 860–61.

3. See *The Kingdom of Art*, p. 269n. and the reference there. In Bernice Slote's *WC: A Pictorial Memoir*, p. 12, part of the manuscript of this essay is reproduced in facsimile.

4. See Alice Hall Petry, "Caesar and the Artist in WC's 'Coming, Aphrodite!' " *SSF,* 23 (1986), 307–14, who, in a perhaps too psychological essay, finds the dog "the medium through which Cather articulates her personal beliefs in regard to creative endeavor and the place of the artist in society." She also finds a possible influence from the dog in "A New England Nun," by Mary E. Wilkins Freeman.

5. David Daiches, *WC,* p. 164, is excellent on Willa Cather's subtle use of this incident for characterization.

6. Loretta Wasserman, "The Music of Time: Henri Bergson and WC," *AL,* 57 (1985), 226–37.

7. In Slote and Faulkner, eds., *The Art of WC,* pp. 201–2.

8. "WC's Uncollected Short Stories," *AL,* 26 (1955): 537–51.

9. *WC's Collected Short Fiction, 1892–1912* (1965 edition), p. xxxvii.

10. Richard Giannone has an excellent comment on this in *Music in WC's Fiction,* p. 88.

11. *The World and the Parish,* vol. 1, pp. 439–41, 491–94.

12. See also her 1901 piece on the Chinese minister, Wu T'ing-fang, ibid., vol. 2, pp. 803–5, and the use of Chinese characters in "The Conversion of Sam Loo" and "A Son of the Celestial." In "The Affair at Grover Station" the villain in half-French and half-Chinese but pretends to be Jewish. There are unpleasant references to "barbarous blood" and clam-blooded Asiatics" and to "the sluggish amphibian blood of a race that was already old when Jacob tended the flocks of Laban."

13. Reprinted in *The World and the Parish,* vol. 2, pp. 782–91. See also Robert M. Cherny, "WC and the Populists," *Great Plains Quarterly,* 3 (1983), 206–18.

14. Sister Lucy Schneider, C. S. J., "Artistry and Instinct: WC's Land-Philosophy," *CLA Journal,* 16 (1973), 485–504.

15. "WC's Uncollected Short Stories," as cited above. These tendencies were not even peculiar to Willa Cather's late years, though age certainly accentuated them. In "WC, Undergraduate — Two Poems," *AL,* 21 (1949): 111–16, John H. Hinz shows that in her poetic tributes to Shakespeare and Columbus, both published before she was sixteen, she was already glorifying the heroic past against the degenerate present and finding consanguinity between the artist and the pioneer.

16. "The Lovely Storm: Sexual Initiation in Two Early WC Novels," *SN,* 14 (1982), 348–58.

17. For more on Julio, see O'Brien, *WC: The Emerging Voice,* ch. 18.

18. See Willa Cather, "The Man Who Wrote 'Narcissus,'" *Ladies' Home Journal,* November 1900; also the many references to Nevin in *The World and the Parish,* especially vol. 2, pp. 626–42, in which the Cather article is largely reprinted. David Stouck's discussion of the "weak" men in Miss Cather's fiction, in his *WC's Imagination,* p. 164, n. 2, is thoughtful and suggestive. Her friendship, largely epistolary, late in life, with a young Englishman, Stephen Tennant, is interesting in view of Edith Lewis's statement that his letters and Sarah Orne Jewett's were the only ones Miss Cather kept. Tennant contributed a long foreword to *WC on Writing,* published two years after her death.

19. A catalogue of the failures would be tiresome. But see Randall's *The Landscape and the Looking Glass,* pp. 90–95.

20. See *The World and the Parish,* vol. 1, pp. 121–27. Willa Cather's 1895 descriptions of the women portrayed in two paintings by Carl Newman and Frank Benson respectively do sound more like a man than a woman; on the other hand, her praise of the physical perfections of Godfrey St. Peter in fiction and Julio in life sound very feminine.

21. In *The World and the Parish,* vol. 1, pp. 5–10, there is an interesting description of various types of religious services as Willa Cather saw them in 1897. In the next year she wrote, "Gospel Hymns have driven more people of taste from the churches than Robert Ingersoll and all his school" (*The Kingdom of Art,* p. 177).

22. Though I assert no indebtedness, this always reminds me of a statement of Anthony Trollope's: "All material progress has come from man's desire to do the best he can for himself and those about him, and civilization and Christianity itself have been made possible by such progress."

Bibliography

The following abbreviations are used in this section and in the Notes.

AAK	Alfred A. Knopf, Inc.
AL	*American Literature*
HM	Houghton Mifflin Company
PMLA	*Publications of the Modern Language Association*
PS	*Prairie Schooner*
SN	*Studies in the Novel*
SSF	*Studies in Short Fiction*
UNP	University of Nebraska Press
WC	Willa Cather

The collected Autograph Edition of "The Novels and Stories of Willa Cather," 13 vols., was published by HM by arrangement with AAK, vols. 1–6 in 1937, vols. 7–12 in 1938, and vol. 13 in 1941. After Miss Cather's death in 1947, AAK published one more volume of fiction, *The Old Beauty and Others* (1948); also *Willa Cather on Writing* (1948), a collection; and *Willa Cather in Europe* (1956), which consisted of her letters to the *Nebraska State Journal* describing her 1902 journey to England and France.

The University of Nebraska Press has reprinted all the stories that the author had not herself collected in *Willa Cather's Collected Short Fiction, 1892–1912* (1965, revised 1970), with an introduction by Mildred R. Bennett, and *Uncle Valentine and Other Stories: WC's Uncollected Short Fiction, 1915–1929*, edited by Bernice Slote (1975). They have also generously sampled Willa Cather's journalistic writings in *The Kingdom of Art: Willa Cather's First Principles and Critical Statements, 1893–1896*, edited by Bernice Slote (1966), and *The World and the Parish*, edited by William M. Curtin, 2 vols. (1970).

My Autobiography, by S. S McClure (Frederick A. Stokes, 1914), belongs in Willa Cather's bibliography, since she wrote the whole of it without notes after long talks with him. He himself stated that he was indebted to her for "the very existence" of the book, and she believed that writing here from a man's point of view helped her when she needed to do the same thing in her fiction.

The following books have been published about Willa Cather:

Ambrose, Jamie. *WC*. St. Martin's Press, 1987.

Arnold, Marilyn. *WC: A Reference Guide*. G. K. Hall, 1986.

———. *WC's Short Fiction*. Ohio University Press, 1984.

Bennett, Mildred R. *The World of WC*. Dodd, Mead, 1951, revised 1961.

Bloom, Edward A., and Lillian D. *WC's Gift of Sympathy*. Southern Illinois University Press, 1962.

Bloom, Harold, ed. *WC*. Chelsea House, 1985.

———. *WC's My Ántonia*. Chelsea House, 1987.

Bohlke, L. Brent, ed. *WC in Person: Interviews, Speeches, Letters*. UNP, 1986.

Bonham, Barbara. *WC*. Chilton Book Company, 1970.

Brown, E. K. *WC: A Critical Biography*. AAK, 1953. Completed by Leon Edel. The authorized biography.

Brown, Marion Marsh, and Ruth Crone. *Only One Point of the Compass: WC in the Northeast*. Archer Editions Press, 1980.

Byrne, Kathleen D. and Richard C. Snyder. *Chrysalis: WC in Pittsburgh*. Pittsburgh Historical Society of Western Pennsylvania, 1980.

Callander, Marilyn. *WC and the Fairy Tale*. UMI Research Press, 1989.

Crane, Joan. *WC: A Bibliography*. UNP, 1982.

Daiches, David. *WC: A Critical Introduction*. Cornell University Press, 1951.

Fryer, Judith. *Fabulous Space: The Imaginative Structure of Edith Wharton and WC*. University of North Carolina Press, 1986.

Gerber, Philip L. *WC*. Twayne Publishers. 1984.

Giannone, Richard. *Music in WC's Fiction*. UNP, 1982.

Handy, Yvonne. *L'oeuvre de WC*. University of Rennes, 1940.

Huff, Linda. *A Portrait of the Artist as a Young Woman*. Frederick Ungar, 1983.

Lee, Hermione. *WC: A Life Saved Up*. Virago Press, 1989.

Lewis, Edith. *WC Living: A Personal Record*. AAK, 1953.

Lothrop, Jo Ann. *WC: A Checklist of Her Published Writings*. UNP, 1975.

McFarland, Dorothy Tuck. *WC*. Frederick Ungar, 1972.

Middleton, Jo Ann. *WC's Modernism: A Study of Style and Technique*. Fairleigh Dickinson Press, 1990.

Murphy, John J., ed. *Critical Essays on WC*. G. K. Hall, 1985.

———. *My Ántonia: The Road Home*. Twayne Publishers, 1989.

Nelson, Robert J. *WC and France: In Search of the Lost Language*. University of Illinois Press, 1986.

O'Brien, Sharon. *WC: The Emerging Voice*. Oxford University Press, 1987.

Randall, John H., III. *The Landscape and the Looking Glass: WC's Search for Values*. HM, 1960.

Rapin, René. *WC*. Robert M. McBride, 1930. A translation from the French and the first book-length study.

Robinson, Phyllis C. *Willa: The Life of WC*. Doubleday, 1983.

Rosowski, Susan J. *The Voyage Perilous: WC's Romanticism*. UNP, 1986.
Schroeter, James, ed. *WC and Her Critics*. Cornell University Press, 1967.
Sergeant, Elizabeth Shepley. *WC: A Memoir*. Lippincott, 1953.
Skaggs, Merrill Maguire. *After the World Broke in Two: The Later Novels of WC*. University Press of Virginia, 1990.
Slote, Bernice. *WC: A Pictorial Memoir*. UNP, 1973.
———, and Virginia Faulkner, eds. *The Art of WC*. UNP, 1974. Report on the International Seminar of October 25–28, 1973.
Stouck, David. *WC's Imagination*. UNP, 1975.
Thomas, Susie. *WC*. Barnes and Noble, 1990.
Van Ghent, Dorothy. *WC*. University of Minnesota Press, 1964. University of Minnesota Pamphlets on American Writers.
Woodress, James. *WC, Her Life and Art*. Pegasus, 1970.
———. *WC, A Literary Life*. UNP, 1987. Revision and expansion of the author's 1970 study. Now recognized as the fullest and most authoritative biography.

Articles about Willa Cather in the periodicals are plethoric. Some are mentioned in the notes hereinafter. For others, consult the bibliographical works noted above, the quarterly and annual listings in *AL* and *PMLA,* and the periodical indexes. The *Newsletter* published by the WC Pioneer Memorial and Educational Foundation contains information not elsewhere available. Margaret O'Connor's "Guide to the Letters of WC," in *Resources for American Literary Study,* 4 (1974): 145–72, is useful.

Index